I0814507

Marie Antoinette

Marie Antoinette

Teen Queen to Guillotine

Melanie Burrows

First published in Great Britain in 2025 by
Pen & Sword History
An imprint of Pen & Sword Books Limited
Yorkshire – Philadelphia

ISBN 978 1 39904 136 2

A CIP catalogue record for this book is available from the British Library.

Typeset by Mac Style
Printed in the UK by CPI Group (UK) Ltd, Croydon, CR0 4YY.

The Publisher's authorised representative in the EU for product safety is Authorised Rep Compliance Ltd., Ground Floor, 71 Lower Baggot Street, Dublin D02 P593, Ireland.
www.arccompliance.com

For a complete list of Pen & Sword titles please contact

PEN & SWORD BOOKS LIMITED
47 Church Street, Barnsley, South Yorkshire, S70 2AS, England
E-mail: enquiries@pen-and-sword.co.uk
Website: www.pen-and-sword.co.uk
or
PEN AND SWORD BOOKS
1950 Lawrence Road, Havertown, PA 19083, USA
E-mail: uspen-and-sword@casematepublishers.com
Website: www.penandswordbooks.com

Contents

Acknowledgements

When I first wrote this book in 2014, I had never written an entire history book before and had absolutely no idea what I was getting myself into. I was an absolute nightmare to live with and felt like I was going insane by the time it was finished but I was incredibly proud of the finished product and despite all of the stress and woe, absolutely determined to do it all again and write another book as soon as possible. I was thrilled to get my first contract with Pen and Sword a year later, to write a biography of Marie de Guise and I haven't stopped writing since. However, as my research skills became more honed and my writing improved immeasurably, I kept remembering this early book and resolved to rewrite and update it for a new audience and to reflect more contemporary research and changing attitudes towards its subject as ten years is a long time in the world of historical research.

I have to say that it has been a genuine treat and delight to revisit Marie Antoinette for this project and am so grateful to Jonathan at Pen and Sword Books for agreeing to let me do this and to Laura and Charlotte for facilitating the whole thing and supporting me as I made a book of which I was already extremely proud, even better. I'm extremely fortunate when it comes to my readers (I can't bring myself to call them 'fans', it's so *gauche*), many of whom have been following my work right from the very start and I hope that they enjoy reading this updated version of my biography of Marie Antoinette just as much as I enjoyed writing it.

Writing may be a singularly solitary occupation but most of us still need a good support network or just one exceptional person to keep us going. I am fortunate enough to have the writer Marc Burrows as my exceptional person and absolutely could not have written this or indeed anything else without him. He is the very best, funniest, cleverest and most generous, wonderful and loving person that I have ever met and the absolute love of my miserable life. He is my rock. My everything. I adore him. This book is for him.

It's also for all of you.

À bientôt.

Chapter 1

The Archduchess 1755–1767

'Born to obey.'

Like most children, the young Archduchess Maria Antonia would love to hear the story of her birth which, according to family legend, had rather inconveniently interrupted the all-important daily business of her mother Empress Maria Theresa[1] – a fact that no doubt delighted the mischievous princess and her siblings, not least because it was almost certainly the only time that she was ever permitted to interrupt the crucial business of governing an empire. The Habsburg Empress had been busily working away at her mountain of official papers and dispatch boxes on All Souls Day, 2 November 1755[2], when the pains of labour finally began to overwhelm her and she was forced to send word to her husband Emperor Francis[3] that the latest addition to their already large family was on their way before retiring to her bed-chamber in the Hofburg Palace in Vienna. It is said that, keen as always to use her precious time as productively as possible, the resourceful Empress also called for her dentist and asked him to pull out a painful tooth, reasoning that she would not notice this additional torment against the pangs of childbirth and although this story may well be as apocryphal as so many others surrounding Marie Antoinette, it is so redolent of what we know of the intimidating Maria Theresa's actual character that it is entirely believable.

The baby, an unusually tiny girl, was born at around half past eight in the evening and after an inspection by her proud parents and the attending physicians, was whisked away to the soft and muted world of the royal nurseries at the Hofburg Palace, which currently housed four older siblings (the last of the Empress' children, the Archduke Maximilian, would be born a year later), while her mother, relieved to have once again survived the perils of childbirth, returned once again to her papers and carried on working. Thirty-eight years old and in the prime of life, Empress Maria Theresa had already given birth to fourteen children, of whom eleven were still living. This new baby was her eighth surviving daughter and although her arrival was undoubtedly pleasing to both her parents, it was not exactly extraordinarily exciting either, although the Empress, who loved gambling, may have experienced an extra little fillip at having won a bet against one of her courtiers, Count Dietrichstein, who had wagered that the forthcoming baby would be a boy.

However, commonplace though the arrival of yet another imperial baby might have seemed, it was still an occasion that required proper and formal celebration and the new baby was duly baptised a day later in the presence of her proud father at the Church of the Augustine Friars in Vienna, where she was given the names Maria Antonia Josepha Johanna and her suitably grand godparents, King Joseph I and Queen Mariana Victoria of Portugal[4] were represented by her eldest siblings Archduke Joseph[5] and

Archduchess Maria Anna[6]. The prefix Maria was a Hapsburg custom, designed to show their reverence for the Virgin Mary, but was never normally used – instead the daughters of Maria Theresa were referred to within the family by their second names, in this instance, Antonia.

While Maria Theresa recovered from the birth and immediately returned to work, her new daughter was being tended to by a troupe of nursemaids in the royal nurseries. Later on she would be under the charge of a governess, who would oversee her education, but for now she was primarily cared for by her wet nurse Constance Weber, a magistrate's wife who had been specially selected as much for her beauty, 'pure principles' and good character (it being rather improperly believed that the appearance and personality of a wet nurse could be imbued along with her milk, which was probably fair enough if one was so unwise as to hire an alcoholic or opium eater for the job) as for the quality of the nourishment that she was expected to provide. Frau Weber moved into the Hofburg with her baby son Joseph, who was just three months older than her royal charge and, as was the usual arrangement, shared her milk between the two with Joseph Weber[7] becoming known as the little Archduchess' '*frère de lait*', her milk brother, a bond that would last throughout their lives.

Although Maria Theresa had no direct part in the upbringing of her daughters, she still kept a close eye on the royal nurseries and personally supervised the appointment of staff and programme of education. The sixteenth century vogue for scholarly princesses as exemplified by the likes of Elizabeth I and Lady Jane Grey was long since over and by the time Maria Antonia was born it wasn't considered important for the imperial Archduchesses to have more than basic literacy, a smattering of Italian and fluent French, the latter being the language most commonly spoken at court due to the Emperor's preference for his mother tongue. The more courtly skills of dancing, music, conversation and singing were considered to be of far more importance for a group of girls who were being carefully groomed for insertion into the most exalted courts in Europe, where women were expected, without exception, to be pleasing to both the eye and ear and would rarely be called upon to participate in anything more onerous than the most basic social chit chat.

However, although the Empress' ambitions for her daughters were extremely grand, their upbringing was rather less so, albeit in the splendid surroundings of the imperial palaces: the stately Hofburg, a massive 2,600-roomed edifice in the centre of Vienna where Maria Antonia was born and the family usually spent their winters; the charming, airy summer palace of Laxenburg and the beautiful and enormous Schönbrunn on the outskirts of Vienna, with its gorgeous gardens and wonderful menagerie of rare and domestic animals, which was a source of great delight to the imperial children. As was the custom, the imperial household moved between their different residences depending on the time of year but they seemed happiest when they were spending time at Laxenburg, which was by far the most informal of all the royal palaces and where the royal children had a beautiful series of playrooms, the walls and ceilings painted with charming rustic scenes and fanciful *trompe l'oeil* birds and flowers. It was here that Maria Theresa and her amiable French-born husband Francis, a grandson of Louis XIV's brother Philippe d'Orléans who had given up his own duchy of Lorraine in order to be allowed to marry her, could mostly fully indulge their taste for an almost bourgeois informality and what the Empress would refer to as '*gemütlich*' or rather 'cosiness', a taste that they would pass on to their youngest daughter, Maria Antonia.

Of course, it was nothing new for a royal family to have a favourite country hideaway which they could visit with a small and very select group of family and close friends. At Laxenburg, everyone was required to follow a strict dress code of red coats for the gentlemen and red gowns for the ladies as they frolicked in a world of bucolic make-believe interspersed with vigorous hunting excursions into the surrounding countryside. Monarchs have always done their best to escape from the pressures of royal life by creating private little bolt holes for themselves of admittedly varying degrees of magnificence and privacy. After all, even Versailles had started life as a hunting lodge before being transformed into a bulging great monstrosity and as the palace grew, the royal family continued to seek ever more ingenious ways of hiding away so that by the late eighteenth century there existed secret little warrens of corridors, staircases, mezzanines and rooms behind the splendid state-rooms, where the royal family could retreat and attempt to enjoy some semblance of a private life.

Luckily for the young Maria Antonia and her siblings, the tone at the imperial court was far more informal than that at Versailles, although they were still capable of putting on a proper and extraordinarily lavish show of almost byzantine magnificence when the occasion called for it, as evidenced by accounts of the weddings of the numerous royal children over the years. Overall though the Viennese court was gossipy and fun-loving, with the imperial family, in particular the numerous royal children, leading the way with their enjoyment of simple pleasures like sleigh rides in the snow at Schönbrunn, picnics on the banks of the Danube river, exchanging gifts at Christmas and dressing up in capes and masks for the famous Viennese carnival. As a young woman, Maria Theresa was almost as light-hearted and pleasure-seeking as her daughters but things changed dramatically after the premature death of her beloved husband Francis at the celebrations in Innsbruck for the wedding of his son Archduke Leopold[8] to the Infanta Maria Luisa of Spain[9] in August 1765. Consumed by grief, she cut off the lovely long blonde hair of which she had been so proud, eschewed the grand and colourful dresses and jewels that she had once loved so much in favour of heavy black mourning, no longer danced at balls or appeared at the theatre and became even more austere and formidable than ever, which must have been rather frightening for her younger children.

If Maria Theresa's intimidating manner, numerous offspring, love of cosy Germanic informality and exclusive and perhaps excessive delight in her husband are reminiscent of her distant relative Queen Victoria, then so too was her all-consuming manner of mourning him as she gave herself wholeheartedly and one might even say with some enjoyment up to grief, noting despondently in her prayer book that her '*happy married life lasted 29 years, 6 months and 6 days; this is 335 months, 1540 weeks, 10781 days and 258744 hours.*' That her beloved Francis had not always been an entirely perfect husband and had indeed been something of a womaniser, who conducted discreet liaisons with much younger women at court, was now tactfully swept under the carpet and forgotten.

The unexpected death of Emperor Francis was to have sad repercussions for all of his children, particularly his eldest son Joseph who now found himself Emperor and in the unhappy position of acting as a rather superfluous co-ruler with his domineering mother at the age of just twenty-three. Meanwhile, his youngest sister, nine-year-old

Maria Antonia was especially distraught as she had long been her father's pet and was said to be his favourite child and most beloved *mignonne*. In later years she would tell her friends about the last time that she saw her handsome, cheerful father when he set out with his gentlemen to travel to Innsbruck for her brother's wedding but then suddenly turned back to embrace her one last time, almost as if, she would later recall, he had somehow known that he would never see her again and had had a premonition of the terrible sorrow that would be her lot in life.

The imperial family's love of simple middle-class living is perhaps perfectly illustrated by an amateur family portrait painted by Maria Antonia's elder sister Archduchess Maria Christina, which depicts the family on St Nicholas Day in 1762. The Emperor is shown very much at his ease before the fire, looking positively rakish in his dressing gown, slippers and nightcap and with a clear stubble on his chin, while his devoted wife, the Empress stands behind his chair in the simple blue dress of a well to do Austrian *hausfrau*, looking pleased as punch as she serves him his morning cup of hot chocolate. Only four of the imperial children are depicted in the painting, with the rest presumably getting up to mischief elsewhere: eight-year-old Ferdinand is shown crying as his pretty elder sister Maria Christina presents him with his Krampus gift of birch rods arranged as a switch in his shoe, obviously a punishment for acts of naughtiness, while the youngest imperial child, six-year-old Archduke Maximilian, who has clearly been much better behaved than his elder brother rather smugly tucks into a delicious looking pile of iced heart-shaped gingerbread biscuits on the carpet. Most charming of all though is the diminutive figure of the seven-year-old Maria Antonia, her father's little pet, who peeps out from behind her mother's skirts and proudly holds her splendidly dressed new doll up to the viewer, clearly thrilled with her latest acquisition.

However, as with the later Victorian court, this near obsession with appearing as middle class and 'ordinary' as possible had a darker flip side in that it also fostered a certain restrictive, stiff-lipped and often depressingly narrow-minded bourgeois attitude towards morality and duty, that would all too often cast a cloud over the lives of Maria Theresa's children and in particular her daughters, who were raised to have an equal fear of both God and their mother, considering both as omniscient and terrifying as the other. As might be expected at the imperial court, there was always a heavy emphasis on religious observation with daily Mass and devotions and strict adherence to the timetable of the church, which included fasting for Lent and being marked with a cross on the forehead on Ash Wednesday. However, after Francis' death, the court quickly became increasingly gloomy – which would have a particularly marked effect on the moods of the young Archduchesses, who now became even more terrified of drawing their mother's censorious eye, which was always so quick to find fault, upon themselves. However, at the same time, they were desperate for her affection and there can be no doubt that for all her scolding and tiresome nitpicking, Maria Theresa loved her children deeply and had their best interests always at heart even if on occasion she would ruthlessly sacrifice them for the best interests of her empire, which would forever be the greatest and truest love of her life.

At the time of Maria Antonia's birth in 1755, there were already seven surviving Archduchesses, the eldest of whom, Maria Anna, was seventeen, old enough to be her youngest sister's mother and would probably have already been married off had she not unfortunately been physically delicate and prone to debilitating bouts of ill health since birth, which rendered her sadly quite ineligible in an age when European princelings were looking about for robust wives who could hopefully provide them with lots of children. Maria Anna was very intelligent though and a great favourite with her father, who shared her taste for science, archaeology and politics – all of which were considered unusual interests for young women at that time, although as she was highly unlikely to ever marry, foibles that might well have been discouraged in one of her more marriageable younger sisters were tacitly tolerated in Maria Anna.

Although Maria Anna was their mother's eldest surviving child, it was her next daughter, Maria Christina, the talented artist of the family who went by the nickname 'Mimi', who was Maria Theresa's undoubted favourite, probably initially because she had the good sense to be born on her mother's twenty-fifth birthday but then later because she was considered to be the most talented, charming and intelligent of the royal daughters. The obvious favouritism shown by the Empress for Mimi was to be a source of contention amongst all of her sisters, who competed for their fearsome mother's approval and attention. Although all of the imperial Archduchesses were made very aware that their ultimate duty was to marry well for the sake of Austrian interests, it was Mimi alone who was permitted the very great privilege of following in their mother's footsteps and marrying for love when she rejected her first cousin Benedetto of Savoy, Duke of Chablais, youngest son of Charles Emmanuel III of Sardinia and the suitor that her parents had chosen for her and instead begged to be allowed to marry another cousin Prince Albert of Saxony, who was virtually penniless and an altogether less eligible match for an imperial Archduchess who was also the favourite daughter of the Empress. However, this favouritism would inevitably win the day for Mimi, when the Empress quickly realised that allowing her daughter to marry a penniless prince would mean being able to keep her always close at hand rather than having to sacrifice her to a grand foreign match, which would in all probability mean never seeing her again. Prince Albert was therefore further ennobled with the Duchy of Teschen, while Mimi was presented with an enormous dowry, which enabled the young couple to live in high style at the imperial court after their marriage.

Even this unusual favour might have been overlooked by the others had not Mimi been a telltale who delighted in reporting her younger siblings' misdeeds to their mother and sowing discord between them all, with the aim, of course, of enhancing her own position of the most favoured child. Maria Antonia, who was thirteen years Mimi's junior, came to loathe her eldest sister whose bossy, high-handed ways and intellectual snobbishness, which was so different to Maria Anna's gentle introverted cleverness, left her with a permanent suspicious dread of what would later be termed 'bluestockings'. For the rest of her life, Maria Antonia would eschew the company of intellectually sophisticated women, such as the cultivated and delightfully louche *salonières* of Paris, in favour of what she regarded as more straightforward friendships with much less challenging companions who shared her interests. When Mimi later visited Maria Antonia, now Queen of France and no longer the despised little sister, the latter took great pleasure in delivering a few small snubs to the elder sister that she had always so heartily disliked.

Mimi was also often at loggerheads with her brother Joseph, who had become Emperor after the death of his father but to his immense frustration was forced to take a back seat to his mother, who retained a firm grip on affairs of state and had no great wish to delegate to her son. Resenting the fact that Mimi was clearly his mother's favourite was one thing but when his own adored Spanish first wife, Isabella of Parma[10], whose mother Louise-Élisabeth of France was a daughter of Louis XV, began to also show a marked preference for his sister's company to the extent that it was suspected that the two were lovers, he clearly decided that enough was enough and the two never really got on again.

The third surviving daughter was Maria Elisabeth, a lively and rather vain little blonde, who was considered to be by far the prettiest of the Archduchesses, despite some stiff competition, particularly from Mimi, Maria Amalia and Maria Josepha. Known within the family as Leisl, she looked like butter wouldn't melt in her pretty mouth but wasn't nearly as nice as she looked. Deprived of what she considered to be her rightful Queen Bee status among the siblings by the continued presence of Mimi after her marriage, she was disliked by the younger girls thanks to her sharp put-downs and tendency to flirt with whatever handsome young men happened to be in the vicinity – which naturally worried her ever-watchful mother, who feared that Maria Elisabeth's flirtations would eventually lead to a scandal that might damage her all-important marital prospects. 'It mattered not if the look of admiration came from a prince or a Swiss guard,' the Empress commented on her daughter, 'so long as someone was doing homage to her beauty, Elisabeth was satisfied.' The princes whose admiration Maria Theresa was particularly interested in was a young trio of Bourbons: Ferdinand of Parma, Ferdinand of Naples and, most grand of all, the Dauphin Louis Auguste of France, whom she had currently set her sights on as the most eligible and potentially useful prospective sons-in-law in the wake of the Seven Years War, which came to an end in 1763.

Charming, intelligent and frivolous with an underlying stubborn streak and undeniably mutinous air, Archduchess Maria Amalia was the fourth surviving daughter of Maria Theresa and one of Maria Antonia's favourite sisters, probably because she could always be safely relied upon not to tell tales back to their mother and also liked to spoil her younger siblings. Maria Amalia had little patience with her mother's controlling behaviour and so, unlike her sisters, was not at all desperate for her approval which meant that they were frequently at loggerheads, particularly when Maria Amalia became of marriageable age and declared that she didn't see why she shouldn't be allowed to follow in her elder sister Mimi's footsteps and choose her own husband. After Maria Amalia there came Maria Johanna and then Maria Josepha, two sweet-natured little princesses born just over a year apart who were as close as twins and shared their rooms and lessons until Maria Johanna, the elder of the pair, tragically died of smallpox at the age of twelve, just as her mother was arranging her marriage to the heir to the Spanish throne, after which attention switched to Maria Josepha. Maria Antonia, who had survived a mild case of smallpox at the age of two and was consequently immune from that point onwards, was seven years old at the time and her elder sister's illness and horrible death would have a profound effect on her. However, it was even more distressing for the shy and rather introverted Maria Josepha, who became even more withdrawn after Maria Johanna's death and, not unsurprisingly, developed a terrible and morbid fear of smallpox.

Of all her sisters, however, it was the mischievous, strong-willed and quick-witted Maria Carolina, known within the family as 'Charlotte', who would always remain closest to Maria Antonia's heart and would be her staunchest ally, best friend and most trusted confidante during her childhood in Austria and beyond. Like their elder sisters Maria Johanna and Maria Josepha, Maria Carolina and Maria Antonia were so close in age, with just three years separating them, that they were brought up together, sharing rooms and lessons and also inevitably paired off together during court entertainments, when the talented imperial children, who were taught music and dancing by the finest masters in Vienna, would sometimes dance and sing for the entertainment of favoured courtiers. However, although the two youngest Archduchesses were outwardly a most delightful pair of girls, all big blue eyes, pretty pink pouts and fair ringlets, they were, by all accounts, a pair of terrors, who led their nurses and governesses a merry dance and were frequently reprimanded by their mother, who would often exasperatedly complain that of all her daughters, the pert, often vexatious and remarkably bright Maria Carolina was the one who was most like herself – and not always in a good way. It's likely that as the more strong-willed and cleverer of the pair, Maria Carolina was very much the ring leader in all of this, but the fact that Maria Antonia would retain a playful, teasing streak for most of the rest of her life suggests that she very much entered into the spirit of things and was not exactly an innocent bystander in her sister's pranks. In the end, however, the Empress made good on her threats to separate the two and in 1768 they were indeed eventually divided and made to take their lessons alone.

Their chief governess during childhood was Countess Brandeis, a kind-hearted woman who was very eager to please and never quite managed to strike a proper balance between indulging her flighty young charges and instilling them with a reasonable level of education. Keen that her daughters should fit into whatever grand spheres that marriage placed them within, Maria Theresa insisted upon a fairly broad education that encompassed literacy, languages (primarily Italian, taught by the famed librettist Metastasio, and French, although some Latin was also optimistically attempted), mathematics, history and geography, none of which were taught to a very vigorous level, it being considered enough that the girls should at least know a smattering of information – enough to render them not entirely ignorant. There was also a heavy emphasis on filial duty, obedience and moral decorum, with Maria Theresa herself declaring that her daughters were '*born to obey*' and ensuring that they were brought up to place their allegiance to Austria above all else, which would naturally cause them to walk a tricky tightrope when their inevitable marriages made them rulers of various other countries, with different and occasionally conflicting interests.

To this end, the Empress insisted upon maintaining a daily correspondence with her children's tutors and governesses, making sure that she was kept informed of everything that happened, however insignificant it might seem. Possibly it would have suited her better to take complete charge of their upbringings herself but as her state affairs and enormous workload made this impossible, she did the next best thing and kept as close an eye as possible on their development, even occasionally summoning them into her presence to discuss their progress with, naturally, particular emphasis on their various failings. Maria Antonia must have absolutely dreaded these conversations with her formidable mother for she was never left in any doubt that her unimpressive intellectual abilities, which to be fair were not entirely her fault, were an enormous disappointment to the exacting Maria Theresa.

It's not that Maria Antonia was stupid, in fact, she was in her own way almost as bright as Charlotte and would later show herself capable of making astonishing progress in quite a rapid amount of time when given a proper tutor. However, her natural inclination tended more towards laziness than application and the good-hearted, undemanding Countess Brandeis proved herself quite unable to inspire and motivate her charge to do any better, probably because she valued winning the friendship of her pupils above their educational attainments. From an early age, Maria Antonia struggled with both her reading and writing, finding the former tedious and the latter just too much like hard work, with the result that her exercises were a mess of blotches, crossings out and misspellings. In the end, the Countess, fearful of the Empress' censure, decided it might be better to do the exercises herself in pencil and get her pupil to trace over the words in ink – a most unsatisfactory way of going about things but definitely the easiest for both governess and pupil, even if it meant that the latter never really quite improved, while the former must have quaked in her shoes at the thought of the Empress finding out about her subterfuge.

A lack of interest in reading could not be so easily rectified or hidden however, especially when coupled with a worrying inability to pay proper attention or concentrate for more than short periods of time. As Countess Brandeis and eventually the court of France were soon to realise, the young Archduchess Maria Antonia had an absolute horror of ever feeling the slightest bit bored and would as a result strenuously avoid anything that forced her to concentrate – which would become something of a flaw in a young girl who might well one day become a head of state and be expected to sit through long state events or make polite conversation about subjects that were of no immediate relevance or interest to her. In not cajoling her young charge to apply herself more, Countess Brandeis, for all her good-natured intentions, did in fact do the young Maria Antonia a grave disservice.

Lessons took up only a small part of the day though (although probably more than enough as far as Maria Antonia was concerned) and the rest of the time was employed with all the delights that the royal palaces could offer to a cheerful and energetic group of young people. Although the elder children were significantly older than their youngest siblings they still, for the most part, all got along together reasonably well and later on Maria Antonia would reminisce happily about afternoons spent skating and sledging with her older brothers and sisters at Schönbrunn and Laxenburg, interspersed no doubt with enthusiastic snowball fights and cups of hot *Viennoise* chocolate and soft warm gingerbread. Riding and hunting were also favourite occupations – the latter being considered an essential part of court life in many countries for both men and women because of its unique opportunities for relatively informal access to the monarch. Many an otherwise obscure nobleman had risen to dazzling favour simply because of his prowess in the hunting field, while displaying superior horsemanship was a well-tried and tested way for ladies of the court to catch the King's eye, as demonstrated by Louise de la Vallière, mistress of Louis XIV.

Music was also extremely important at the imperial court as both Maria Theresa and Francis passed on their love of music to their children, all of whom learned to play an instrument and took singing lessons, which was particularly important in the case of the girls in an age when women were expected to be entertaining adornments who must always be ready to be called upon to please and divert their companions with an impromptu musical interlude. In time the royal children were numerous enough to form a small orchestra and would play both at private family gatherings and to a much bigger audience at court events. Maria Antonia made her first public debut at not quite four years old, singing French couplets at a court gala to celebrate her father's name day in October 1759, followed by her brother Ferdinand enthusiastically playing the kettle drums, Joseph performing with his cello and Maria Elisabeth and Maria Christina showcasing pieces on the piano. Although her academic progress was rather less than stellar, music was something that Maria Antonia really excelled at and she would show particular aptitude with the harp and singing as well as being able to sight-read music.

Where there is music there must naturally also be dancing and it was in this most essential of courtly arts that Maria Antonia, who naturally managed to hit just the right balance of grace and enthusiasm, was held to particularly dazzle. It's likely in fact that her exquisite dancing and polished deportment went a long way towards excusing her lack of skill in other arenas, particularly the intellectual, as the ability to strike an impressive pose on the dance floor was considered of tremendous and indeed paramount importance at the time. Certainly, the young Maria Antonia would frequently be called upon to take the starring role in performances with her siblings, enchanting everyone at court with her precocious poise. It's little wonder therefore that she takes a prominent position, her arms elegantly extended and small feet placed just so, in the lovely Meytens painting of some of the imperial children dancing together in the Gluck operetta *Il Parnasso Confusio*, which was composed and performed in honour of her brother Joseph's second marriage to Josepha of Bavaria, which took place in January 1765 when she was just nine years old. Certainly, Maria Antonia herself was fond enough of this painting to ask for a copy to be sent to her in France and it took pride of place in the Petit Trianon, acting as an endearing reminder of what she was pleased to recall as a most happy and carefree childhood, even if beneath the surface it was often anything but this.

The physical well-being of the entire imperial family was under the care of Gerard van Swieten, a Dutch-born educationalist and physician who was to become something of a lifestyle guru to Maria Theresa and was closely involved in helping to plan and supervise the upbringing of the imperial children. An enlightened man who would also be responsible for improving health care for all classes of society, Van Swieten took an almost Rousseau-like line when it came to his young charges, recommending plenty of fresh air and outdoor exercise to build their strength and health, as well as a nourishing and simple diet of noodle soups, eggs, fresh vegetables, fruit, fish and very little in the way of rich red meats, possibly influenced by the Habsburg tendency, shared with their Bourbon counterparts, to become alarmingly overweight as the result of overindulgence. His optimistic attempts to put Maria Theresa, whose own mother had ballooned to such tremendous proportions in later life, probably because of a diet that her physicians recommended in order to boost her fertility, that she eventually completely lost the use of her legs, on a diet were unsuccessful but he had better luck with her children, with Maria Antonia, in particular, retaining abstemious eating habits throughout her life.

At Schönbrunn, Maria Theresa constructed two new wings to house her growing family, with the Archdukes and their households being housed in the new right-wing, which became a riot of rampaging adolescent boys squabbling, playing pranks, duelling in the gardens and wrestling in the galleries. Meanwhile, their sisters lived rather more decorously in the left wing in a cosy and comforting feminine fug of hot chocolate, rosewater and floral scent, although one wonders how harmonious their apartments actually were with eight young women of such varying temperaments living so closely together. At the age of five, each of the girls graduated from the royal nursery and was presented with their own small suite of five rooms, which followed the formal pattern of their parents' apartments – with an outer audience chamber where guests could be formally received, after which the rooms became increasingly more private as they approached the inner sanctum of the bed-chamber.

Just as her apartment at Versailles would become a colourful and beautiful riot of flowers, drawings, precious little objects and dogs, so too were her rooms at Schönbrunn, which she filled with the things that she loved best. Picking flowers in the gardens was a favourite pastime of the youngest Archduchesses and the vases in their rooms would have overflowed with the sweet-scented fruits of their labours, especially in the summer. Encouraged like other girls of high station to always have some embroidery to hand to keep herself occupied, there would have been cushions and other small pieces worked by her own hand and those of her sisters, as well as sketches and paintings. Maria Theresa took great delight in her daughters' artwork and even had one of the rooms at Schönbrunn entirely decorated with examples of their prowess, with prime position, naturally, being given to the work of the talented Mimi.

Fully aware that her children would find it of benefit to be able to mix with people from all stations, Maria Theresa encouraged them to make friends with young people from outside their family circle, including the children of their wet nurses, whom they were brought up to regard as foster siblings, and other servants. Other friends were, as might be expected, drawn from amongst the children of nobles and officials at their mother's court, with both Maria Carolina and Maria Antonia becoming especially friendly with the Princesses Frederica[11], Louise[12] and Charlotte[13] of Hesse-Darmstadt, the three eldest daughters of Prince George William of Hesse-Darmstadt, who were distant cousins of the imperial Archduchesses. In 1768, Frederica, the eldest of the Hesse girls, would marry the Grand Duke of Mecklenburg-Strelitz, brother of Queen Charlotte, and her daughters would include Queen Louise of Prussia and Frederica, Queen of Hanover. Maria Antonia would refer to this pleasant bevvy of Hesse-Darmstadt girls as her 'dear princesses' and would become particularly fond of Princess Charlotte Wilhelmine, the middle daughter, who was three days younger than herself, to the point that she even at one point paid her the signal honour of picking up her pen in order to labour through a heartfelt letter to the princess, in which she concluded that, '*I can't convey to you the depth of my feeling for you*'. Based on this, it seems that Princess Charlotte was the first in a series of close and warm female friendships with which Maria Antonia would find comfort, acceptance and succour throughout her life and the Hesse-Darmstadt princesses would remain her close friends until the very end with Maria Antonia treasuring their letters and portraits and excitedly enjoying their company whenever they visited France.

Although by our modern standards, we may consider Maria Antonia to have been pampered, perhaps even a little spoilt by the grandeur of the surroundings that she grew up in and the comforts of her everyday life, it's likely that she herself would have been surprised by this as she would always in later life contrast the relative informality and happiness of her childhood in Vienna with the stifling etiquette and endless discomforts of her married life at Versailles. There was also her loathing of the almost total lack of affection that existed within the French royal family, which had left her husband riddled with insecurity and awkwardness, while she herself shimmered with the confidence and vitality that came from being raised in the heart of a loving and supportive, if often maddeningly controlling and meddlesome, family in an atmosphere of Germanic frankness rather than French obfuscation.

On 27 November 1763, Isabella of Parma, the twenty-one-year-old wife of Maria Antonia's handsome eldest brother Joseph, died of smallpox just five days after giving birth to a daughter who also died but not before she was given the name Maria Christina in honour of her aunt Mimi. The unfortunate Isabella had sadly possessed a rather morbid and undoubtedly depressive personality, which was quite at odds with the lively good humour of the imperial family, although they were all very fond of her. In private, the young woman confided that she longed for death, writing at one point that '*Death speaks to me in a distinct voice that rouses in my soul a sweet satisfaction*' but her faith prevented her from doing anything to harm herself. She also, more worryingly from a dynastic point of view, developed a horror of the sexual act, which devastated her adoring husband, who then had to watch as his wife shunned him in favour of his own sister, Mimi, who shared her illicit love and to whom she wrote[14] more than two hundred ardent notes in French, in which she professed to '*love you to the point of worship*' and informed her sister-in-law that '*I love you like a mad woman, in a holy way or diabolically, I love you and will love you to the grave.*' After Isabella's death, Mimi chose to show her grieving brother the amorous and extraordinarily passionate letters that his dead wife had written to her over the years, thinking that they might alleviate his terrible grief by proving that Isabella had not been worthy of it – a plan that naturally backfired and only served to increase the rift between the two siblings.

Despite their issues, Joseph and Isabella had still managed to do their duty and produced a daughter, Maria Theresa, a lively little thing who was born in March 1762 and named for her doting grandmother (who had with her usual domineering high-handedness declared that all of the first-born daughters of her offspring should be named after herself). This was not enough to secure the succession though and the Empress relentlessly pressed her highly resistant son to marry again as soon as possible until the heartbroken and completely bereft Joseph was forced to capitulate to his mother's demands that he do his duty and provide himself with a male heir. Deciding that he couldn't possibly love anyone as much as he had loved Isabella and thwarted in his original plan to marry her younger sister Maria Luisa[15], who was already betrothed to the heir of the King of Spain, he declared that one princess was as good as another, refused to take any part in the hunt for a second wife and left the decision entirely in the hands of his mother, who duly selected a second cousin of impeccable lineage for the task. Docile, good-natured but rather boring, Maria Josepha of Bavaria was not an unattractive young woman but from the very first she failed to appeal to Joseph, who professed himself horrified by her 'charmless' figure, pimpled face and bad teeth. However, although Joseph was clearly far from enamoured with his new wife, whom he married in 1765, he still gritted his teeth and made the best of things, leading what he referred to as a 'bachelor' life and avoiding her company as much as possible. So unhappy was the marriage and so miserable and lonely was poor Maria Josepha that his sister Mimi, who did not mince her words, once declared that if *she* had the '*great misfortune to be Joseph's wife, I would run away and hang myself from one of the trees at Schönbrunn*'. To the surprise of absolutely no one at all, the couple had no children.

A much more congenial and popular sister-in-law was the gregarious Infanta Maria Luisa of Spain, who married Maria Antonia's elder brother Archduke Leopold in 1765 and whose wedding celebrations in Innsbruck were cut so dramatically and tragically short by the death of her new father-in-law Emperor Francis. Sadly for everyone however, the newlyweds, who became Grand Duke and Duchess of Tuscany upon Francis' death, moved to Florence immediately after their wedding and returned to Vienna only once in the spring of 1770, shortly before Maria Antonia's wedding, which meant that the two sisters-in-law, Maria Luisa and Maria Antonia had very little time to get to know each other before the latter left Austria forever.

By the end of 1767, the question of the youngest girls' marriages became of even more pressing moment as Maria Theresa worked hard to fix the rapidly crumbling friendship that had sprung up between Austria and France in the wake of the alliance formed by their common enemies England and Prussia during the Seven Years War and which had been sealed with the Treaty of Versailles in 1756. However, Austria and France were not natural allies and in the face of Louis XV's increasing apathy, Maria Theresa desperately tried to bring about an alliance in the time-honoured fashion of a marriage between one of her daughters and Louis' heir, his grandson Louis Auguste. At the same time, she was keen to further reinforce the friendship between Austria and the Bourbons by marrying two other daughters to Ferdinand, King of Naples[16] and Ferdinand, Duke of Parma[17], both of whom were descendants of Louis XIV, while the latter had the additional benefit of also being yet another grandson of Louis XV as well as the brother of the late and very lamented Isabella of Parma.

At first, it was proposed that Maria Amalia should marry Ferdinand of Naples and Maria Carolina should marry Louis Auguste of France, which seemed ideal as his grandfather, Louis XV was her godfather, while their elder sister Maria Elisabeth, the loveliest of them all, could potentially marry the French king, whose Polish wife Marie Leszczynska was ailing and eventually died in June 1768. However, Ferdinand's father Charles III of Spain objected to the first of these matches on the grounds that Maria Amalia was too old for his son, who was five years younger. It was therefore arranged that he would instead marry her younger sister, the sixteen-year-old Archduchess Maria Josepha while Maria Amalia was instead to be betrothed to Ferdinand of Parma, who was also five years younger than her but, on the advice of his grandfather Louis XV, who took the pragmatic view that one princess was much like another when it came down to it, declared that he wasn't about to be fussy about which Archduchess he married as they all seemed to be more or less the same.

Nevertheless, it transpired that Maria Amalia, the social butterfly of the family and most stubborn of Maria Theresa's daughters, had other ideas. Encouraged by her sister

Mimi's love match with Prince Albert of Saxony, she had fallen helplessly in love with yet another handsome young cousin Prince Charles, Duke of Zweibrücken[18], who was, as far as the smitten Maria Amalia was concerned, the embodiment of a Teutonic hero with blond hair, steely blue eyes and chiselled good looks. Upon being informed of her upcoming marriage to the Duke of Parma, she declared that she would be doing no such thing and would instead be marrying the Duke of Zweibrücken, arguing that it was not such a bad match as the handsome Charles was heir of his childless cousin, the Elector of Bavaria and indeed was more eligible than Mimi's husband had been. However, as far as Maria Theresa was concerned, a putative heir was in no way competition for a prestigious Bourbon princeling who was already in possession of his inheritance and so she insisted that Maria Amalia renounce Charles and do her duty by marrying Ferdinand.

It seems odd perhaps that Maria Amalia, who was usually so strong-willed, should have bowed her head and given in to her mother's demands, instead of defying her and perhaps running off with her handsome prince in the dead of night. However, princesses in real life rarely behave like the ones in romantic novels and having been brought up since childhood to worship at the altar of filial duty and to regard the word of her mother as tantamount to the word of God himself, there was no question of Maria Amalia seriously disobeying Maria Theresa in such an important matter, however much she may have secretly wished to do so. There were threats and tears and shouting of course, Maria Amalia being one of the more emotive and demonstrative of the Archduchesses, but it was all so much hot air and everyone, including young Maria Antonia who was observing all of this with the full and no doubt apprehensive awareness that one day it would be her turn, knew it.

Chapter 2

The Ingénue 1767–1770

'I pity Antoinette, who still has all of this to face.'

Not for nothing is 1767 sometimes referred to as Maria Theresa's '*annus horribilis*', for just as she was able to congratulate herself on having pulled off a frankly incredible coup with the triple alliance between her family and the Bourbons, disaster struck in the form of her daughter Mimi giving birth three days after her birthday to a daughter, who was also named Maria Christina and lived for just one day, and then falling dangerously ill with puerperal fever. As if this was not bad enough, there was also yet another outbreak of smallpox, that most dreaded of eighteenth-century diseases, which had already claimed the lives of her daughter-in-law Isabella, her daughter Maria Johanna and, in January 1761, her favourite son Charles Joseph. This time the disease killed Maria Theresa's poor unloved daughter-in-law Maria Josepha and left her daughter Maria Elisabeth permanently disfigured, which removed all possibility of marriage with the fastidious Louis XV, whose taste for pretty young women was well known throughout Europe. If Maria Elisabeth had been a great heiress then perhaps suitors would have been able to overlook her sadly ruined looks, but as just one of several Habsburg Archduchesses, her value on the royal marriage market took a serious blow.

However, most disastrous of all was the fact that Maria Theresa herself was struck down by the disease, almost certainly while giving her daughter-in-law Maria Josepha a farewell kiss, and indeed came so close to death that the Last Sacrament was given and her family went into a panic, unable to comprehend the possibility that they might be about to lose her. Luckily though, the indomitable Empress pulled through and made a full recovery, to the tremendous relief of everyone, although it's possible that her eldest son Joseph was not a little disappointed to see his chance to take total charge come to an end, delighted though he was to see his mother, whom he revered as much as he was frustrated by her, recover.

Plans for the marriages carried on as before, with Maria Josepha due to leave Vienna in October 1767 to make the journey to Naples. However, shortly before her departure her mother insisted that she spend a night praying and keeping vigil in the imperial crypt of the Capuchin church in Vienna where her sister-in-law Maria Josepha had recently been interred alongside other members of the imperial family. To an impressionable young girl, already terrified of disease and death, this must have been an appalling ordeal and it was probably of no surprise to anyone when she collapsed and had to be carried back inside the palace afterwards. Sadly, her collapse was quickly found to have far more sinister reasons than simple adolescent squeamishness but instead proved to be the first symptoms of smallpox, perhaps caught from noxious gases seeping from Maria

Josepha's improperly closed tomb but more likely, based on the inoculation period of the disease, caught before she had even descended the steps to the crypt.

The unfortunate Maria Josepha died on 15 October, the very day that she had been scheduled to leave Vienna for Naples. Instead, as Leopold Mozart, who was in Vienna for the wedding celebrations, gloomily noted, '*the Princess Bride has become the bride of a heavenly bridegroom*'. Elsewhere, the news of Maria Josepha's sad and untimely death was greeted with dismay as the Kings of Spain and France were now as keen as Maria Theresa to see this union between Austria and Naples sealed for good. Her prospective bridegroom on the other hand amused himself by dressing one of his friends in a dress and putting sweets on his face to represent smallpox spots before parading him through Caserta palace, telling everyone that it was the Austrian Archduchess' funeral procession. He did not object when he was informed that he was still to be married, only this time to Maria Josepha's younger sister, Maria Carolina, who had been hastily offered as a replacement, inheriting her sister's spectacular bridal trousseau as compensation for having to permanently forgo the grand match with the Dauphin of France that she had been cheerfully anticipating for several months.

Like her elder sister Maria Amalia, Maria Carolina loudly and forcefully protested at being so summarily packed off to Naples but in the end she too was forced to give in and obey, although not at all meekly. Maria Carolina was married to Ferdinand of Naples in a lavish proxy wedding on 7 April 1768 at the church of the Augustine Friars in Vienna, with one brother, Joseph walking her up the aisle and another, Ferdinand standing in for her absent groom. She left for Naples the same afternoon, taking public leave of her family in front of the entire court but then stopping her coach as it pulled away from Schönbrunn in order to jump down and embrace her beloved Maria Antonia, who was distraught, one last time. During her long journey to Naples, the devastated and apprehensive Maria Carolina wrote to her former governess, Countess Lerchenfeld, to ask that she should '*write to me everything that you know about my sister Antonia, down to the tiniest detail, what she says and does and even what she thinks... Beg her to love me, for I am so passionately concerned for her.*' Later on, after her disappointing wedding night, she would write more ominously that, '*I pity Antoinette, who still has all of this to face. When my sister has to confront this situation, I shall shed many tears.*'

Maria Amalia's wedding took place just over a year later on 27 June 1769, again in the church of the Augustine Friars and following the same procedure as Maria Carolina's nuptials, with Joseph walking her down the aisle and Ferdinand standing in for the absent Duke of Parma. A few days later she departed Vienna for her new life in Italy, dropping a dutiful but chilly curtsey to the mother who had destroyed her happiness and forced her against her will into a marriage that she despised, before she left. They would never see each other again. Her disappointed suitor, Charles of Zweibrücken, would later, in an ironic twist of fate, marry Maria Amalia of Saxony, a first cousin of the Dauphin Louis Auguste, who had once been suggested as a prospective bride for the French heir by his mother, who was her aunt.

With Maria Carolina and Maria Amalia now safely married off, albeit resentfully, attention now turned to the most glittering prize of all – the Dauphin Louis Auguste of France. Although his parents had been implacable enemies of the Austrian alliance and would have preferred their son to be married to a German princess like his mother, they were both dead by 1767, leaving the way clear for negotiations between Louis XV and Maria Theresa to move on in earnest. Although the first choice was Maria Carolina, Louis' goddaughter, when she was betrothed to the King of Naples attention naturally turned to her hitherto unmentioned younger sister, Maria Antonia, who turned thirteen in November 1768 and was just over a year younger than the French prince. This French match was extremely close to Maria Theresa's heart and she must have wondered just why it was proving so hard it was proving to arrange, considering that Louis XV had made a rather less than dazzling match to a Polish princess and then married his own son to a relatively obscure princess of Saxony. Surely a match with imperial Austria was far more impressive than both of these alliances?

For Louis XV's part, although he was open to the idea of a match between his heir and the Archduchess Maria Antonia and more than awake to the extraordinary grandeur of such a marriage, Louis XV was also painfully aware of both his own sharply declining popularity in France and the antipathy directed towards their Austrian allies, who were regarded with great suspicion and hostility by the French populace. In short, he wasn't sure if he could survive antagonising them with what was bound to be an extremely unpopular marriage. However, he listened to Maria Theresa's approaches and instructed his Ambassador in Vienna, the Marquis de Durfort to discreetly inspect the thirteen-year-old princess before dispatching not altogether glowing reports of the girl, whom he deemed to be pretty but childish and rather badly educated, back to Versailles.

Eager to advance the marriage as much as possible, Maria Theresa now took a close look at the education of her youngest daughter. She had already had plenty of reasons to bemoan Maria Antonia's lack of aptitude and concentration in the past but had taken no real measures to rectify this. Now, however, the grooming of Maria Antonia to become a worthy morsel for French delectation became of paramount importance to the Empress and she bent her considerable energies to this end, overseeing every detail and overlooking nothing in her quest to transform her daughter into a perfect French Dauphine both in appearance and actuality.

The first thing to receive attention was Maria Antonia's previously desultory education, which even by the lax standards of the time was clearly in no way suitable for a future Queen of France. Upon investigation, Maria Theresa discovered that not only was her daughter's native German execrable but her French was also appalling and would require a great deal of work to get it up to scratch. At first, two actors, Messieurs Aufresne and Sainville, were employed to get the young Archduchess up to speed but when Versailles, appalled that a prospective Dauphine was learning her French from a pair of common thespians, intervened, another, more worthy tutor was engaged for the unenviable task of ironing out all the problems with Maria Antonia's education.

Charming, urbane and erudite, the Abbé de Vermond was a perfect choice to act as the Archduchess' new tutor as he had the knack of teaching without really seeming to and also managed to quickly earn his young pupil's admiration and trust thanks to his gentle manner and conversational method of introducing subjects to her attention so that lessons were more like informal little chats than lectures. When he first took charge of her education in late 1768, Maria Antonia spoke terrible French and was almost illiterate when it came to reading and writing both French and German, while her general knowledge of history and geography was poor to non-existent. However, by the time she left Vienna in May 1770, matters were much improved to the extent that she now spoke fluent French, could read and write properly and was able to converse with relative confidence about the histories of both Austria and France, although there were still great gaps in her knowledge that might never be adequately filled.

While the Abbé de Vermond was taking charge of Maria Antonia's education, the ladies were scrutinising her dress and appearance. Up to this point, her everyday clothing had been relatively simple dresses of light cotton in the hottest part of summer, especially in the laid-back surroundings of Laxenburg, and silk and velvet for the rest of the year, with her grandest dresses, trimmed with cascades of lace, pearls and ribbons being reserved for the grandest court ceremonies and galas. Versailles, however, was very different and a much grander wardrobe would be required if Maria Antonia was to impress the fussy French with her *toilette*. Thus a steady stream of fashion dolls, known as Pandoras, began to make their way from the finest dressmakers in Paris to the palaces of Vienna, where their exquisite dresses were replicated for the Archduchess in different colours and patterns. A particular problem was caused by corsetry which, entirely understandably, the young girl was totally unwilling to wear tightly laced or even at all and some persuasion was required to get her to wear a restrictive whalebone corset in the French style, thus creating the elegantly slender silhouette that was required for her lavish new dresses.

Maria Antonia's hair was also a problem as, although it was very thick and a lovely strawberry blonde colour, it had been totally neglected and was often allowed to hang loose about her shoulders, drawn back from her face by a simple black hairband and was only worn up when she was likely to be seen in public, when it was pinned up, powdered and decorated with diamonds. Once again, such informality was considered totally inappropriate by Versailles standards and so Maria Theresa appealed to the Duc de Choiseul, Louis XV's First Minister of State, who was the chief supporter of the union between their two nations. Choiseul's intimidating sister Béatrix, Duchesse de Gramont eventually came to the rescue and despatched her own hairdresser, Larsenneur to the Hofburg, where he modified and updated the simple chignon style that had been favoured by the late Madame de Pompadour, raising it slightly so that it would disguise the Archduchess' high forehead and uneven hairline while the relative simplicity of the style accentuated her youth.

Rather less pleasantly, the Archduchess' crooked teeth were also deemed to require correction and in 1768, a pioneering French dentist by the name of Pierre Laveran arrived in Vienna bearing what probably appeared at first sight to be a terrifying torture device but turned out in fact to be an eighteenth-century precursor of the modern dental brace, which had been invented by Pierre Fauchard. Poor Maria Antonia was forced to wear this hideous device every day for three long months until her teeth were judged to be straight enough to pass muster. We can only imagine how much she complained about the indignity of this.

Of course, Maria Antonia's transformation was not just sartorial – there were also hours of dancing and etiquette lessons with the great dancer Noverre[1] to be endured as he taught her all of the dances that were performed at the French royal court as well as how to curb her natural instinct to run and romp and instead behave in the manner that would be expected of her at Versailles, where her every gesture and expression would be closely observed and commented upon. Already naturally very graceful, the Archduchess now also had to master the peculiarly gliding way that the ladies at the French court walked as they cautiously navigated the slippery highly polished parquet of the palace's state rooms in their high-heeled mule shoes – she would eventually become the absolute mistress of this and the swan-like serenity with which she glided, apparently effortlessly and without once lifting her feet, through the palace state rooms would be the subject of much admiration from visitors and courtiers alike.

Decked out in the very finest Parisian style with her hair tamed and exquisitely dressed and her brand new smile glittering and perfect, Maria Antonia was then paraded like a prime piece of livestock in front of the French Ambassador, with her mother losing no opportunity to point her out, pressing the unfortunate Ambassador to admire her daughter's graceful carriage and winsome appearance and dropping increasingly unsubtle hints about her suitability as a future Queen of France. To all intents and purposes, Maria Antonia now looked, moved and behaved like a French woman and could even sound a bit like one too, although she never quite lost all traces of her German accent – however, would the exacting French agree?

The favourable reports of both the beleaguered Monsieur de Durfort and the Abbé de Vermond, who was by now completely captivated by his graceful but indolent pupil, made a great impression on Louis XV and his advisors, who thought that the great efforts that had gone into schooling Maria Antonia for a French marriage did not at all count against her, proving as they did her malleability and quickness to learn and adapt to circumstances. Versailles, as they were fond of reminding themselves, was very different to Vienna and it would make life exceedingly uncomfortable for everyone should the princess prove herself unwilling to accept this.

In the summer of 1769, the French court were finally able to get a glimpse of this paragon for themselves when a portrait of the Archduchess Maria Antonia arrived at Versailles for the inspection of her prospective future family. Painted over five arduous sittings by the French royal artist Ducreux who had been despatched along with Madame de Gramont's hairdresser from Versailles for this very purpose, the portrait depicted the princess as enchantingly pretty with precisely the sort of Dresden shepherdess fairness that was most admired at Versailles at that time. Unsurprisingly, Louis XV, who had a well known penchant for blue eyed, blonde ingenues, agreed with the consensus that the Archduchess of Austria was utterly adorable for he now announced himself to be fully in favour of the match. No one seems to have cared what the prospective bridegroom, Louis Auguste thought, however. Durfort, who had been anxiously awaiting further instruction in Vienna, finally received word that the marriage was to go ahead and on 6 June 1769, no doubt to his great relief as his position in Vienna was becoming increasingly awkward, he made a formal application to Maria Theresa for her youngest daughter's hand in marriage.

Maria Theresa was utterly elated to have her dearest heart's desire delivered to her at last and excitedly assured her daughter, who was bewildered, frightened and exhilarated in equal measures by the delight that her long expected betrothal was causing, that '*if one is to consider only the greatness of your position, you are the happiest of your sisters and all princesses.*' It was easy to be excited when she was still at home and surrounded by her family and friends but whether Maria Antonia would agree that she was indeed the happiest of all her sisters once she embarked on her new life far away in France was an altogether different matter.

The royal wedding was scheduled for the following May and preparations for the forthcoming marriage soon gathered pace as both sides hammered out the terms that would make up one of the most important marriage contracts of the period, which would hopefully cement the peace between France and Austria forever. In the meantime, Maria Theresa kept an even closer watch over Maria Antonia. Perhaps feeling that she did not properly know her youngest daughter who had suddenly been propelled into the limelight, one of Maria Theresa's first actions after the betrothal was officially announced was to take Maria Antonia with her on a private pilgrimage to the basilica at Mariazell in northern Styria, where mother and daughter could take communion and pray together at a shrine devoted to the Virgin Mary. Then as now, a road trip was considered an excellent way of getting to know someone better and Maria Theresa would have been watching her daughter closely during their time together, assessing her character as she dispensed advice about her future life. For her part, Maria Antonia was no doubt delighted to be suddenly spending so much unprecedented time alone with her mother, whom she had always idolised as much as feared. She had once told Mimi that she was envious that her eldest sister saw so much of their mother and now, to her delight, she had her all to herself.

When they returned to Vienna in the autumn of 1769 it was to find preparations for the royal wedding gathering pace and while Maria Theresa turned her attention to the tiresome details of dowries, jointures, titles, contracts and precedence, Maria Antonia in her turn was enveloped in the excitement of choosing her enormous trousseau, which was to cost her mother 400,000 livres and being provided by the best dressmakers in Paris. Even more delightfully, she spent hours daydreaming about her fiancé, about whom she knew very little other than that he was tall, had blue eyes and was extremely fond of books. The latter point being probably of very little recommendation to a girl who never so much as touched a book unless she absolutely had to, but the other details probably gave her plenty to moon about as wedding fever gripped the imperial court over the winter of 1769.

Just as the public obsessed about every detail of Lady Diana Spencer's life before the royal wedding in July 1981 so too did the Austrians and French clamour for images and information about Archduchess Maria Antonia, whose wedding was already being lauded as the precursor of a period of the greatest peace and prosperity for both their nations. Prints and medals depicting either Maria Antonia on her own or with her fiancé Louis Auguste were issued in their thousands, while anyone who had ever had even the slightest bit of contact with the Archduchess could no doubt dine out on the fact for weeks on end as everyone wanted to know every single thing about her. When it was announced that Maria Antonia would be attending a masked ball in December 1769, almost four thousand people turned up, desperate to catch a glimpse of her as she did the rounds of the room on her mother's arm, bowing gracefully to the other dignitaries and occasionally dancing with one of her brothers.

Maria Antonia handled being suddenly thrust into the spotlight with enormous aplomb and was much complimented for her confident poise and charming manners, even while being rudely stared at by hundreds of people. To a casual observer it must have seemed as though she was enjoying the fact that the spotlight was now very firmly fixed upon her after a lifetime spent as the youngest and least known of the imperial Archduchesses – however, behind the scenes she was riddled with anxiety, apprehension and, above all, the terrible fear of disappointing her mother. Although her lessons with Abbé de Vermond continued, she was now also expected to participate in the social life of the court and began attending the twice weekly card parties that were held in her mother's apartments, where her brothers taught her how to play cards and gamble, an essential skill at the royal courts where everyone was expected to join the candlelit card tables in the evening and indulge in a little good-humoured gambling for relatively small stakes. In time the monotony of adult court life would wear Maria Antonia down but at first, it was extraordinarily thrilling to be allowed to stay up late with her family and the other courtiers, to make small bets on the turn of a card with money out of her own special velvet gambling purse and to be praised and admired by all – heady stuff for a girl who had until recently rarely been seen in public.

Of course, it wouldn't be a Habsburg celebration without some sort of terrible tragedy occurring and this duly came to pass in January 1770 when Maria Antonia's beloved little niece Maria Theresa, who was the only child of her brother Joseph and his wife Isabella of Parma, died. The little girl was just seven years old and as the youngest royal child at the imperial court was the pampered pet of her grandmother, father and the various aunts and uncles still living at home. Joseph was completely devastated by her death as he had regarded her as his last bond with her beloved mother, while for her part Maria Antonia too was very much distressed as she had loved to play with her niece.

Shortly after the little girl's extremely sad funeral, another more intimate but equally momentous event occurred when Maria Antonia woke up on 7 February with the ominous cramps that signified the beginning of her first period. An important occasion in any girl's life, this was of even more enormous significance when that girl was destined to become Queen of France and Maria Theresa lost no time in communicating the happy news to Louis XV, keen to assure him that her daughter enjoyed normal fertility and would presumably have no trouble providing his grandson with a whole bevvy of fine, healthy children.

Although nowadays the subject of menstruation, rightly or wrongly, is considered a private one that might perhaps only be discussed with a close group of friends, the periods of a Dauphine of France were very much public property and would be openly talked about by literally everyone. Living in such close quarters at Versailles, surrounded at all times by attendants and servants and having barely a moment to themselves, the basic bodily functions of the royal family were considered fair game and open to open scrutiny. It was a situation that Maria Antonia, in particular, could never quite reconcile herself to and she was no doubt mortified by the gleeful chatter about her menses, although she never failed to dutifully inform her mother of the arrival of 'Générale Krottendorf', as the ladies of her family referred to their periods. Not much is known about the unfortunate Générale who lent her name in such a way, but it must be assumed that she was not, after the first visit at least, considered the most welcome of guests. When the lady died at the end of 1779, Maria Theresa would write to her daughter, who was trying to have another baby at the time, that '*the Générale Krottendorf has just died. I hope that she will stop visiting you…*'

Maria Antonia was due to leave Vienna on the morning of 21 April and the rest of the month passed in a whirl of glorious celebrations and last-minute preparations for her departure. As with any other wedding then and now, there were all the usual last-minute hitches, panics and small triumphs, all of which were massively amplified by the international significance of the whole event. Maria Theresa, now faced with the prospect of seeing her youngest daughter, to whom she had become extremely close in recent months, leave for good now became rather flustered by the prospect and decided to move the girl into her own rooms for the last few weeks of her time at home so that she could spend as much time as possible with her before she left.

This signal honour, which had been accorded to none of her sisters, must have been both an incredible treat and an awful torture for poor Maria Antonia, who was thrilled to be so close to her mother and to have the comfort of her reassuring presence at such an emotional time, but also exhausted by the Empress' punishing routine which she was now expected to share – up at 4 am every morning and then late to bed in a bracingly cold room with all the windows open, as was Maria Theresa's custom. There were also lengthy and often mortifying lectures to be endured about queenship, behaviour, religion and, most embarrassingly of all to a young girl of just fourteen, married life. The Empress drew on the example of her own happy and fruitful marriage in order to embellish her advice and homilies, wilfully forgetting of course that she had condemned all but one of her children to loveless marriages of state, which were in no way comparable to the close and intimate relationship that she had enjoyed with her own husband, whom she had married for love.

Maria Antonia must have felt hideously awkward as she shivered in her little camp bed in the gloom of her mother's opulent but freezing cold bed-chamber, which had been hung with black velvet since the death of her husband, and listened to Maria Theresa's voice rambling on about the delights of the marriage bed. However, it was fortunate for her that she didn't know just yet quite how inappropriate and sadly inadequate her mother's well-meaning advice about sex and marital relations actually was. Less embarrassingly, Maria Antonia also began to have weekly private audiences with her eldest brother Joseph, who did his best to instil some political understanding in his flighty little sister. As Maria Antonia had always rather hero-worshipped Joseph, she actually, probably to everyone's surprise, enjoyed these meetings enormously, especially as he followed Abbé de Vermond's lead and structured them as cosy little chats rather than more intimidating lessons, hoping by this measure to at least vaguely capture her capricious interest. It's doubtful that Maria Antonia proved herself a satisfactory pupil to Joseph but she took away enough information to make him feel at least relatively confident that she wouldn't show herself up at Versailles and could be relied upon to work for Austrian interests after her marriage.

The days before Maria Antonia's departure were marked with a series of splendid court entertainments, including a gala hosted by her mother on 16 April when she was finally presented with two portraits of her fiancé Louis Auguste. Delighted to finally set eyes on her future husband, she asked to have one placed by her bed where she could see it at all times and immediately fastened the other, a miniature surrounded with diamonds, to the front of her dress. Although the French prince was not quite the handsome prince of her daydreams and most fervent imaginings, he did at least look kind, which counted for a great deal more if the veiled hints of marital disappointment and discord in the letters of her sisters Maria Amalia and Maria Carolina were anything to go by. If she no longer sighed over her prince then at least she could look at his likeness and feel reasonably reassured that she was not being sent to a monster.

The next day, Maria Antonia formally renounced all of her rights to both her mother's imperial lands and also the territories formerly owned by her father in Lorraine. After which her brother hosted an enormous supper party for 1,500 guests at the Belvedere palace, where Maria Antonia took the place of honour during the feast and then led the dancing at the masked ball afterwards, which was attended by a further six hundred people, the very crème de la crème of Viennese society. The ball went on until seven in the morning with the guests fuelled by a sumptuous supper and copious amounts of alcohol as well as lemonade, hot chocolate and coffee. The Archduchess Maria Antonia, thrilled and excited by all of this attention, danced until three in the morning when she finally allowed herself to be whisked away to her little bed in her mother's chilly room in the Hofburg.

The following evening there was another enormous party, this time hosted by the French Ambassador, Monsieur de Durfort, at the Liechtenstein Palace, where again the Archduchess danced alongside several hundred guests until well past midnight, after enjoying a splendid firework display accompanied by Turkish music. It was Maria Antonia's last night as an unmarried Archduchess of Austria and as she looked around at the other guests, which included people that she had known her whole life, she must have felt a tinge of sadness at the prospect of leaving them all behind, while they in turn were sorry to be losing such an enchanting addition to the Austrian court before they had a chance to get to know her.

The proxy wedding of Maria Antonia and the absent Dauphin Louis Auguste, so hotly anticipated by everyone, finally took place at six o clock on the evening of 19 April in the church of the Augustine Friars, where her parents and sisters had been married. Her brother Archduke Ferdinand yet again stood in as proxy bridegroom, but this time it was not her elder brother Joseph but, in a token of extreme honour, the Empress herself who led the blushing bride, dressed in a gorgeously opulent gown of silver brocade and lace, up the aisle past the entire imperial court to where the Papal Nuncio, Monsignor Visconti was waiting to officiate. After the wedding ceremony, Maria Antonia, now officially Dauphine of France and henceforth to be known by the French form of her name: Marie Antoinette, was escorted back to the Hofburg for a splendid wedding banquet, where once again she took the position of honour although sadly with her brothers rather than her groom at her side. Did she wonder how the Dauphin Louis August was feeling far away in Versailles, knowing he was now officially husband to a girl he had never met? Probably not – at just fourteen and every bit as silly, selfish and shallow as any other girl of her age, Marie Antoinette (ironically perhaps for someone who has been the subject of so many novels written in the first person) was almost certainly not given to such moments of introspection and if her mind did indeed wander to the as yet unknown boy sitting in his grand apartments at Versailles, she probably didn't dwell on him all that much.

Marie Antoinette departed Schönbrunn forever early in the morning of 21 April and like her sisters before her, was expected to say her last farewell to her mother, whom she knew that she might never see again, in front of the entire court, who had gathered together before the great palace to see her off. The departures of her sisters Maria Amalia and Maria Carolina had been hideous occasions, punctuated by a great deal of indecorous sobbing and fuss. To the relief of everyone, however, Marie Antoinette behaved extremely well and did her best to hide her nervous dread as she embraced each of her family in turn before falling to her knees before her mother for a final blessing. It was an emotional moment for them both and even Maria Theresa could not restrain her tears as she hugged her daughter one last time, saying, 'Farewell, my dearest child, a great distance will separate us' and extolling her to 'do so much good to the French people that they will say that I have sent them an angel.' Her mother's weeping set Marie Antoinette off as well and they clung together sobbing until finally Archduke Ferdinand picked his sister up in his arms and deposited her in the luxurious and beautifully decorated carriage, more like a gorgeous jewellery box than a vehicle, that had been sent from France to collect her. As the carriage made its way down the avenue at Schönbrunn, the golden flowers decorating its roof waving gracefully as it went, the little Dauphine was seen to be hanging half out of the open window, sobbing and waving to her family before finally her head popped back inside and she was gone for good.

No detail of Marie Antoinette's journey to France had been overlooked, with special attention being paid to the furnishings of her bed-chambers at her numerous stops along the way. In keeping with her newly exalted station, it was decreed that all furnishings, including her commode should be covered with imperial red and gold and that her curtains should be made from gorgeous crimson taffeta. Such magnificence was not at all to Marie Antoinette's taste, which tended more towards light pastels and the pretty muted hues of sugared almonds and spring flowers, but for this most important journey, perhaps the most significant of her life, it was accepted that proper attention must be paid to her status.

Also of great importance was the huge entourage that was to accompany the Dauphine to the French border and which would amount to a travelling court in its own right, designed to ensure that the princess had every conceivable comfort during her long journey and also render all who saw it awestruck by the might and magnificence of the imperial court. To this end, fifty-seven coaches were put into service to carry all of the ladies in waiting, officials, courtiers, doctors, cooks and dressmakers considered necessary for such a great undertaking, while twenty thousand horses were commissioned to ensure that there were enough available for each stage of her long journey. To further ensure the smoothness of the journey, orders were given in October 1769 to completely repair all of the roads that Marie Antoinette was to travel over so that not a single pothole would disturb the tranquillity of her voyage as she played cards and gossiped with her dear friend, Princess Louise of Hesse-Darmstadt, who had been selected to accompany her to the border.

The first stage of Marie Antoinette's journey was a mercifully short one and involved an overnight stay at the grand monastery at Melk, where she was reunited with her brother, Joseph, who did his best to cheer her up while at the same time heavily impressing upon her that she ought to be grateful for the position that she had found herself in, albeit thanks to a series of family tragedies and disasters. For her part, Marie Antoinette was too exhausted and emotionally wrung out after the ordeal of having to say goodbye to her mother to really pay much attention and was observed to look morose and bored at the obligatory after-dinner entertainment: an opera performed by the monastery's pupils.

Her journey to the French border continued the next day and would cover several thousand miles, taking two and a half weeks to accomplish. This arduous journey, which was spent cooped up in the confined splendour of the carriage, would have tested the patience of even the most seasoned eighteenth-century traveller and must have seemed like an interminable torture to a young girl used to spending her days rushing about the gardens of Schönbrunn, practising her dancing for hours on end or playing with her dogs in the splendid, echoing galleries. Her chief companion during the journey was the fifty-one-year-old Princess Paar[2], one of her mother's dearest friends, who was entrusted with the care of the Dauphine until she was handed over to the French. However, this much older lady was no substitute for the mother that Marie Antoinette had left behind in Vienna, whose parting gift had been a small gold watch, which the Archduchess now kept on her person at all times and would be one of her most precious possessions for the rest of her life.

This long and extremely tiring journey, which was the most that Marie Antoinette would ever see of her own native country, was enlivened with several stops along the way so that the Dauphine and her party could stretch their legs and be splendidly feted by the inhabitants of the various towns that they passed through, who pulled out all the stops and spared no expense in order to show their great respect for this scion of the Habsburg dynasty. There were also pleasant opportunities for Marie Antoinette to meet with relations from both sides of her family, such as her mother's cousin Maximilian III Joseph, Elector of Bavaria, who treated her to a sumptuous couple of days at the exquisite Nymphenburg Palace in Munich, where she was housed in the Amalienburg Pavilion, a delightful rococo masterpiece in the grounds that had been built for her host's mother, Maria Amalia of Austria[3], who had been the Empress' first cousin. Later, she would also spend some time with her father's sister Anne Charlotte of Lorraine, the Abbess of Remiremont and Mons, who was actually travelling in the opposite direction on her way to visit her sister-in-law Maria Theresa in Vienna. Anne Charlotte would have been able to offer her niece some interesting if perhaps outdated insights about the French court as her mother, Élisabeth Charlotte d'Orléans, had been the niece of Louis XIV and she herself had been taken to France in the autumn of 1722 in order to attend the coronation of her cousin, Louis XV although alas her mother's subsequent scheming to secure her future by marrying her to Louis and making her Queen of France came to nothing.

Marie Antoinette's last night on German soil was spent at Schüttern Abbey on the edge of the Black Forest on 6 May. A few days earlier, she had had the great joy of receiving a letter from her mother, which had been written by the Empress after her departure from Schönbrunn and followed her across Germany until it finally made it into her hands. Already desperately homesick and feeling extremely apprehensive about what lay ahead, Marie Antoinette treasured this last link with her formidable mother even if she was perhaps disappointed by the fact that the letter was not so much a reminder of her mother's love and concern for her as a lengthy list of advice and instructions entitled '*Regulation to Read Every Month*', which chillingly reminded the little Dauphine, who was already trembling at the thought of what the next few days would bring that '*All eyes will be fixed upon you.*'

Chapter 3

The Bride
1770

'All eyes will be fixed upon you.'

All of the grand celebrations and tense discussions about precedence had centred on this one moment, when Marie Antoinette would formally take leave of her own country and step across the border to France to begin her new life as Dauphine and wife of the future King. A highly important ceremonial event, it had been the focus of many fraught hours of negotiation as both sides deliberated the proper etiquette for such a momentous occasion, keen that there should be no loss of dignity on either side and that proper and equal honour should be paid to both Austria and France.

Whereas an ordinary bride would probably find herself being carried over the threshold of her new home by an enthusiastic bridegroom, the arrival of a new Dauphine required rather more ceremony and although both her mother and Louis XV had been extremely caught up in discussions about how best to preserve their *own* dignity, they seem to have mostly disregarded that of Marie Antoinette, the fourteen-year-old pawn in their machinations, who was now required to literally strip herself of every link to her homeland before being permitted to step across to France.

The grand handover took place on an island in the middle of the Rhine, on exactly the same spot where the Dauphin Louis Auguste's mother Maria Josepha of Saxony had been ceremoniously handed over to the French over twenty years earlier. The building used on that auspicious occasion had unfortunately tumbled down during the intervening years and so a new wooden pavilion was constructed in its place. Designed to look like a French château, it was furnished with five rooms – the two Austrian chambers that Marie Antoinette would enter, the grande *salle de rémise* in the centre where the official handover would take place and then two French chambers on the other side where she would eventually emerge as the fully-fledged Dauphine of France. This charming edifice was furnished with suitably splendid furniture and tapestries, one of which shocked observant onlookers by depicting the rather inauspicious marriage of Jason and Medea, which ended in a mess of recrimination and infanticide. It's unlikely however that Marie Antoinette, who never opened a book unless she could help it and had endured an extremely patchy Classical education, would have recognised the story on the tapestry even if she hadn't been entirely preoccupied with the distressing necessity of saying goodbye to the friends that had accompanied her from Vienna.

Before it was time to say goodbye, however, Marie Antoinette was required to be formally stripped of everything that linked her to her former life in Austria, specifically her clothes and accessories. It didn't matter that everything she wore had been made for her by the finest Parisian dressmakers, it still had to come off and everything from her silk gown to her hated corset to her fine cotton shift was removed, leaving the Dauphine shivering and naked in the middle of the room while sounds of thunder and approaching rain emanated ominously from the Black Forest. She was then quickly dressed again in a splendid new cloth of gold dress, part of the expensive trousseau that her mother had ordered for her from Paris while her hair was re-powdered and face and cheeks painted with the heavy cosmetics worn at the French court, an entirely unnecessary garnish for a fresh-faced young girl whose complexion was universally praised as '*literally blending lilies and roses*'. However, at Versailles all the ladies wore a thick layer of white paint on their faces and sported comical little circles of pink rouge high on their cheeks and so Marie Antoinette, who had been warned by her mother to do everything in her power to fit in with her new court, duly followed suit.

Marie Antoinette's original 'Austrian' outfit was destined to be parcelled out between her ladies in waiting, who regarded gaining possession of the Dauphine's hand-me-down clothes as one of the juiciest perquisites of their job. One can't help but hope that someone had the sense to plan ahead and choose Marie Antoinette's least favourite new gown for the occasion so she would suffer no qualms when she later saw it being worn around Versailles by one of her new ladies.

Fully transformed into a proper *femme Française*, the little Dauphine, who was suffering from a cold caught during her long journey, which had often involved rather inadequate accommodation, was then escorted into the central *salle de rêmise* where she was now expected to say her goodbyes to her Austrian companions before stepping across to the other side of a long table covered with red velvet, which represented the border between France and Austria. Here, she was introduced to her new French attendants, most of whom were mature ladies who had previously been in the household of Queen Marie Leszczynska of France and had therefore been without an official court function since her death in June 1768. Chief amongst them was the Comtesse de Noailles[1], who was to be Marie Antoinette's *dame d'honneur* and a figure of great importance during her early years at Versailles.

Madame de Noailles was a quintessentially stiffly upright, etiquette fixated and glacially snobbish denizen of Versailles, a pretentious and rather humourless woman utterly obsessed with precedence and thanks to her arrogant and condescending manner in no way suited to attract the affection and confidences of a candid and warm-hearted young girl like Marie Antoinette. However, to the latter, now forcibly separated from the last friendly faces of home, shivering with cold and still feeling pinpricks of humiliation as a result of being stripped of her clothes in front of a not wholly sympathetic crowd of witnesses, the much older Madame de Noailles, who was forty-one, must have seemed like an oasis of comfort in the midst of so much misery. Emotionally overwhelmed by the situation that she had found herself in, exhausted by all the long weeks of travelling and desperate for a scrap of human kindness, Marie Antoinette burst into tears, threw herself at Madame de Noailles and gave her a spontaneous hug, no doubt hoping that here was the substitute mother that she had doubtless been hoping to find in France. Instead, there was a gasp of dismay and probably some stifled giggles too from the onlookers as the haughty Comtesse stiffly disengaged herself from the young Dauphine, leaving her in no doubt that she had committed a terrible *faux pas*. In some situations it is naturally considered to be something of an honour to be hugged so publicly by royalty but this was neither the time nor the place and the frosty Comtesse made it clear that she was horrified by such a social solecism, which had the effect of making the already unhappy Marie Antoinette feel even more awkward and miserable. Nonetheless, she managed to make a graceful apology: 'Forgive me, Madame, for the tears that I have just shed for my family and my homeland. From this day forward, I shall never again forget that I am a Frenchwoman.'

Amongst the other ladies in waiting who had travelled to meet their new mistress at the border, there was also her *dame d'atours*, mistress of robes, the Duchesse de Villars[2], who was in her mid-sixties, as well as the fifty-four-year-old Marquise de Tonnerre-Breteuil[3], who must both have seemed very old to the young Dauphine. Fortunately, there were a few younger and less intimidating faces in the throng – for instance, the Duchesse de Cossé-Brissac[4], who was in her late twenties, the thirty-one-year-old Marquise de Tavannes[5], as well as the twenty-five-year-old Marquise de Duras[6], who was the daughter of Madame de Noailles and said to be one of the cleverest ladies at court due to her intellectual interests, and the twenty-two-year-old Marie-Jeanne de Talleyrand-Périgord, Comtesse de Mailly-Haucourt[7], whose mother had been one of Marie Leszczynska's favourite ladies in waiting. Madame de Mailly-Haucourt was extremely popular at Versailles where, like most of the extensive Talleyrand clan she was known for her wit and good nature and she soon became very friendly with the young Marie Antoinette, who was badly in need of friendly faces during her first puzzling weeks at Versailles. It's likely that if the unfortunate Marie Antoinette had hugged the kindly Madame de Mailly-Haucourt instead of the fearsome Madame de Noailles, then she might have received a warmer and far more sympathetic response.

Also present to greet the new arrival was the very pretty twenty-six-year-old Marie-Paule-Angelique d'Albert de Luynes, Duchesse de Picquigny[8], another former lady in waiting of the dead Queen who had been transferred to the service of the new Dauphine. Quiet, refined and rather shy, Madame de Picquigny was an object of interest and some mild ridicule at Versailles thanks to it being well known that her marriage to Monsieur le Duc, an austere and rather remote young man who had once been betrothed to the daughter of Madame de Pompadour and whose mother was famously promiscuous, had never been consummated, a fact signalled by her habit of never wearing anything other than virginal white.

As soon as the all-important introductions were over, it was time to clamber back on board her splendid coach, this time with the thin-lipped and clearly disapproving Madame de Noailles and the Duchesse de Villars for company rather than the cheerful and comforting Princess Paar, and make the journey to Strasbourg for her first official welcome to France. Marie Antoinette stared apprehensively out of her rain-splattered carriage windows at the countryside, her mother's watch, which she had somehow managed to keep out of the hands of the ladies as they removed all of her Austrian possessions, hidden about her person. The only relief must have been the fact that it was against etiquette for anyone to directly address a member of the royal family unless they had already been spoken to and so she didn't have to talk to the disagreeable Madame de Noailles, who sat silently opposite her, unless she absolutely wanted to.

Nonetheless, by the time they arrived in Strasbourg, a charming border town which must have seemed reassuring Germanic to Marie Antoinette's eyes, equanimity was clearly restored and she was seen to chat quite affably with her ladies as she settled into enjoying her first impressions of France. In Strasbourg, the smiling Dauphine was greeted by cheers, shouts of welcome and crowds of children dressed up as shepherds and shepherdesses or in the picturesque local costume, who showered her with flowers, which we are assured that she received and held as '*the goddess Flora herself might have done*'. The Franco-Austrian alliance may have been the cause of some suspicious raised eyebrows and apprehension closer to Paris but here on the German border, where for centuries the people had regularly found themselves caught in the midst of conflict between the two great nations, it was greeted with tremendous joy. The cheers and acclamations only increased when Marie Antoinette stopped an official as he began to make a speech of welcome in German, saying, 'Don't speak to me in German. From now on I want to hear no language but French.' Unschooled and, on occasion, gauche though she may still have appeared to the critical French courtiers, it nonetheless seemed to everyone that the little princess had a hitherto unsuspected ability to say just the right thing when the occasion called for it.

That evening, Strasbourg's magnificent cathedral, built from local sandstone which took on a glorious rose pink hue at sunset, was lit up and the great and good of the city filed silently past the new Dauphine as for the first time she took part in the '*Le Grand Couvert*', which involved dining in solitary splendour in front of a crowd of gawking onlookers. Never a hearty eater at the best of times and prone to going pink about the ears when stared at, Marie Antoinette nonetheless handled this very well and pleased everyone with her graceful manners and appearance of not appearing not notice that she was being watched like an animal at the zoo. Eating in public would always be a torture to her though and she would never manage to emulate the famous aplomb of her grandfather-in-law Louis XV, who liked to perform tricks like smoothly using his knife to swipe the top off his boiled egg to please the crowds that had gathered to watch him eat.

After supper, there was a performance at the theatre to sit through, followed by a ball, where she was introduced to all the local nobility and danced until past midnight before falling into her bed in the splendid episcopal palace of Cardinal de Rohan, where beneath her windows there was a floating garden created by a flotilla of illuminated boats, all heaped with sweet smelling flowers. In the morning she went to Mass in the splendid cathedral, yawning behind her hand as the Cardinal's handsome and extremely ambitious nephew Prince Louis de Rohan[9] gave a speech welcoming the Dauphine and fulsomely praising her mother, whom he described as 'the admiration of Europe'. Perhaps more worthy of admiration than the dread Empress, although Marie Antoinette may well have disagreed, was Strasbourg Cathedral itself, which at the time was the tallest manmade structure in the world – a title that it held for an astonishing 227 years until 1874.

After this it was time to say goodbye to Strasbourg and hop back in the gorgeous carriage, which was more window than wall so that she might be better seen by the populace, for the journey to the city of Nancy, where her father Emperor Francis had been born in 1708. Marie Antoinette had been especially looking forward to this leg of her trip as it was a unique opportunity to see the lands of the Lorraine family, which her father had been so unwilling to give up as a condition of his marriage to her mother. Although Marie Antoinette had been raised to take pride in her Austrian background, she had also been encouraged to feel a connection to her Lorraine roots as well and visiting Nancy, where she was to lodge in the ducal palace where her father had been born, would no doubt have been of great comfort to her at this time. This visit to Nancy would also have served as a reminder of Marie Antoinette's own French heritage as her grandmother, Élisabeth Charlotte d'Orléans had been the only daughter of Philippe d'Orléans and had furthermore been born near Paris at the Château de Saint Cloud, which Marie Antoinette would later own. Due to the vast and complex web of intermarriage that characterised European royalty at the time, it's not really surprising that Marie Antoinette and her new husband Louis Auguste were cousins due to both being descended from Philippe, known to history as 'Monsieur', the controversial younger brother and only sibling of Louis XIV. Philippe was a complex character, famed for his liking for pretty young men and passion for fashion and the more byzantine complexities of court etiquette as well as his bravery in battle.

Perhaps fittingly, Louis Auguste was the great great-great grandson of Philippe and his flighty, pretty, delicate first wife, Princess Henrietta Anne of England, youngest daughter of the troubled Charles I, with whom Louis Auguste would alas, turn out to have more than one thing in common. Marie Antoinette, on the other hand, was the great grand-daughter of Monsieur and his second wife, the sensible, forthright and rather tomboyish Protestant princess Elizabeth Charlotte (known as Liselotte), who was the grand-daughter of Elizabeth of Bohemia, daughter of James I and so, like Philippe's unfortunate first wife Henrietta Anne, yet another sprig from the Stuart family tree. However, while the Stuarts, with the possible exception of James II, tended to have a certain glamorous charisma, they were also famously unlucky – with perhaps the most striking example of this being their enigmatic common ancestress Mary, Queen of Scots, who had once briefly been Queen of France. Louis Auguste, who loved his history and was a big fan of Hume's *History of England*, was fascinated by his Stuart, Tudor and Plantagenet ancestors and while Marie Antoinette had no interest in the past, she might still have been just a little bit intrigued by the glamorous and romantic personages of Mary Stuart and her granddaughter, the Winter Queen of Bohemia, both of whom were still being discussed and written about in the late eighteenth century.

It was her immediate ancestors, however, that Marie Antoinette was more interested in as she met her father's relatives in Nancy, earning herself a sharp reprimand from Madame de Noailles, whom she already heartily detested, for showing them too much familiarity. Lighthearted, carefree and informal in a way that must have brought to mind her own similarly pleasant father, she very much enjoyed spending time with them in surroundings that would have instantly recalled to mind Francis' stories about his youth and all too brief time as Duke of Lorraine. Spared the hideous ordeal of keeping vigil alongside her Habsburg ancestors in the imperial crypt of the Capuchin church in Vienna, Marie Antoinette took pleasure in praying at the tombs of her Lorraine ancestors in the church of Saint François des Cordeliers, which served as a necropolis for the Ducal family of Lorraine and included the tomb of her grandmother Elisabeth Charlotte d'Orléans as well as the wonderful Ligier Richier recumbent effigy of Philippa of Guelders, formidable great grandmother of Mary Queen of Scots. Her father Francis had been laid to rest in the imperial crypt in Vienna, there to await the eventual entombment of her mother beside him, but Marie Antoinette would felt his comforting presence everywhere around her in Nancy and it must have been a tremendous wrench to have to leave and continue with her journey west towards Compiègne, where she was to have her first meeting with her new husband Louis Auguste and, perhaps more importantly, his grandfather Louis XV.

What must Marie Antoinette have felt as her glorious carriage drew ever closer to the appointed meeting place in the heart of the royal hunting forest of Compiègne? Her new ladies in waiting had been acquainted with the Dauphin for many years, some of them had even known him all his life – did she ask them what he was really like and did they raise their eyebrows and shake their heads at each other behind her head? To Maria Theresa, the personality of the French prince had been of as little importance as the identity of the precise Archduchess to be sent to marry him had been to his grandfather and Marie Antoinette, raised to put her absolute trust in the superior judgement of her mother, had probably not wondered too much about it either. However, as her carriage sped along the muddy forest tracks and her ladies fussed about her, primping her in preparation for this all-important meeting, the new Dauphine must have felt extremely apprehensive about the boy who was currently just as nervously waiting for her in the forest clearing.

When the carriage pulled up, the Duc de Choiseul, Chief Minister of France, who had been the chief architect of her marriage, was waiting to greet her. 'I shall never forget that you are responsible for my good fortune,' Marie Antoinette told him with a charming smile. 'Madame, the good fortune is that of France,' the gallant Duc replied with a graceful bow before leading her to where the royal party were descending from their carriage. The meeting had been originally envisaged as an intimate family affair, but word had naturally sped with the result that there were many witnesses to the touching scene that followed as the Dauphine, impatient to meet her new family left the Duc de Choiseul and ran lightly forward before sinking into an exquisite and extremely well-schooled curtsey before the King, a still handsome man with the bold black eyes of his Medici ancestors and the Roman nose and refined manners of his great grandfather Louis XIV, from whom he had inherited the throne at the age of just five.

King Louis was a complex man. Orphaned in infancy, he was exceedingly reserved almost to the point of shyness and, although charmingly urbane and never anything less than beautifully polite on the surface, actually quite hard to get to know – as his exquisite but now sadly recently departed mistress Madame de Pompadour[10] had often had cause to bemoan. He was completely obsessed with maintaining his privacy, to this end building up a warren of small rooms beneath the eaves of Versailles where he could retreat and be perfectly alone with his latest mistress and closest friends. His passions were private but it was well known that besides hunting, which was perhaps his most favourite pursuit, he was also fascinated by astronomy, loved to read and had amassed an enormous collection of several thousand books in his private library. He also enjoyed writing and kept up an enormous correspondence with several members of his scattered family, in particular his grandson and *protegé* the Duke of Parma, who was the husband of Marie Antoinette's sister Maria Amalia. Another passion, perhaps surprisingly, was cookery, which prompted him at the age of sixteen to take lessons from a chef in a specially constructed kitchen at Versailles, where he learned to make perfect omelettes while wearing one of twelve specially commissioned aprons, each one exquisitely embroidered with the double V of Versailles.

Always a discerning connoisseur of female beauty, the sixty-year-old Louis XV was completely charmed by his grandson's young wife, who had the pink and white complexion, huge blue eyes and bouncing strawberry blonde hair of the nymphs in one of his favourite Boucher paintings and was not really all that dissimilar in type to the young girls, not much older than she was, who populated the private brothels he frequented in the town of Versailles. Knowing this, there was no doubt a great deal of discreet nudging and winking going on from the courtiers as they watched the wily old King greet his new granddaughter, kiss her rouged cheeks and look her over in the French style: swiftly, from head to toe and back again before he gracefully motioned for his grandson, her husband, to step forward and be introduced.

If the fifteen-year-old Dauphin bore little resemblance to the miniature portrait that Marie Antoinette had received with such excitement only a month earlier, she gave no sign as she politely curtseyed and replied to his mumbled greeting then offered her cheek for an unenthusiastic kiss, while the Dauphin's libertine grandfather watched in sad resignation and almost certainly wished that it was he who was to be the bridegroom instead. Although not a monstrous spectacle by any means, Louis Auguste was overweight with heavy dark eyebrows, his grandfather's prominent Bourbon nose and an awkward manner. Phlegmatic by nature and schooled since early childhood to hide his emotions, he also gave no sign of his feelings about his new wife, which left Marie Antoinette, used to flowery praise and admiration wherever she went, feeling doubtful and somewhat bewildered.

Louis Auguste was the fourth child and second surviving son of Louis XV's eldest son, the Dauphin Louis of France[11] and his second wife Maria Josepha of Saxony[12], who was affectionately known as 'Pépa'. The royal couple had been considered unusual at Versailles for their domestic harmony and frank and open adoration of each other in a court where it was considered bad form to be openly affectionate towards one's spouse. The Dauphin was a complicated character: he wrote to a friend that his soul was '*always gay*' and indeed there was a liveliness and cheerfulness about him that made his company much sought after. However, he had also inherited the morbid nature of his parents Louis XV and his devout Polish wife Marie Leszczynska and was obsessed with death and dying, much as his cousin Isabella of Parma had been during her time in Vienna. His mother kept the skull of the celebrated seventeenth-century courtesan Ninon de L'Enclos[13] on her desk, garlanded with flowers and grinning toothily upon a velvet cushion. She called it '*Ma chère mignonne*'.

In the early days of their marriage, the young Saxony princess Maria Josepha had been horrified to witness her new husband and his sisters spending evenings dressed in black and walking slowly around a dim candlelit room murmuring, 'I am dead, I am dead, I am dead' in a continuation of a favourite game from childhood. It all seemed very weird and unacceptably morbid to a young princess who adored dancing, laughter, being outdoors, having fun and celebrating life. It didn't help matters that the young Dauphin had been married once before, to the Infanta Maria Teresa Rafaela of Spain[14], who was four years his senior. The court had giggled behind their spangled and painted fans at the young bride's plain face and unfashionable red hair, but the Dauphin had fallen immediately and violently in love with her and was thrilled when she became pregnant. '*I can hardly believe that I am so soon to be a father!*' he wrote to a friend, his delight echoing that of every young father throughout the centuries.

In July 1746, at the age of twenty, Maria Teresa gave birth to a daughter Marie-Thérèse and died four days later. Her young husband, just sixteen years old at this time, was genuinely devastated with courtiers likening his grief to that of '*an inconsolable child*', which in many ways he was. The little princess, his only link with his deceased love, was to live for just two years and would die in April 1748 after being given an emetic in an attempt to alleviate the pain of teething.

No one knew quite what to expect when the Dauphin, who had made it quite clear that he had no wish to ever take another wife, was forced to marry Maria Josepha less than a year later in February 1747, and she must have been mortified when on their wedding night he collapsed in tears into her arms and sobbed about his dead wife, which must have been somewhat awkward to say the least. The marriage seemed doomed to failure until the Dauphin caught smallpox and his wife insisted on nursing him back to health herself. It is said that she took such great care of him that a short-sighted doctor, unused to the court and therefore unable to recognise Maria Josepha, said to the Dauphin, 'You have an excellent little nurse there. Never get rid of her.' The Dauphin made a full recovery and filled with gratitude, he fell in love at last with his wife.

The young couple consequently enjoyed a blissful life together, almost a second honeymoon in fact, and were to be seen at their devotions together in the Versailles chapel every morning, before taking the air together on the terrace by the Orangerie. They shared exactly the same taste for music, reading and gardening and their life together was wholesome and busy. The Dauphin was a talented musician and played the violin, organ and spinet as well as singing in a very fine baritone. He was also a talented actor, capable of reducing an audience to fits of uncontrollable laughter with his comedic roles.

Their lives were not just devoted to wholesome pleasures, however. Both were keen philanthropists, who loved to assist the needy. They instructed their children's tutors that the princes and princesses should be taken to the houses of the poor and needy of Versailles so that they could see for themselves how their grandfather's less fortunate subjects lived. '*They must learn to weep. A prince who has never shed any tears cannot be good*,' the Dauphin explained. He also took his sons to view the baptismal register of the parish of Versailles, where their names were written alongside those of more humble infants. 'Look, my children, look at your names written after the name of a pauper. The only thing that can establish any difference between you is virtue,' he said. One can imagine the effect of all this on his sensitive second son, the young Louis Auguste.

When Louis Auguste was born in the Dauphine's bed-chamber on the ground floor of Versailles in the boiling hot summer of 1754, the royal nursery at the palace was already home to Marie Zéphyrine, who was born in August 1750 and Louis Joseph, who was born in September 1751. Another son, Xavier, had recently died in February 1754 at the age of six months. Typically, Maria Josepha was determined not to make a fuss when she went into labour at around four in the morning and, believing she simply had colic, had got up and spent the next few hours alone before waking her husband who in his turn alerted the servants. Their new son was born at quarter to seven and immediately passed into the care of Madame de Marsan[15], who was already governess to his elder brother the Duc de Bourgogne and a most imposing presence at court where she was one of the few granted the rare distinction of being allowed to sit in an actual chair in the presence of royalty and also use an oval silver chamber pot instead of the usual round one.

The baby's grandfather was hunting at his nearby estate at Choisy when the news arrived that his daughter-in-law had delivered a child and he immediately rushed back to Versailles to inspect the baby. There had been some concerns about the healthiness of the Dauphine's progeny as her three earlier babies had all appeared to inherit her own rather sickly constitution, however, this new baby boy delighted everyone by being gloriously plump, healthy and loud. According to court protocol, he was immediately baptised, presented with a tiny blue watered silk sash of the Order of the Holy Spirit and given the title of Duc de Berry which would be publicly used instead of a Christian name for several years – it was the custom at the time for royal sons to only be known by their titles (which could be recycled if they died in infancy) until they were officially christened with their actual names later on.

The first six years of Louis Auguste's childhood, which passed under the strict but loving care of Madame de Marsan, were relatively normal. There was all of the usual concern about weaning, teething and learning to walk as well as the occasional small childhood illnesses, of which Louis Auguste remained mercifully virtually untouched. Naturally, any sign of illness was regarded with suspicion lest it turn out to be the dreaded smallpox but fortunately, Louis Auguste and his siblings managed to avoid that most feared and hated of eighteenth-century diseases. During the late 1750s, the French succession must have seemed not just secure but also in exceptionally good hands – Louis Auguste's father was the very picture of health and his elder brother, the Duc de Bourgogne was considered by all to be a very promising child who would one day make an excellent monarch. Bourgogne actually sounds completely insufferable but there can be no doubt that he was an extremely precocious little boy – at the age of seven, he presented his doting grandpapa Louis XV, who shared his passion for mathematics and science, with a book of geometry problems that he himself had worked out.

Unfortunately, at the age of nine, Bourgogne became ill with tuberculosis and it soon became clear that he would not survive – at which point it was decided that his younger brother, who was then aged six, would leave the comfort and security of his nursery a year early and begin the lessons and training that would prepare him to take his place as heir. Until this point, Louis Auguste had, as was traditional, still worn dresses and had been cosseted and fussed over by Madame de Marsan. Now, however, he was expected to dress like a miniature adult, live with his brother in a splendid apartment and be raised under the care of his new governor the Duc de la Vauguyon, who was part of a court faction that was vehemently opposed to the alliance with Austria and consequently brought him up to be instinctively suspicious of anything Austrian, particularly its reportedly lovely bevvy of Archduchesses.

Poor Louis Auguste was completely miserable as he was now also expected to spend all of his time with his elder brother Bourgogne, whose already sharp nature had not sweetened one whit during the rapid onset of his illness. Quite the reverse in fact – he had become even more difficult and imperious and also quite terrifyingly pious, which can't have been much fun to be around. He did not have to endure this situation for long, however, as his brother died in March 1761, casting the entire court into mourning. Difficult, haughty and often irritatingly precocious though the boy had been, there is no doubt that his family and much of the court saw in him the last great hope for the future of the Bourbon dynasty, regarding him as a prospective king in the mould of the great Louis XIV.

For his younger brother Louis Auguste, the sudden rise to prominence as heir to the throne of France was devastating and confusing. Whereas Bourgogne had been flattered, admired, encouraged and adored from the moment of his birth, Louis Auguste had been regarded very much as 'the spare' and had received no such public adulation, although at least his parents treated him with affection. Furthermore, he had been raised to consider himself inferior to his elder brother in every possible way so when he suddenly took centre stage, he didn't know how to act and certainly didn't have the carefully fostered high opinion of himself that Bourgogne had. This awkwardness and lack of confidence would remain with Louis Auguste for the rest of his life, balanced by his rather un-Bourbon attributes of a warm heart, sensitivity and, eventually, uxoriousness as Marie Antoinette, his new bride, casting him covert glances from beneath her eyelashes in the sunlit clearing at Compiègne, would soon discover for herself.

Also present that afternoon were Louis XV's three surviving unmarried daughters, who remained with him at Versailles, where they inhabited enormous, splendidly decorated apartments on the ground floor. Familiar to us as charming, winsomely smiling young princesses in the flattering portraits of Nattier, the three maiden princesses were by now in their thirties and not nearly so delightful to look at as they had been in their fresh-faced youth. There had originally been eight princesses born to Louis and his Polish wife Marie Leszczynska, only one of whom, Louise-Élisabeth, had escaped into marriage (becoming the mother of Isabella and Ferdinand of Parma), while the rest remained at Versailles to adorn their father's court, attend to their mother and cause trouble for the royal mistresses, whom they wholeheartedly loathed and regarded as jumped up rivals for their adored father's affections. For his part, the King was carelessly fond of his unattractive trio of daughters and would make a point of visiting them every day to make hot chocolate and enjoy some court gossip, of which they always seemed to have an enormous store.

After the death of his beloved mother Maria Josepha, the orphaned Louis Auguste had turned to his aunts for comfort and by 1770 was in the habit of regarding them as substitute mothers, always willing to listen sympathetically to his troubles and offer advice. However, they had been avowed opponents of his match with an Austrian Archduchess, seeing this as a chance to make trouble for his grandfather's mistress Madame de Pompadour who had been very much in favour of it and had therefore done much to poison the vulnerable boy's mind against the dangers of such a match. Most worryingly, they had done everything possible to make him personally suspicious of his putative bride who, they spitefully suggested, could never be anything other than an avowed enemy of France and an agent of Austrian interests.

The eldest of the trio of aunts, Madame Adélaïde[16], who had been considered rather lovely in her youth, was their undisputed leader, by dint of her seniority and also due to respect of her strong-willed, bold and extremely formidable personality. It was said of

Adélaïde that as a child of eleven, at the height of yet another war between France and England, she had been caught sneaking out of Versailles with her pin money, declaring that, 'I am going to make all of the English lords sleep with me, which they will be honoured to do, and then bring back their heads to my Papa.' Intelligent, energetic and forceful, she very much ruled the roost at Versailles and resented any other woman who challenged her dominance within the family.

The other two daughters, plump and pretty Madame Victoire[17] and the nervously blinking and rather plain Madame Sophie[18], who were spitefully described by Horace Walpole as '*clumsy, plump, old wenches*', were much less intimidating than their daunting elder sister but although they seemed more inclined to treat the new Dauphine kindly, they followed the domineering Adélaïde in everything and so did their best to remain aloof. The three women, whose position at Versailles was already rather undignified thanks to their unmarried status were given unflattering nicknames by their father – Adélaïde was 'Loque' (Rags), Victoire was 'Coche' (Piggy) and Sophie was 'Graille' (Scrap). A fourth princess, Madame Louise[19], whose nickname was 'Chiffe' (bad silk), had recently scandalised the court by running away at dawn to a convent with the intention of praying for her father's lost and blackened soul. When Madame Adélaïde was informed that her youngest sister, who was by far the most coquettish and sociable of the group, had left the palace, she immediately assumed that Louise had eloped and asked 'Who with?'

Once the introductions were over, Marie Antoinette cheerfully clambered into the royal coach between the King and her silent, grumpy-looking young husband and they made their way to the lovely château of Compiègne, one of the royal family's favourite summer residences, to meet the princes of the blood, headed by the Duc d'Orléans[20] and his son the Duc de Chartres[21], who was seven years older than his cousin Louis Auguste. Marie Antoinette was also introduced to the seventeen-year-old Duchesse de Chartres, Louise Marie Adélaïde de Bourbon, daughter of the Duc de Penthièvre and a great-granddaughter of Louis XIV and Athénaïs de Montespan.

The premature death in May 1768 of Louise Marie's only brother, the irredeemably dissolute Prince de Lamballe[22], had left her in possession of an immense fortune and sole heiress to one of the most enormous and fabulous fortunes in all France, if not all Europe, bringing her lucky husband a dowry of 6 million livres (which made Marie Antoinette's dowry look positively measly) and an annual income of 240,000 livres, which later doubled to almost half a million livres a year. No wonder then that the ambitious and extremely intelligent Duc d'Orléans, originally so unwilling to marry his eldest son into an illegitimate branch of the royal family, had changed his mind after the death of the Prince de Lamballe and hastened to secure this jewel for their family. For her part, the Duchesse was madly in love with her husband even if he had allegedly already returned to the dissolute carousing of his bachelor life. Accompanying the Duc and Duchesse de Chartres, was Maria Teresa Luisa of Savoy[23], the widow of the Duchesse de Chartres' dead brother, the Prince de Lamballe. The twenty-year-old half-German and half-Italian Princesse de Lamballe must have been a figure of some romantic interest to the young Marie Antoinette as she was just six years older, had already experienced personal tragedy and was also extremely pretty with soft blue eyes and very long auburn hair, of which she was extremely proud. Naturally, the two young women hit it off straight away.

The next day the royal party travelled to the small pleasure château of La Muette, a glorified hunting lodge in the Bois de Boulogne, a stone's throw away from the centre of the French capital. However, it was unlikely that anyone present would have been so tactless as to remind the King of this fact. Once so popular that he was hailed by his people as Louis *le bien-amé*, the best beloved, he was now so universally loathed that he had not dared to show his face in his own capital for several years and discouraging his family from also going there.

At La Muette, Marie Antoinette was introduced to the younger members of the royal family, first of all Louis Auguste's two younger brothers, Louis Stanislas Xavier, Comte de Provence[24] and Charles Philippe, Comte d'Artois[25]. Provence, the elder, was almost exactly the same age as his new sister-in-law (he was fifteen days younger) and superficially resembled his elder brother, the Dauphin although he was not nearly so nice. He was instead intelligent and rather spiteful, although he took some pains to hide this behind an amiable, amusing chatterbox veneer. Meanwhile, Artois, the youngest brother, was twelve and was the only one of the brothers to have inherited the charm and good looks of their suave grandfather which meant that he was fully expected to one day be a serious hit with the ladies. Naturally, he and Marie Antoinette got on like a house on fire.

Marie Antoinette was charmed by La Muette and it was to remain one of her favourite summer residences, where she could enjoy a close proximity to all of the pleasures of Paris with just a small group of friends. After retiring to her rooms to freshen up, Marie Antoinette rejoined the others for a private supper party attended by her new family and a few very select courtiers, most of whom Marie Antoinette had already met. However, when she entered the room it was to a tense atmosphere, quite at odds with the mood of cheerful celebration that had predominated over the past few days. This uneasy feeling only increased when Marie Antoinette glanced up the table to where the King was sitting and noticed him deep in conversation with a beautiful blonde woman she did not recognise. Seeing that the King was roaring with laughter at something that this lady was whispering in his ear, she asked the Comtesse de Noailles, who was rigid with disapproval, who she was. 'That is the Comtesse du Barry,' was the bland reply, no doubt uttered in a tone intended to deter any further enquiry.

'She is very pretty,' the Dauphine observed. 'What is her function at court?'

'To amuse the King,' Madame de Noailles' mischievous nephew, the Duc d'Ayen said with a wink at his dumbstruck aunt.

Marie Antoinette, too innocent to properly understand his meaning, laughed. 'Then I should like to be her rival,' she remarked.

Born Jeanne Bécu in Vaucouleurs in August 1743, the future Madame du Barry was said to be the illegitimate daughter of a gorgeous seamstress and a friar – a shocking beginning to what was to be a scandalous life. Jeanne, dragged up by her mother before being fortuitously sent to a convent school by a wealthy benefactor, was to grow up to be exceedingly beauteous with a lovely face, tumbling blonde hair and meltingly seductive violet eyes. Sadly, her prospects were not at all promising and when an initial attempt to attain at least some vague semblance of respectability by training as a milliner went awry, the young Jeanne found herself working in a casino, which was actually little better than a brothel.

She was 'rescued' from this life by a noted roué, the spurious Comte du Barry who installed her as his mistress and then launched her on a career as a high-class courtesan, which suited her just fine as she had been blessed with a budding taste for expensive luxuries. She did very well for herself until 1768 when she came to the attention of another aged roué, Louis XV who, always prone to depression, had been in a protracted state of bored gloom ever since the death of his exquisite mistress Madame de Pompadour. He'd ignored all of his courtiers' attempts to divert his attention with various beautiful and well-born ladies of the court and instead consoled himself with the less demanding charms of servant girls and the stream of young women who passed through his private brothel in Versailles.

He was instantly smitten by Jeanne, however, and it wasn't long before her lover's brother, the Comte du Barry, was forced to marry her in order to make her position more respectable and give her a title – a necessity for an entrée to Versailles. After this, there was no stopping her and to the horror of everyone, the King even installed her in apartments in the palace. No one in Versailles had any illusions about the origins of the latest favourite though, lovely thought she was. They'd all sneered at the middle-class origins of the exquisitely refined Madame de Pompadour, so their feelings about having the undeniably low-born Madame du Barry prancing around in their midst, dressed up in pink silk and exquisite lace and covered in the flashy diamonds that she adored so much, were more than their aristocratic sensibilities could bear. That a trollop like Jeanne du Barry should be invited to such a prestigious event as the intimate supper party designed to welcome the new Dauphine to the royal family was considered to be an insupportable insult to everyone, but most especially to Marie Antoinette herself, who luckily for the moment remained innocent of all of this – although not for much longer.

Chapter 4

Madame la Dauphine 1770

'The only real happiness in this world is a successful marriage.'

The 16 May 1770 dawned bright and beautiful – perfect weather for a royal wedding day. The King, Dauphin and their attendants left just after dawn to make the three-hour carriage journey back to Versailles, leaving Marie Antoinette to follow them a few hours later. Extremely excited to be finally getting her first glimpse of the most magnificent and famous palace in all Europe, the one that had served as the model for all others ever since its inception just over a century earlier, she beamed with delight at the immense crowds that had gathered on the road from Paris to watch her pass. Although their initial suspicion about this unpopular Austrian match would never quite disappear, there had been enough glowing reports of the little Dauphine's prettiness and charm to make the Parisians take her to their hearts, incapable as always of resisting the appeal of an attractive young woman.

Another huge crowd awaited the Dauphine at Versailles where, although admission was strictly by ticket only for the day, well over six thousand people had turned up to swell the ranks of the court and see as much as they could of the royal wedding day. Everyone was dressed in their finest clothes while the ladies of the court, many of whom had been up since 6 am in order to have enough time to get ready, had been laced into their finest court dresses, the famous *grand habit* with its bared shoulders, ruffled and flounced lace sleeves, wide panniered skirts and sumptuous decoration, which had been introduced as court dress by Louis XIV in 1670 and barely changed since other than with the barest of nods to contemporary fashion. For Marie Antoinette her first sight of Versailles, which would be her chief residence for the next nineteen years, was awe-inspiring and emotional as her carriage drove through the imposing gilt-covered gates and deposited her in the courtyard. As the Dauphine looked up at the splendid gleaming facade of the palace she would have seen dozens of courtiers crammed into all of the windows, all staring down curiously at this small girl who would one day, God willing, be their Queen.

Without further ado, Marie Antoinette was swept off to the Dauphine's apartments on the palace's ground floor, where she was to be temporarily housed until the much grander Queen's apartments on the first floor, which were being renovated, were ready for her. The Dauphine's apartments, which incorporated two antechambers, a cabinet, two sitting rooms, an oratory, a large bed-chamber and a bathroom, had not been inhabited since the death of Maria Josepha of Saxony in 1767 and were gloomy, sparsely decorated and rather lacking in privacy, giving out as they did straight on to the gardens, although a small area of the terrace had been fenced off during the former Dauphine's residence there. However, they had the bonus of being directly next door to the rooms inhabited by Louis Auguste, which meant that they could see each other easily – should they wish to do so.

Waiting in her bed-chamber, where her new husband had been born, were her wedding presents from the King, arranged on the pale blue silk cushioned drawers of a three-foot high and six-foot wide crimson velvet coffer specially designed by the architect Belanger. Chief amongst the gifts was a beautiful diamond *parure* set from the King as well as a diamond-encrusted fan and other ornaments, including a diamond bracelet set with a miniature portrait of the King which she immediately snatched up and put on her wrist, prompting an onlooker to say that '*she loses no occasion of seeking to please him.*' More importantly, though, Marie Antoinette was presented with the jewels traditionally owned by the Dauphine of France, which had last belonged to her husband's mother Maria Josepha of Saxony. Valued at over 2 million livres, they included a wealth of pearls, diamonds and other fabulous jewels and would have made Marie Antoinette's eyes widen with amazement as she stared at them as they were equally as fine, if not finer, as the jewels that she had seen her mother wearing before she went into mourning and eschewed such worldly splendour. As there was currently no Queen of France, she was also given a beautiful pearl necklace that had once belonged to Anne of Austria, the mother of Louis XIV, and which had been handed down to each successive consort.

Also waiting for Marie Antoinette were her ladies in waiting, headed as always by Madame de Noailles and the Duchesse de Villars, and also her shy little sisters-in-law Clotilde and Élisabeth. Clotilde, the elder was just ten years old and, like her elder brothers, so chubby that she was known, rather unkindly, at court as '*Gros Madame*'. Later, her future husband, Charles Emmanuel IV of Sardinia, would say that he adored her generous figure as it meant that 'there is more of her to love'. The other sister Élisabeth, was just six and still in the nursery. She was a delightful but rather naughty child who hero-worshipped her elder brothers, especially the dashing Comte d'Artois.

The Princesses' governess Madame de Marsan, whom Marie Antoinette had been warned about as an arch schemer and to whom she was to take one of her childishly quick and unyielding dislikes, was quick to push her favourite pupil, Madame Clotilde forward but Marie Antoinette, always fond of small children, instead immediately knelt in front of the smallest princess, Élisabeth and gave her a quick hug before she was led away by her ladies to prepare for the wedding.

Sadly, Marie Antoinette's wedding dress vanished during the chaos of the French Revolution, but enough contemporary descriptions exist for us to know that it was a gorgeous confection of cloth of silver, white brocade and fine lace, encrusted with diamonds and pearls. The still extant wedding dress worn by another royal bride Hedwig Elizabeth Charlotte Holstein-Gottorp when she married her cousin, the future King Charles XIII of Sweden in July 1774, just over four years after Marie Antoinette's wedding day at Versailles, gives some sort of clue as to how it may have looked though. Hedwig's romantic silver tissue gown was made for her in Paris, just as Marie Antoinette's had been, and was designed to accentuate her dainty 19" waist while maintaining all the hallmarks of a royal wedding dress of this period – the low neckline, exposed shoulders and frothy lace sleeves above enormously wide panniers. However, in the case of Marie Antoinette, either she had grown since the dress was made or the measurements were wrong for it turned out that her dress was a tad on the small side for the petite Dauphine, which resulted in a bit of a fuss as the ladies hastened to hide the resulting overly wide lacing at the back.

However, what is a wedding day without a hitch or two and Marie Antoinette was sufficiently over-awed by her surroundings and eager to please her new family to make no complaint about the fact that her dress didn't quite fit properly. With perfect dignity and her head held proudly erect, she mounted the stairs past hordes of staring courtiers to the King's apartments where the procession to the chapel was due to begin. This was to be Marie Antoinette's first glimpse of the famous Hall of Mirrors and other splendid state rooms of the palace, a wonderland of crystal, gilt, marble and fabulous paintings and sculptures. Having grown up in Schönbrunn, she was obviously not a stranger to such magnificence but had still never seen anything quite so beautiful as Versailles in all its wedding day splendour, crammed to bursting with courtiers decked out in dazzling jewels and fabulous silk dresses and with sunlight streaming through the tall windows on to the highly polished parquet floors.

The Royal Chapel at Versailles is perhaps one of the most beautiful rooms in the whole palace, a gorgeously light and airy space with a wonderful painted ceiling that evokes thoughts of Heaven itself to the fortunate worshippers gathered below. As Marie Antoinette approached the high altar and then gracefully knelt beside the Dauphin, himself resplendent in cloth of gold encrusted with diamonds, she was observed to look serene as the Archbishop of Rheims, Grand Almoner of France, performed the ceremony and then led the nuptial Mass afterwards. In contrast, her new husband visibly trembled as he placed her ring, which had been selected from a choice of several presented to her upon her arrival at Compiègne, on her finger and then went quite pink about the ears as he said his vows.

Once the deed was done, there was nothing more to do but sign the marriage contract, which Louis Auguste did with neat aplomb after his grandfather, while Marie Antoinette messily blotted her own clumsily sloping signature. After this, the court enjoyed the celebrations, which kicked off at six in the evening and then went on for nine whole days of parties, concerts, balls and firework displays. For Marie Antoinette, the celebrations began with a card game, during which she sat beside the King in the place of honour at a green baize-covered table placed in the Hall of Mirrors. As with *le grand couvert*, courtiers and other suitably dressed members of the public were at liberty to silently file past as the royal family played an excruciatingly dull game of *cavagnole* while blithely pretending not to notice that they were being stared at by the hundreds of people on the other side of the gilt balustrade. In Austria, royal weddings were somewhat riotous affairs marked with massive public balls, wine flowing in the streets, parties and all manner of light-hearted and joyous fun, here at Versailles, however, they were altogether more sedate and much less enjoyable.

After this endurance test, there was the wedding banquet, which took place in Gabriel's newly completed theatre, where supper was served to the royal family on a table placed on the stage, while the rest of the court crammed themselves into the stalls, galleries and boxes to watch. This must have been an exceedingly unnerving occasion for Marie Antoinette as she sat with the King on one side and her new brother-in-law Artois on the other, while her husband Louis Auguste was opposite her on the other side of the enormous white linen-covered table. Also in attendance were the Duc and

Duchesse of Chartres and the Princess de Lamballe, who was at the other end of the table, opposite her father-in-law the Duc de Penthièvre. Madame du Barry was not in evidence, although she was in one of the boxes overlooking the stage, enjoying the spectacle and perhaps also some choice dishes sent up to her by her adoring royal lover. Everyone else at the table was already known to Marie Antoinette and she must have taken some comfort from that while doing her best to ignore the stares of the courtiers who watched them eat as though they were literally performing on the stage.

The banquet went on for several excruciating hours and as the heavens broke outside and the revellers outside in the gardens were forced to take shelter from the rain, the numbers of spectators in the theatre also increased. Marie Antoinette ate very little of the wonderful food placed before her but across the table the Dauphin was seen to be enjoying himself perhaps a little too much, heaping his plate high with delicacies until finally his grandfather leaned towards him and whispered, 'Go easy, my boy.'

The Dauphin looked surprised, perhaps even pausing with a fork of food halfway between plate and mouth. 'Why?' he asked, as his brother Provence giggled beside him. 'I always sleep better after a good meal.'

When the banquet finally came to an end, the royal family, many of whom were more than a little inebriated, got up to escort the newly married couple, who had barely spoken more than perhaps half a dozen words to each other since their wedding, to Marie Antoinette's bed-chamber. The Archbishop of Rheims sprinkled holy water on the bedsheets before the couple retreated to their own sides of the bed and were ceremoniously helped into their nightclothes in front of an intimidatingly large crowd of spectators, with the King handing his visibly terrified grandson his nightshirt, while the Duchesse de Chartres, who was the highest status lady present, helped the blushing Marie Antoinette into her lace-edged and embroidered nightgown.

The young couple then clambered into the bed and sat there stiffly side by side as the heavy brocade bed curtains were closed for a moment and then pulled open again to symbolise the consummation that everyone optimistically hoped would ensue after the King and courtiers gravely said goodnight and departed. The King paused for a moment in the doorway and gave the little Dauphine a sad last look, no doubt fully aware that his shy and ungainly fifteen-year-old grandson, whom he had described 'as not a man like others' would almost certainly not be making any attempt to consummate his marriage. However, although he was saddened and rather perplexed by the boy's apparent lack of interest in his bride, his letters reveal that he was at least still relatively sanguine that he would in time grow to appreciate Marie Antoinette's undoubted charms. After all, how could he not?

The Dauphin had already departed by the time Marie Antoinette was woken up the next morning to face her first formal *levée* at Versailles. The *levée* was an old tradition whereby the foremost members of the royal family, specifically the King and Queen formally got up in the presence of their households. It was considered a tremendous honour to participate in this, either by holding a basin or handing over an item of clothing, as Marie Antoinette would eventually find to her cost when on one occasion she was left naked and shivering by the side of her bed as first the Duchesse d'Orléans and then the Comtesse de Provence arrived one after the other, delaying the moment when the highest ranking woman present could hand her a shift with which to cover herself, while Marie Antoinette muttered furiously about how utterly preposterous the whole affair was. On the morning after her wedding however, Marie Antoinette was still too bewildered and intrigued by Versailles to raise much complaint as she was chivvied out of bed and then dressed in front of her ladies before the maids stripped the bedsheets, raising their eyebrows when they saw that they were perfectly clean and that there had therefore presumably been no consummation – a fact that they wasted no time in reporting to their superiors.

It didn't take long for rumours about the Dauphin's lack of amorous performance to spread through the gossip-crazed court and for the next few days no one could talk about anything else as the silent, embarrassed-looking young prince squired his enchanting young bride through the exhausting series of opulent court events that had been arranged to celebrate their marriage. There were more concerts, plays and banquets to be endured as well as a splendid state ball in the new theatre, where Marie Antoinette and the Dauphin led a stately minuet in front of the entire court before the Dauphin glumly departed to the dais beside his grandfather and his bride gave herself up to the enjoyment of dancing with his far more amusing cousin the Duc de Chartres, who was rather bored by her childish conversation but still very much admired her glowing good looks.

While the courtiers danced the night away in the splendid surroundings of the new theatre, over 200,000 people were enjoying a fabulous *bal champêtre* in the palace gardens, which were entirely thrown open to the public and filled with all manner of revelry, such as orchestras playing in the lantern illuminated groves, dancing on the lawns; decorated gondolas wafting slowly across the great canal; jugglers, acrobats, troupes of actors and fire breathers on the splendid parterres and then finally a wonderful firework display, which Marie Antoinette watched from a window in the Hall of Mirrors, no doubt desperately longing to be either outside enjoying the fun or, better still, on the palace roof where her lively brothers-in-law had gone with their friends to get a better view of the display.

The celebrations were due to conclude with a huge public fireworks display in Paris at the end of May which Marie Antoinette, to her tremendous joy, was permitted to attend in the company of her husband's three aunts while the Dauphin, perhaps sensitive to his grandfather's lack of popularity in the capital, preferred to remain behind at Versailles. Other than her brief overnight stay at La Muette, Marie Antoinette had not yet caught a single glimpse of the famously beautiful French capital and she was thrilled to be finally going there. However, before her carriage had even arrived at the grand Place Louis XV[1] they were greeted by the screams and cries of the terrified crowd as dozens of people confused by the darkness fell into trenches that had been left open on the Rue Royale, which was still under construction, there to be crushed and suffocated as the crowd continued to surge overhead and carriages still tried to force their way through. The result was wholesale panic and the disappointed and terrified Marie Antoinette was obliged to turn around and return to Versailles.

Horrified and deeply distressed by what she had witnessed, the Dauphine was greeted at Versailles by her young husband who, hitherto so silent and morose by her side, now astonished her by listening sympathetically to her account of what happened. The next morning he sent his entire monthly allowance to the Minister of Police with a note saying simply, '*This is all I have to dispose of. Use it as best you can. Help those who need it most.*' Deeply touched by his concern and generosity, Marie Antoinette immediately did the same with her own allowance which had the effect of making both instantly lauded by the Parisians as angels of benevolence, which both pleased and piqued the King, whose own generous donation had received no such commendation, in equal measure.

Horrible though the tragedy in Paris undoubtedly was, it had the effect of drawing the young Marie Antoinette and her husband a little further together, although he would never quite forget his governor Vauguyon's lectures about the untrustworthiness of Austria. Their tastes might be very different, with Marie Antoinette being of a far more lively and sociable bent than her shy and retiring husband, who loved books and history and many other occupations that she found incredibly tedious, but here at least, in their shared compassion, kind-heartedness and instinctive philanthropy, they found some common ground and were able to begin building a friendship if not a romance. Just a few weeks after their wedding, things had even progressed enough for Marie Antoinette to be able to write to her mother that her husband had '*changed very much for the better. He is very friendly towards me and beginning to confide in me. Also the King could not be kinder and is full of attentions. I love him dearly, but it is pathetic to see how weak he is with Madame du Barry, who is the silliest and most impertinent creature imaginable.*'

Their shared hostility towards Madame du Barry was fanned by Louis Auguste's troublemaking trio of aunts who naturally absolutely loathed this parvenu upstart who had somehow managed to infiltrate their family circle. They would perhaps have been less pleased had they known that it would have the effect of bringing the young couple further together as the Dauphin was pleased to discover that beneath his new wife's frivolous exterior, she was as morally fastidious as he was himself and equally inclined to look upon the activities of his grandfather's low born mistress with a censorious eye. However, while Marie Antoinette showed her displeasure by refusing to speak or even so much as look at Jeanne du Barry when they found themselves in the same place, the Dauphin had to at least maintain the appearance of civility for the sake of good relations with his grandfather – especially as Madame du Barry presided over the intimate little suppers that the King hosted after his hunting parties which the Dauphin, himself an ardent devotee of the hunt, would usually attend.

Thrown together in marriage at such a tender age, Marie Antoinette and Louis Auguste were barely beginning to know themselves before they were expected to get to know each other as well and it is little wonder that they were at first rather standoffish with each other. Although Marie Antoinette gave the appearance of being a light-hearted social butterfly, she was at heart also rather shy and, like her new husband, much preferred the company of a few like-minded and well-chosen intimates to a great crowd of people. They also shared a taste for the simple life, fostered in the case of Marie Antoinette by her cheerful, informal Austrian upbringing, while Louis Auguste looked to the quiet, affectionate, comfortable life enjoyed by his own parents as a model of how a marriage should be. These were things that they were able to find out about each other over the following few years though, as their tentative friendship deepened and a mutual respect and regard flourished between them.

Emboldened both by her success with his grandfather, who thought she was delightful and petted her in a manner that recalled to mind the way that Louis XIV had lavished attention on Marie Adélaïde de Savoie, Duchesse de Bourgogne[2], when she first arrived at Versailles as a girl of ten, and the increased friendliness of the Dauphin, Marie Antoinette began to treat her husband with the same careless, breezy affection as she treated everyone else, spontaneously hugging him when he visited her rooms and chattering away about her day. She also kept in mind her mother's advice that: '*a woman should be in all things obedient to her husband and have no other thought but to please him and carry out his wishes. The only real happiness in this world is a successful marriage. I know what I am talking about. All depends on the woman, if she is willing, loving and amusing.*' Unwilling and bewildered at first, the Dauphin, so starved of affection since the death of his mother, soon came to appreciate her efforts and in time even returned her affection – at first with a punctilious politeness that soon gave way to genuine warmth and then, on his part at least, actual love.

In the bed-chamber, however, things remained much the same as they had done on that very first night and although the Dauphin soon proved himself willing to embrace his wife and even on occasion kiss her cheek in front of the court, there was very little more going on in the all-important marriage bed, where every night the shy young couple would bid each other good night then chastely go to sleep beside each other. Although it was commonplace for young courtiers of the Dauphin's age to have been introduced to amorous adventures by one of the experienced older ladies of the court or a pretty and, one hopes, disease-free young courtesan, Louis Auguste had shown no taste for such affairs and was almost certainly still a virgin at the time of his marriage. However, even if he was not naturally inclined towards sex, he was still very much aware of his duty as heir to the throne of France and his marriage's lack of consummation almost certainly weighed as much on his mind as it did on Marie Antoinette's.

They were both very young though and although both King Louis and Maria Theresa were impatient for the deal to be sealed and matters to advance between them, it was also accepted that there was still time for a sexual relationship to develop naturally once the couple had got to know each other a bit better. Besides all this, Louis XV was still only sixty years old and to all intents and purposes seemed to be in the very prime of life – there was plenty of time to go before his grandson and his little Austrian wife would be expected to take up the mantle of real authority or were under real pressure to produce an heir.

As well as getting acquainted with her new husband, there was also the equally peculiar and often confusing Versailles for Marie Antoinette to get used to – enormous, splendid and falling apart at the seams, it was an extraordinary and rather ridiculous mausoleum, completely over the top, built on a massive scale and always full to the rafters of people, many of whom really had no business being there at all. It had swelled and become bloated in size since its heyday a century earlier and was now home to almost four thousand people, only the most privileged and favoured of whom were accorded a small and exceedingly cramped suite of rooms, while everyone else had to make do with squalid little chambers beneath the eaves. Not that anyone cared – to be housed at Versailles was still considered to be the most immense honour and if the uninsulated rooms were freezing cold in the winter and intolerably hot in the summer then no one was going to be so ungrateful as to complain about this.

During the day the palace's residents were also joined by dozens of merchants and hawkers who set up their stalls on the staircases, along the corridors and out in the gardens, selling their goods to the courtiers and also the hundreds of visitors who crammed into the palace every day, much as they do now, to stare at all the magnificence and perhaps even catch a glimpse of royalty passing by on their way to Mass or sitting down for dinner.

As Marie Antoinette, always accompanied by two ladies of waiting, made her way from her rooms to the chapel for Mass or out to the gardens to walk her badly trained and completely spoilt little dogs, she did so past a vast crowd of people, who were held back by the palace guards but still permitted to stare at her and even call out comments as she went by. Her every gesture, word and look were closely observed and then discussed at great length, particularly those that were considered to confer favour on other courtiers. Louis XIV had made himself the sun that all the court must revolve around and although the prestige of the royal family had been somewhat tarnished since the glory days of the great Sun King, they were still the central focus of the court with everyone clamouring for whatever scraps of attention and favour they could get from the royal hands.

Also hoping for scraps from the royal hands were the palace dogs, which roamed the galleries and splendid rooms in snarling, barking packs. Most of the royal family had pet dogs (while Louis XV, contrary as always, had an enormous, extremely unpopular and bad-tempered white Siamese cat), ranging from the pampered and badly trained little spaniels of the aunts to the bigger hounds that the princes kept for hunting. There were also the pets of the courtiers, which ran underfoot everywhere in the palace, howling, barking, snapping at ankles, begging for morsels of food and relieving themselves in the gardens and courtyards. High up in her beautiful new rooms, which had finally been finished shortly after her wedding, Marie Antoinette was cut off from most of the noise, dirt and squalor that assailed much of Versailles but she would still have been able to hear the distant shouts of the vendors as they plied their trade on the staircases and outside on the terraces, the barking of dozens of dogs, the ringing of the chapel bells and the endless chatter of the courtiers as they went about their business, their aristocratic high heeled shoes, the soles traditionally painted red in a style since emulated by Christian Louboutin, clip-clopping on the polished floors.

Chapter 5

The Butterfly
1770–1774

'It is possible to be virtuous and at the same time to be gay and sociable.'

Although Marie Antoinette had been welcomed with warmth, albeit of varying degrees of sincerity, to the French court by the royal family, she still felt isolated and lonely in her new life. Used to being part of a large and boisterous young family, life seemed to have a very different flavour at Versailles, where everyone was in total thrall to an excessively constraining system of etiquette that had been laid down over a century before. As Dauphine, Marie Antoinette now found herself at the very centre of this system, heading up an enormous household of her own, most of which had been inherited from the deceased Queen and former Dauphine. Besides her *dame d'honneur*, Madame de Noailles, there was also the Mistress of the Robes, Madame de Villars, and twelve chief ladies in waiting, the *dames du palais*, all of whom were exceedingly highly born and well connected. Below the noble ladies of the household, there were *femmes de chambre*, who were less well-born but would have had to have been no less well connected to have been able to secure such sought-after positions at court, while beneath them there were the Dauphine's maids, known as the *femmes rouges* due to the red dresses that they always wore, whose duty it was to perform the most menial tasks in Marie Antoinette's rooms, such as bringing her daily outfits, looking after her clothes and making her bed. Besides all of these ladies, there were also pageboys, valets, equerries, cooks, surgeons and general lackeys; all of whom devoted their lives to making the existence of this one pampered individual run as smoothly as possible.

Shortly after her marriage, Marie Antoinette wrote a description of her daily routine in a letter to her mother. Although the Dauphine sounds typically chipper and upbeat about the relentless boredom and loneliness of her life, it also reveals a great deal about her growing closeness with her husband, which would have pleased the Empress very much, and the amount of influence that his aunts were beginning to hold over her, which would perhaps have been much less pleasing to her mother.

> *'I get up between nine and ten o'clock, and having dressed say my morning prayers, then have breakfast and go to visit my aunts, where I usually find the King. This lasts until about ten thirty. At eleven I have my hair dressed. After which everyone is allowed to come in – that is, everyone who has the right of entry. I put on my rouge and wash my hands in front of them all. Then the gentlemen go away, while the ladies stay and I put on my formal dress. Mass is at midday, and if the King is at Versailles I go with the King and my husband. If he is not there then I go alone with the Dauphin. After Mass, the two of us dine alone, but anyone who cares to can come and watch us. As we both eat very quickly we have finished by half past one, and I go back with the Dauphin to*

his apartments, but if he is busy I go back to my own where I read or write or work, for I am embroidering a waistcoat for the King, which is not making much progress, but by the Grace of God I hope to get it finished in a few years. At three o clock I go again to my aunts, where I usually find the King. At four, the Abbé (Vermond, who continued in her household in France) comes to see me and at five there is the music master, who stays until six when I either return to my aunts or go for a walk. I must tell you that my husband almost always comes with me to visit the aunts. At seven we sit down to cards, but if it's fine then I go again for a walk. At nine we have supper and if the King is not there the aunts come and have supper with us. Otherwise we go to them where after supper we wait for the King, who usually appears at about a quarter to eleven. But while waiting I put myself on a comfortable sofa and sleep until he arrives. When he is not there we go to bed at eleven.'

It's interesting that she mentions reading when the Dauphin was 'too busy' to spend time with her in the afternoon – perhaps the efforts of Abbé de Vermond, who had travelled to Versailles in her wake to take up the position of Reader in her household there had finally paid off or maybe she was hoping to please her bookish husband? Alternatively, this could simply have been an attempt to pull the wool over her mother's eyes by pretending to spend her time in more worthy occupations than just lazing on a sofa while chatting about fashion and hair feathers with the Princesse de Lamballe, who was by now her best friend at court.

Besides the devoted Abbé Vermond, Marie Antoinette also saw a great deal of the Austrian diplomat Mercy d'Argenteau, a highly educated, urbane man, utterly devoted to Maria Theresa, who was to become something of a father figure to her daughter over the next few years. It was Mercy's job to help the young Dauphine avoid the pitfalls of life at Versailles and give her advice, which often involved acting as a mouthpiece of her mother, who sent him a constant stream of commands and advice to be passed on to the unfortunate girl. He also acted as a sort of unofficial spy, delicately using his diplomatic skills to pump the unsuspecting Marie Antoinette for intimate information about her relationship with the Dauphin, the King and other members of the royal family before secretly passing it all on to her mother who then terrified the Dauphine by seeming to have an alarming omniscience when it came to her daughter's most private affairs.

It was also Mercy's duty to facilitate the correspondence between mother and daughter which flourished during this most interesting time. Before her departure from Vienna, Marie Antoinette had been ordered to write home once a month to give her mother a full and up-to-date report of all her activities, including an update about her irregular menstrual cycle and the ongoing efforts to make the Dauphin consummate their marriage. To these sadly blotched, misspelt and crossed out missives, Mercy would then attach his own secret reports giving a bit more context to the Dauphine's letters and adding little titbits from his own close observations of Marie Antoinette and her circle.

It was Mercy's shrewd opinion that the aunts, outwardly so benign and welcoming of this newcomer to the royal circle, exerted far too much influence over Marie Antoinette and were in danger of effectively estranging her from the King by encouraging her to snub Madame du Barry. Marie Antoinette may have been blissfully unaware of the aunts' true feelings towards her, but it had not escaped Mercy's attention that they had been bitterly opposed to the Austrian marriage from the outset and had taken to privately referring to their new niece-in-law by the mocking soubriquet of 'L'Autrichienne'. They were, moreover, busily spreading rumours about her while all the while smiling and welcoming her to their apartments several times a day and commissioning portraits of her to hang there, including the famously delightful Krantzinger one of her dressed 'à l'Amazone' in her red masculine cut riding habit and tricorne hat, which delighted her mother when a copy was sent to Vienna in 1771. However, as the Dauphin remained so fond of his aunts there was nothing to be done but hope that his affection for his pretty young wife would eventually supersede the one that he still retained for this triumvirate of unpleasant, embittered women, whose chief remaining pleasure in life seemed to be making trouble for everyone else and were, besides this, motivated by a terrible personal jealousy of Marie Antoinette herself who was already such a favourite with their adored father.

However, for now, they accepted that she was their best chance to oust the hated Madame du Barry and so encouraged her visits to their rooms, while at the same time filling her pretty little ears with poison about their father's mistress, sparing no detail while regaling the rather prim girl, Mama's perfect daughter who was more like the Empress than either might have cared to admit, with stories about Madame du Barry's scandalous past. For her part, Madame du Barry initially made friendly overtures towards the Dauphine but was so soundly snubbed that she had taken to loudly making fun of her with her catty friends and even nicknamed her 'Carrots' due to her strawberry blonde hair. The Dauphine's careless manner of dress was also picked apart by the fashion-obsessed Du Barry who told everyone that Marie Antoinette was nothing but a dowdy little prude. It was even said that the Dauphine, while passing beneath the favourite's windows at Versailles, was splattered with ordure from a chamber pot that one of her maids was emptying from the window (not an unusual incident, sadly) and had gone to the King to complain that it had been done deliberately. Louis, bored and fed up with being once more caught between bickering women, refused to get involved.

It *was* true, however, that after her marriage, Marie Antoinette had fallen back into the old careless habits of her youth and was once again paying very little attention to her appearance. There was an ongoing battle with the Comtesse de Noailles about her unwillingness to wear a restrictive corset beneath her dresses and she barely had the patience to sit still for long enough to have her hair done. She was encouraged in this by her husband's aunts, who never got properly dressed unless they could help it and would hide their state of lazy *déshabille* beneath voluminous silk mantles when their father came to visit.

Naturally, thanks to Mercy, it didn't take long for all of this to come to the ears of her mother, who immediately fired off a letter to her rebellious daughter. '*I beg you not to neglect your appearance. It is very wrong to do so at your age, and even worse when you are in your position… Which is why I keep pestering you on the subject, to warn you against letting yourself go and ending up like the French royal family, who have no idea how to present themselves or to set the tone, or even to amuse themselves in an honest way… It is possible to be virtuous and at the same time to be gay and sociable.*'

All of this was small fry, however, when placed alongside the fact that the aunts were maliciously encouraging Marie Antoinette to be as rude as possible to Madame du Barry at a time when that lady's ascendancy over her royal lover was increasing by the day. In vain did Mercy berate Marie Antoinette, informing her that her own position at court was not yet so secure that she could afford to completely alienate the King's mistress and through her, the King himself. He reminded her that with each passing month that her marriage remained unconsummated, her position at court became increasingly difficult as the enemies of the already unpopular Franco-Austrian alliance plotted to get rid of the unsatisfactory Dauphine, whose marriage could still be summarily dissolved and whose position was further weakened by the dismissal of the Duc de Choiseul, who had been the chief architect of her marriage, and his replacement with the Duc d'Aiguillon, who was no friend to Austria and, worse, belonged to the cotérie of Madame du Barry.

However, Marie Antoinette, who had become accustomed to endless admiration and flattery had not yet properly learned that behind honeyed words and empty smiles there often lay far darker thoughts and purposes and so could not quite believe that she had actual enemies at the French court, who would be more than happy to see her ignominiously packed off back to her mama in Vienna. She had no idea of the nasty rumours and gossip that were already circulating about her, much of it emanating from the gilded apartments of the aunts that she trusted so much, and above all, she refused to believe that the King, who seemed to adore her, was not entirely pleased with how his grandson's marriage was progressing.

Maria Theresa was exasperated by her daughter's intransigence and wrote her furious letters, demanding that she show more favour to Madame du Barry as the current stand-off was seriously endangering relations between Austria and France. '*What is all this fuss and bother… of addressing as much as a word to people whom you have been advised to speak to, the inability to say good morning, or make a compliment or exchange some other triviality. All these tiresome caprices for no other reason than that you have allowed yourself to become so enslaved by your aunts that you have forgotten both reason and a sense of duty… What excuse have you got to behave in this way – none whatsoever! You are only required to know Madame du Barry as a lady who has an entrée at court and who is admitted to the society of the King of whom you are the first subject. It is the King to whom you owe obedience and submission, as an example to the court and to see that his orders are carried out. No one has asked you to become intimate or to indulge in any kind of familiarity, all that is required is an impartial word, a certain regard not for the lady herself but for your grandfather, your master and your benefactor, whom you have let down on the first occasion when you could have obliged him and shown him your attachment.*'

Astounded and rather frightened by such heated missives, Marie Antoinette promised Mercy that she would do her best to oblige the King in this matter and let it be known that she would address a word to the Comtesse after the evening card game at Compiègne, where they were staying that summer. However, just as Madame du Barry drew near, pleasantly smiling as she anticipated this mark of rare favour from the silly snobbish little Dauphine, Madame Adélaïde, the most troublemaking of the aunts, who was keen to scupper this reconciliation, rudely stepped in front of her and whispered to Marie Antoinette that they were late and it was time to retire and wait for the King in her apartments. Flustered, Marie Antoinette did as she was told and ran off in Madame Adélaïde's wake leaving the royal favourite chagrined and mortified while the rest of the court hid their malicious smiles behind their painted and bejewelled fans.

The King was absolutely furious when this sorry tale reached his ears and even the meek Dauphin, who had no liking for Madame du Barry either but knew better than to be anything other than pleasant to her face, upbraided his aunt for her interference in this matter, motivated chiefly by concern for his wife. Although the King did not personally chastise Marie Antoinette for her behaviour, he let his displeasure be known and there was another round of furious letters from Maria Theresa and lectures by Mercy, who did his best to point out just how malign the influence of the aunts actually was. In the end, it took quite a few more months before Marie Antoinette agreed to try again and this time the aunts did not dare interfere as the Dauphine turned to Madame du Barry on New Year's Day 1772 and lightly remarked that 'There are a great many people at Versailles today.' Everyone was delighted, especially the King, but Marie Antoinette would later bitterly inform Mercy that: 'I have spoken to her once, but I am determined to leave things there. That woman will never again hear the sound of my voice.'

Basking in the King's renewed favour, Marie Antoinette now began to have more fun at Versailles. She started to throw weekly balls in her apartments where the men came in full court clothes and all the ladies wore white, which must have looked delightful. The Comtesse de Noailles, in her position as chief lady in waiting, also held the occasional ball for her royal mistress so that she could get to know the other young people at court. To Marie Antoinette's great delight, the Dauphin insisted upon taking dancing lessons so that he wouldn't show her up at these affairs and instead of shyly retreating into the corner would now happily partner her in the occasional quadrille.

As well as dancing, Marie Antoinette also took up riding. Naturally, she had learned the rudiments of horse riding in Vienna but had been discouraged from taking a greater interest by her mother who believed that excessive horse riding was injurious to reproductive health and that long hours spent in the saddle were ruinous to the complexion. She was enraged to hear that King Louis had been encouraging her daughter to learn to ride properly on a donkey and then, dressed in a charming riding habit that showed off her slender figure, to follow the royal hunts, although even she had to concede that taking an interest in the Dauphin's most beloved pastime was probably a good idea under the circumstances. Marie Antoinette delighted in these occasions and would often provide a sumptuous picnic for her husband and his friends which they would take informally beneath the trees of the royal hunting forests.

As Mercy had predicted, the toxic influence of the aunts began to lessen as Marie Antoinette increasingly dominated her husband and weaned him away from them. The widening of their immediate family circle over the next few years also contributed to this as Louis Auguste's sisters left the nursery and his brothers got wives of their own, which meant that there were more young people of their own age on hand to socialise with and the prospect of spending yet another dull evening listening to Madame Adélaïde's ill-natured gossip became far less enticing.

As her young sisters-in-law Clotilde and Élisabeth grew up, Marie Antoinette did everything that she could to make life more fun for them both, hosting concerts, parties, picnics and making sure that their circle included young people of their own age. Marie Antoinette was especially fond of her youngest sister-in-law Élisabeth and they became quite good friends over the years, despite the age difference between them and the fact that Élisabeth was a lot more devout and more interested in reading, science and other intellectual matters than her flighty sister-in-law. However, despite their differences, both girls loved to have fun and liked nothing better than playing silly practical jokes and romping around the palace with their dogs and maids in hot pursuit. On a deeper level, both girls almost certainly felt a little out of place in the huge sprawling palace, where barely a day passed without one of them being told off by Mesdames de Noailles and Marsan and, crucially, neither felt as though they were loved as much as they wished to be. Rouget de l'Isle, later to be the writer of the Marseillaise, encountered the two princesses shortly after Marie Antoinette became Queen and recalled that '*I was fifteen years of age and… on holiday with a lady who was a relation of mine, who had her lodgings at Versailles. All of a sudden, I heard the door of her apartment in which I was, being struck in a certain manner, and my relation, very much upset, said to me: 'Ah, Dieu, my child, hide quickly, here's the Queen!' And at the same time she pushed me into the next room, quickly pulling the curtains over me. And indeed, Marie Antoinette and Madame Élisabeth came in, and soon, freed from the yoke of etiquette, they began to jump, to run and to chase one another.*'

While Marie Antoinette was busy getting acquainted with her new life at the French court, arrangements were in full swing for the marriage of her eldest brother-in-law, Louis Stanislas, Comte de Provence to the Princess Maria Giuseppina of Savoy, a cousin of the Princesse de Lamballe, which was to eventually take place at Versailles in May 1771, almost exactly a year after her own wedding. Naturally, as the second son, Provence's wedding was not quite so grand as that of the Dauphin and nor was the wife chosen for him nearly as prestigious, but still Marie Antoinette was delighted to have another young woman of about her own age (Maria Giuseppina, known in France as Marie Joséphine, was two years older than both her husband and Marie Antoinette) join the royal circle, even if her mother and Mercy were worried that Marie Joséphine might both supplant their protégée in Louis XV's affections and, worse still, produce an heir, which meant that they had serious reservations about the match.

They need not have worried though – the Savoyard princess turned out to be not nearly so pretty as Marie Antoinette, with a nose that Louis XV described to his nephew, the Duke of Parma as '*villainous*'[1]. She was also, even by the rather lax standards of eighteenth-century France, rather lazy when it came to personal hygiene to the point that a discreet word was dropped in her father's ear by the French ambassador, asking him to have a word with his daughter about cleaning her teeth more often, having more baths and attending to her unkempt hair. Compared to the exquisite Marie Antoinette, who was also something of a natural scruff at this time but was at least naturally very pretty, scrupulously clean and always scrubbed up well when it was expected of her, Marie Joséphine had no chance and yet the girls managed to become friends of a sort, drawn together by homesickness and a certain wry amusement at the absurd goings-on within the family circle that they had found themselves within. Marie Antoinette, who was still so desultory when it came to her lessons, was also rather envious of Marie Joséphine's intelligence and even demanded a new library, which Madame de Noailles feared would remain sadly untouched, when the new Comtesse, who had endeared herself to Louis XV by also being a voracious reader, was presented with one upon her arrival at Versailles. However, Marie Antoinette needed to bear in mind that the Comtesse de Provence, who was outwardly so friendly to her face, was also far better versed in the hypocritical arts of courtly dissimulation than she was – as evidenced by the fact that she had been entertaining the despised Madame du Barry to supper in her apartments while at the same time agreeing with Marie Antoinette that she was the worst woman in the world.

When it came to the production of an heir, there was no need for concern either. The Comte de Provence, who was still just fifteen, was almost certainly impotent at this time, possibly because he was already well on the road to obesity but perhaps also because of an undiagnosed lymph gland disorder that may also have affected his elder brother and sister Clotilde. However, whereas Louis Auguste scuttled about the court, red-faced and mortified by the amused chatter about his lack of sexual ardour, Provence, an entirely different kettle of fish, brazened it out with magnificent indifference and went about the place loudly boasting of his prowess and claiming to be bedding his plain little wife several times a night. It was all lies of course but his bravado was certainly impressive.

As for Marie Antoinette and Louis Auguste, although they were now very fond of each other and took a great delight in each other's company even if she never quite got to grips with Louis Auguste's peculiar interests, which included making locks in his personal forge and reading history books, matters had still not progressed all that much in the bed-chamber, although the Dauphin's willingness to at least *try* to have sex with his wife had naturally increased along with his affection for her, as it will tend to do. They were sadly hampered however by a mutual lack of experience and also much clumsy embarrassment, which meant that the Dauphin would fumble around a bit, perhaps even climb on top of Marie Antoinette, but then quickly give up and retreat, mortified, to his own side of the bed before anything of any significance actually happened. He promised several times, often before the court moved to the smaller palaces of Marly or Compiègne for the summer, that he would complete the deed but each time whatever plans he may have had were always scuppered either by illness or his excessive fatigue upon returning from the hunt, which left him feeling too tired to perform. It's probable that the timid Louis Auguste was utterly intimidated by the thought of performing such an intimate act at Versailles or Fontainebleau, where everyone from top to bottom knew everything that occurred in the royal bed-chambers almost as soon as it had happened and so he preferred to make his attempts at the less populated and more informal royal residences, where he had always felt more at ease and where life in general was far more laid back.

Towards the end of 1772, King Louis, who was usually so outwardly sanguine about the whole situation, decided to take matters in hand and asked his tactful and kindly physician Dr Lassonne to examine the young couple and discover what was hindering the Dauphin from doing his duty. As with Maria Theresa, it was inconceivable to Louis that his grandson, who was after all a Bourbon, should be so backwards when it came to sex, however, he was reassured by Lassonne's subsequent report that there was nothing physically wrong with the young couple but rather that their issues were all down to inexperience and the Dauphin's '*surprising nonchalance and laziness*' in bed – in that he made no effort to arouse his wife and then gave up the attempt to penetrate her far too quickly, put off by the painful sensation.

However, gently encouraged by Lassonne, the prince began to put more effort into his nighttime endeavours and soon, in May 1773, Marie Antoinette was able to report to her mother that her husband was '*a little more forward than usual*', a delicate way of saying that he had started paying her more attention in bed. Just a couple of months later, in July, Marie Antoinette was able to excitedly report to her mother that '*my affairs have taken a very good turn… and that I consider my marriage to be consummated; even if not to the degree that I am pregnant.*' A few days later the young couple went together to King Louis and the Dauphin proudly introduced Marie Antoinette to his grandfather as his 'wife' in fact as well as name. The King was absolutely delighted and the happy news quickly spread through the court, temporarily ending all rumours that Marie Antoinette would be packed off back to Vienna and replaced with a different princess, although naturally, the talk would soon begin again when the Dauphine still failed to become pregnant.

On one occasion, shortly before the marriage of Louis Auguste's youngest brother, Marie Antoinette tried to tell him how upset she would be if her new sister-in-law, the Comtesse d'Artois, became pregnant before she did. 'But do you love me?' her husband asked. 'You must know that I do,' Marie Antoinette replied rather sadly. 'I love you sincerely and respect you still more.' The Dauphin then kissed her and promised to renew his efforts, but sadly it was still in vain and the new sister-in-law would indeed have a child before her.

It had been intended for a long time that Louis Charles, Comte d'Artois should be married to the very pretty Louise-Adélaïde de Condé, daughter of the Prince de Condé, who had recently come to court after leaving the exclusive Parisian convent school Panthémont and become a close friend of Marie Antoinette's sister-in-law Élisabeth. Artois was certainly all in favour of the match as he had long been madly in love with Louise-Adélaïde and, even more importantly, it had the approval of his grandfather, as Louise's father was a prince of the blood and yet another descendant of Louis XIV and Athénaïs de Montespan. However, after Provence's marriage to the Princess of Savoy, it was decided that to further cement the union Artois should marry Marie Josephine's younger sister Maria Teresa and forget all about the lovely Louise-Adélaïde, who had been nicknamed 'Hebé-Bourbon' in tribute to her extreme beauty. They were both heartbroken by this, as were Élisabeth and Marie Antoinette, who would have dearly loved to have had Louise-Adélaïde as a sister-in-law, but Artois like his brothers had no choice but to give in and was duly married to Maria Teresa of Savoy in November 1773 with Marie Antoinette performing the office of handing the blushing little bride her nightgown on the wedding night at Versailles.

Although she was certainly no great beauty, Maria Teresa, known in France as Marie Thérèse, was still considered far more attractive, although much less clever, than her elder sister and was therefore potentially more of a rival to Marie Antoinette. This rivalry was further compounded by the fact that Artois, unlike his two elder brothers, was already experienced with women and had no problems consummating his marriage straight away to the smug delight of his bride who naturally knew all about the problems that the other two couples were having. She and her sister formed quite a formidable little unit at court and although they were outwardly friendly to Marie Antoinette, they saw her first and foremost as their rival and were as fond as the aunts of gossiping about her behind her back and causing trouble for her whenever they could, assisted by the Comte de Provence, who secretly loathed his elder brother and his wife, even if he too pretended to be friendly to their faces. On one occasion though his carefully maintained mask slipped when the Dauphin, always clumsy, accidentally broke one of Provence's most treasured pieces of Meissen china and, enraged, the Comte lunged at his elder brother and knocked him to the ground. What at first looked like one of the usual play fights that the brothers liked to indulge in, soon became far more serious and in the end, Marie Antoinette, who received some scratches for her trouble, was forced to intervene and pull them apart.

However, when they were able to put all their rivalries aside, the grandchildren of the King and their spouses and friends formed a merry little cotérie at Versailles and were often to be seen enjoying picnics together in the park, playing cards and billiards, which Marie Antoinette was extremely good at, or simply enjoying each other's company in their enormous and exquisitely decorated apartments in the palace. The Comte de Provence and the two Savoyard Princesses may have had malicious tongues and a tendency to look askance at the fun of the others but the rest of the group, particularly the Comte d'Artois and Marie Antoinette, wanted nothing more than to enjoy life to the full and enjoy the delights of being rich, rather foolish and young at one of the most dazzling courts in the world. In this, they were encouraged by their grandfather Louis XV who made no attempt to involve his grandsons in politics and did not even properly prepare his heir, the Dauphin for his future responsibilities.

Instead, he encouraged the young people to spend money like water, enjoy themselves and generally be an idle, silly lot. Possibly he was afraid of ending up like his Hanoverian cousins across the Channel who lived at cross purposes with their ambitious heirs, but his apparent lack of interest in giving Louis Auguste any guidance when it came to his future Kingship was certainly a tremendous oversight. He was fond of his trio of granddaughters-in-law though, probably because he had always felt more comfortable in the company of women, and in 1773 commissioned a beautiful pair of paintings of Marie Antoinette and the Comtesse de Provence from Drouais. The fashion for classical conceits in portraiture was definitely on the wane by the mid-1770s but luckily lingered for just long enough for us to be treated to Marie Antoinette posing as Hebé, the messenger of the Gods, graceful in champagne-coloured silk and holding a Grecian ewer and a goblet while Marie Joséphine looks equally becoming as the goddess Diana, dressed in blue silk with a leopard pelt draped across her shoulders.

Another favourite pastime was to indulge in amateur theatricals, with Marie Antoinette and her small circle performing short plays on a quiet mezzanine behind the scenes at Versailles. Here, it was the sharp-tongued and malicious Provence who excelled as he had a prodigious memory and was naturally a very talented actor. Marie Antoinette was rather less talented but made up for this with great enthusiasm while her husband, still so shy and awkward, refused to act at all but instead learned the plays and acted as an enthusiastic audience (reserving his loudest cheers and applause for his wife) and prompt for the others, particularly Artois who was as lazy and un-bookish as his sister-in-law Marie Antoinette and so never bothered to learn his lines properly.

The atmosphere of this little circle, outwardly so friendly but secretly so riddled with rivalry and deceit is very well conveyed by a letter written home to her parents by Marie Joséphine, the Comtesse d'Artois, describing her frantic preparations for the annual summertime departure to Compiègne. '*I don't know why I haven't gone crazy. I'm surrounded by caskets, papers, books on the floor; my casket is ready; now it's been knocked over. I must start all over again. I get angry, they laugh, they grab the paper from me… I'm in a little corner, surrounded by baggage. Madame la Dauphine is knocking everything over, the Comte de Provence is singing, the Comte d'Artois is telling a story that he's already started telling ten times and he's shouting at the top of his voice and laughing loudly, and on top of everything, Monsieur le Dauphin is reading a tragedy out loud. I think he thinks we're deaf. There are also two birds singing and three dogs making a deafening racket, one is mine, two are Madame la Dauphine's.'* A normal cheerful family party of boisterous, mischievous teenagers, all determined to make themselves heard and share their enthusiasms with the others. Used as she was to being part of an enormous happy family herself, Marie Antoinette thoroughly enjoyed all of this noise and chaos and didn't concern herself with what might be simmering underneath the surface.

Added to all this there were now also the joys of Paris, which had seemed like an unattainable dream, so near and yet so far away, for the early years of Marie Antoinette's residence at the French court. However, although King Louis, who was so unpopular himself in his capital, generally discouraged his family from going there, he graciously gave his permission in February 1773 for the Dauphin and Marie Antoinette and the Provences, to secretly attend a masked ball at the Opéra House in the last week of the Parisian carnival. The Dauphin and Provences were less than enchanted by the ball, which thanks to its masked and public nature involved a great amount of freedom between the sexes, but Marie Antoinette was in her element, thrilled both by the unusual anonymity of being able to mingle with the public in her mask and also by the wild dancing, the air of flirtatious excitement and the unprecedented freedom of being away from the endless dreary etiquette and protocol of the royal court. Amused by her clear delight the Duc de Chartres invited the incognito royal party to continue the fun at what would doubtless be an extremely wild after-party at his Parisian residence, the Palais Royal but Marie Antoinette was sadly forced to decline his invitation, knowing that her husband would not approve and also a little alarmed by the fact that they had clearly been recognised by other revellers. In the end, the royal party arrived back at Versailles at seven in the morning, just in time to hear Mass before collapsing into their beds, worn out by their frivolities. Later on, the Dauphine would proudly recount her adventures to her mother, adding that '*everyone appears to be delighted by the fact that Monsieur le Dauphin should have consented to come to the ball, for he usually has an aversion to this kind of party.*'

Marie Antoinette, like so many other women before and since, had fallen madly in love with Paris and would not rest until she could taste its pleasures again. She was therefore delighted when King Louis, belatedly realising that his own sadly diminished popularity could potentially get a much-needed boost from the clear affection that the Parisians had for the younger members of his family, agreed that it was about time she and the Dauphin made their official entry to the capital, after which they would be free to openly visit whenever they liked. The 'Joyeuse Entrée' of Marie Antoinette and Louis Auguste took place on 8 June 1773 when dressed in formal magnificence they travelled by carriage to the gates of the capital where the Duc de Brissac, Governor of Paris was waiting to formally present them with the symbolic keys and freedom of the city. After this, they travelled through streets lined with enormous cheering crowds to Notre Dame where they heard Mass before inspecting the newly completed church of Sainte Geneviève (now known as Panthéon) and returning to the long abandoned royal palace of the Tuileries which had barely been used since the young Louis XV, brought up there by his regent, the old Duc d'Orléans, had taken the court back to Versailles in 1722.

In the gloomy and faded surroundings of the old Tuileries palace Marie Antoinette and Louis Auguste dined in solitary state, attended only by the Dauphine's ladies. A gallery overlooking the chamber was open to respectably dressed members of the public though and they silently filed past as the young couple affected not to notice their presence. Less easy to avoid, however, were the shouts and bawdy catcalls of the Parisian market women who were allowed inside in deference to their traditional position as unofficial and extraordinarily outspoken mouthpieces of the general populace and who now began to good-naturedly heckle the Dauphin and his pretty wife about the lack of an heir. Luckily, Louis Auguste and Marie Antoinette were sufficiently buoyed up by their enthusiastic reception to find this more amusing than offensive and it all ended well on both sides with the market women congratulating the Dauphin on his pretty wife and him happily agreeing with them.

After this interlude, the royal couple went out on the balcony overlooking the Tuileries gardens, there to receive the acclaim of the huge crowd that had gathered there while they were eating. Marie Antoinette took a step back, astonished and a little frightened by the sight of so many people, nervously whispering, 'There are so many of them' to the Duc de Brissac, who immediately replied, with great aplomb: 'Madame, I hope that Monsieur le Dauphin won't be jealous when I say that here, you have two hundred thousand lovers.'

Delighted by this, Marie Antoinette then insisted upon going down to the terrace to mingle with the people, taking her husband's arm as she went so that the Parisians would see for themselves just how affectionate the young couple were towards each other. The Dauphin was equally keen to be seen and gave orders that the people must be allowed to come as close as they liked and were not to be pushed away by their guards or hurt in any way. The couple then walked as far as they could until the tremendous press of the cheering, clamouring crowds forced them to return to the palace. A few days later, a still over-excited Marie Antoinette would write to tell her mother all about it. '*Last Tuesday I had a day which I will never forget as long as I live; we made our entrance into Paris. As for honours, we received every conceivable one; but although this was very well, it was not what touched me the most, but rather the tenderness and eagerness of the poor people, who, in spite of the taxes which oppress them, were carried away with joy on seeing us. How fortunate we are, in our position, to have been able to win the love of our people so cheaply. And yet there is nothing more precious and I will never forget it.*'

Marie Antoinette also had the tact to inform Louis XV, who listened rather wistfully to her tales of their great success, that their popularity in Paris was entirely due to him, telling him that 'Your Majesty must be very much loved or we would never have received such a welcome.' They both knew the sad truth of the matter but it was typical of Marie Antoinette's thoughtfulness that she should try to smooth any potential awkwardness over.

Now that the Dauphine was free to visit Paris whenever she liked, she threw herself into the social life of the capital with enormous delight: visiting the opera, theatre and public balls in the city, making excursions to factories, fairs, artistic studios and museums and basking in the adulation of the crowds that always turned out in their hundreds to see her. To her great pleasure, the Dauphin usually accompanied her on these excursions, prompted both by his growing love for her and also the fact that he was all too aware that as future King of France, it was necessary for him to win the affection of the notoriously fickle Parisian populace. In this at least, though, he seemed to be having no difficulty as the Parisians looked all set to take both Louis Auguste and his wife to their hearts, seeing in them the hope of a more golden age once the vice-riddled regime of Louis XV came to a much longed for end.

Drawn into a new pleasure-loving world and encouraged by her friends the Princesse de Lamballe and the Duchesse de Chartres, Marie Antoinette began to see Paris as the perfect antidote to the problems that she faced at Versailles. Now in her late teens, she felt the full weight of her mother's disappointment about her continued childlessness, a situation that she too found deeply distressing as she increasingly longed for a baby of her very own. In the past, she had sought distraction by asking her ladies and even the lesser servants to bring their children to her apartments so that she might play with them and spoil them with treats and small presents. Now, however, all the years of endless reproaches from her mother and the unfulfilling nighttime fumblings from her husband had worn her down completely and left her desperate for distraction, for some form of escape. She was flattered and pleased by her husband's growing love for her and the shy way that he tried to appeal to her by trying to participate in her interests even if she couldn't quite bring herself to entirely reciprocate. However, her own feelings for Louis Auguste, although affectionate were not romantic.

It was the silly, frivolous Duchesse de Chartres, who had the enormous wealth of both her husband and her father at her disposal, who first introduced Marie Antoinette to the gaming tables of Paris, where far more exciting games than cavagnole were played and for much higher stakes. It was also the Duchesse who introduced the Dauphine, previously so careless of her appearance that she had needed not one but two interventions, to the workshop of a certain Rose Bertin, a Parisian dressmaker and milliner whose immense talents matched the tremendous cost of the outfits and headpieces that she designed for her aristocratic clientele. Fed up with what felt like the endless frustrations of her life at court, frustrated by her mother's complaints, frightened that Madame du Barry's coterie would have their way and get her sent back to Vienna and beginning to wonder if she would ever experience for herself what she considered to be the supreme joy of motherhood, the deeply unhappy Marie Antoinette sought to distract herself with all the fashionable, extravagant frivolities that Paris could offer her.

It was at a masked ball at the Opéra on 30 January 1774 that she was to meet Axel von Fersen for the first time. She had gone to the ball with her husband and the rest of their usual party and then, as was now her custom, had wandered off to have delightful little chats with the other partygoers, who politely pretended not to know who this pretty little blue-eyed *ingénue* was. However, Axel von Fersen, as rich and handsome as the hero of a romantic novel and newly arrived from his native Sweden, genuinely had no idea of the identity of this ravishingly dressed stranger who accosted him by the dance floor and so enjoyed several minutes informal conversation with her before he realised whom he had been flirting with so delightfully. The giggling little Dauphine was whisked away by her companions and beyond being a little flattered to have been so singled out, he thought no more of it and nor did Marie Antoinette.

Besides, she had other matters to distract her as she had been encouraged by her mother to champion the cause of her former music tutor, the already celebrated German composer Gluck who wished to have his groundbreaking opera Iphigénie in Aulide performed in Paris but was having no luck persuading the snobbish directors of the Paris Opera to accept the piece. However, with Marie Antoinette's patronage, a performance slot was secured and when the Dauphine announced that she would be attending the premiere on 19 April, tickets began to sell like hotcakes as, already, where the Dauphine led everyone else must surely follow. The sold-out performance was, unsurprisingly, a resounding success and for the first time, Marie Antoinette was able to consider herself a patroness of the arts – something that she found immensely pleasing.

However, in the wake of this great public triumph came enormous tragedy when on 27 April, Louis Auguste and Marie Antoinette were informed that their grandfather Louis XV had been taken seriously ill at the Petit Trianon, his pleasure pavilion in the grounds of Versailles, and that they must prepare themselves for the worst.

Chapter 6

The Little Queen 1774–1776

'Dear God, guide us and protect us. We are too young to reign.'

King Louis fell ill while out hunting with Madame du Barry during a romantic getaway to the Petit Trianon, their little pleasure pavilion in the grounds of Versailles. At first, the King insisted that he just had a cold, but when his symptoms took a more serious turn, his mistress summoned a physician, who insisted that he return to Versailles immediately, telling the ailing King: 'Sire, you *must* be ill at Versailles.' Although there was not any immediate reason to fear the worst, it was clear to everyone that should the King's illness take a dire turn then it would be far more dignified to die amidst the baroque splendours of his bed-chamber at Versailles than in his mistress' pretty boudoir at the Petit Trianon. Even when they were dying, etiquette appeared to rule the lives of the French royal family.

King Louis was whisked back to Versailles, where it was soon confirmed that he had fallen prey to that most feared scourge of royal families across Europe: smallpox. For the good of his soul, he was ordered to send the terrified Madame du Barry, who had never had smallpox and so had not acquired immunity, away but instead insisted, rather recklessly, that she remain beside him, which to her credit she did. Marie Antoinette, who had survived smallpox as a child and so was immune, also offered her services as a nurse but was ordered, along with her husband and his siblings, to remain in the safety of her apartments. Only the three aunts, who had never had smallpox but nonetheless insisted upon remaining with their father, were permitted to remain by his side and nurse him through his illness.

At first, the doctors were fairly sanguine about the King's prospects of making a full recovery but by 4 May it became clear to everyone that he was dying and when once again, he was asked to send his mistress away so that he could confess and make his peace with God, he did not refuse but instead ordered her to leave and entrusted her to the care of his Chief Minister, the Duc d'Aiguillon. The distraught Madame du Barry, who realised that her luxurious life at court was over as soon as Louis Auguste and Marie Antoinette, the girl that she had mocked and schemed against ever since her arrival in France, succeeded to the throne, left Versailles in the early hours of the morning in a plain carriage – she was almost as unpopular as her royal lover and it was feared that she might be attacked by the large crowd, which was more curious than sad, that had begun to gather outside the palace as soon as news of the King's illness began to spread.

On the morning of 7 May, the libertine King, by now in a terrible state and lying on a camp bed in his bed-chamber, made his first confession for almost thirty years, the holy sacraments having been brought to his chamber by a long state procession headed by the Grand Almoner of France and the devastated Louis Auguste and Marie Antoinette, who waited in the adjoining council chamber as the King confessed then received communion, promising to 'uphold the faith and his religion and dedicate himself entirely to the welfare of his people' should he make a miraculous recovery.

For Marie Antoinette the next few days were a nightmare as, barred from approaching the King's rooms which were filled with a stench of oncoming death so terrible that his servants fainted, she waited for news. Louis Auguste was also in a terrible state and spent most of the time praying for his grandfather's soul, when he wasn't weeping helplessly in her arms. Despite all of his faults he had truly loved King Louis and could not yet bring himself to contemplate the fact that his succession to the throne, which he did not feel at all prepared for, was imminent. 'I am the most unhappy man in the world,' he told his wife as they waited together.

When Louis XV, hideous beyond all recognition and in horrible pain as he appeared to rot while still alive, finally died at quarter past three on the afternoon of 10 May, a candle placed in his bed-chamber window was symbolically snuffed out to signal to the world that his life was at an end. Immediately, an immense crowd of courtiers, who had been loitering around the state rooms of the palace, rushed down the beautiful Hall of Mirrors, making *'a terrible noise, exactly like thunder'*, to the Salon of Peace at the start of the Queen's rooms, where they found Louis Auguste and Marie Antoinette, pale, tearful and clinging together like children, waiting for them. 'Dear God, guide us and protect us. We are too young to reign,' Louis Auguste whispered as they fell to their knees and led the court in a prayer. He was just nineteen years old while Marie Antoinette, his consort and the new Queen of France, was eighteen.

After receiving the homage of their new court, the new King and Queen of France were hustled out of the palace, where over a dozen people had now died of smallpox, and packed off in a carriage to the royal château at Choisy, which had been a favourite love nest of the now dead King and Madame de Pompadour and was a precursor in laid back, airy elegance to the Petit Trianon. Sharing their carriage were Louis Auguste's brothers and their wives, who all sat in stunned silence until the Comtesse d'Artois, only relatively recently arrived in France and still not in full command of the language, chanced a remark which because of her comical mispronunciation sent everyone off into fits of laughter, thereby breaking the solemn mood.

Pretty, relatively simply furnished and secluded, Choisy was the perfect place for the bereft, confused and frightened young royal couple to come to terms with both their loss and also the tremendous change in their circumstances. They remained there for several days, while in their absence from Versailles, the old King's body, which was believed to be highly contagious, was driven with all speed and very little ceremony to the royal necropolis at Saint-Denis, where it was quickly buried. The rather undignified haste with which his *cortège* made the journey gave rise to mocking shouts of 'Tally ho!' from the crowd that had gathered to watch him go, who showed a distinct lack of regret about his passing and were instead looking forward to what they hoped would be an era of happiness and prosperity under the new *régime*, blissfully unaware that their new monarchs, whom so few had seen in public, were a pair of frightened adolescents, considered by even their closest family and advisors to be in no way fit to rule.

On the surface, however, the new reign started well with the new King sending 200,000 francs of his own money to be distributed among the Parisian poor and then graciously turning down the increased income that was automatically given to him upon his succession. Marie Antoinette immediately followed suit by refusing to accept the Queen's traditional *droit de ceinture*, an allowance dating from Medieval times named for the girdles that the Queens of France had traditionally worn in the Middle Ages. 'Girdles are no longer in fashion,' the little Queen airily explained, shrugging her scented shoulders. There was no need to add that conspicuous expenditure was also out of style – everyone knew that the royal coffers had been left in the parlous state by the extravagant Louis XV and that the country itself was teetering on the brink of bankruptcy.

The philanthropic gestures of the new Louis XVI (the 'Auguste' of his youth was now dropped) and Marie Antoinette had long since made them favourites in Paris, where they had the habit of responding with prompt generosity to any pleas for assistance from the populace and, indeed, were often the only members of the royal family to do so. Their open-handedness was seen as further proof that this new reign would be very different to the last, as was the young couple's obvious fondness for each other. Previous Kings of France had squandered astronomical sums on a series of rapacious, expensive mistresses and their children while more or less ignoring their wives, who led quiet lives out of the public eye, content to be trotted out on state occasions in between doing their duty and producing heirs. Now though there was a morally wholesome King who appeared to be entirely in love with his wife and had eyes for nobody else. How could this be anything other than an augur for happier, more prosperous times to come? The days when unruly Kings had been kept in line by threats of Papal excommunication and an interdict on their kingdoms were in the dim and distant past but even so, away from the enlightened circles that existed at court and the main cities, the eighteenth-century was still a superstitious age and it was felt by many of his people that a sinful King was indicative of a more general rot at the very heart of the nation itself.

Nonetheless, not everyone was happy with this new and rather unusual status quo. For all their unpopularity, and most of them had been very unpopular indeed, the King's mistresses in the past had almost always been French and, court factions and tiresome personal vendettas and squabbling aside, therefore perceived as being entirely loyal to France and its interests. There had never been a foreign *maîtresse en titre* (although in Madame de Maintenon there had once been a French morganatic wife to the King) and the prospect of an Austrian mistress-queen with an absolute and unrivalled influence over the King that would not be diluted by the presence of an unimpeachably French mistress, was both unprecedented and, in many quarters, disquieting.

It didn't help matters that Louis XVI, so bumbling and clumsy but always so well-intentioned and fundamentally kind, had always been dismissed at court as something of a weak reed with none of his ancestor Louis XIV's greatness nor even the saving grace of Louis XV's indisputable charm. It now belatedly occurred to some people that more should have been done to check Marie Antoinette's growing influence over such a clearly susceptible young man and that, perhaps, efforts should have been made to throw a few pretty young ladies in his way in order to distract him from his wife. Not that it would probably have worked – Louis appeared to be entirely impervious to the charms of all women, with the exception of his wife, and her ladies giggled behind their painted fans at his awkward manner and habit of never making eye contact when addressing them, preferring instead to stare either down at the floor or at a point somewhere above their shoulder. However, it would be wrong to entirely dismiss the possibility that Louis XVI never had a mistress or even any sort of casual dalliance with other women – there may not be any evidence that he did so but it might be that he was exceptionally discreet in order to not hurt his wife's feelings. It's still unlikely but not *impossible*.

Nonetheless, the main question was would Marie Antoinette, so outwardly outgoing, fun-loving and popular, be content to relinquish her social life and the small influence she had acquired over her husband in order to retire to the quiet, rather dull and dutiful life normally expected of a Queen of France? It seemed very unlikely. Apprehensive though she undoubtedly was about her new and unexpected pre-eminence at court, it was also quickly becoming clear that the new young Queen, like a kitten just beginning to show its claws, was beginning to relish her new power. One of her first actions was to encourage her husband to banish Madame du Barry and then dismiss her creature, the hated Duc d'Aiguillon from his position of Chief Minister. However, her attempts to have the Duc de Choiseul, whom she still revered as the one responsible for having doggedly arranged her marriage in the face of what she now knew was a lot of opposition from the court and within the royal family itself, reinstated to his former position came to nothing. The King, who personally disliked Choiseul and had vowed never to reinstate him, also showed his mettle and instead, on the advice of his meddlesome aunt Adélaïde who was determined to usurp Marie Antoinette's position at her nephew's elbow, appointed the elderly Duc de Maurepas as his chief advisor.

Marie Antoinette was furious and also not a little hurt and humiliated to have her wish in this matter so summarily snubbed by her husband, who was normally so eager to please and obliging. It seemed to her that in refusing to support Choiseul, to whom she felt so much gratitude, he was harkening back to the anti-Austrian teachings of his malicious old governor, the Duc de Vauguyon. However, there was nothing she could do about it and Maurepas at least had the benefit of being unaligned with any of the court factions and was indeed well known to be a man entirely devoid of ambition – an unusual stance perhaps in a royal minister but one that was greatly appreciated by his new master Louis XVI who, with extraordinary humility for a Bourbon King of France, frankly acknowledged himself to be lacking *'both knowledge and experience'* in his first letter to his new advisor.

That the new King, who had been almost entirely excluded from the government of the nation by his grandfather, was desperately unprepared and in need of advice was an indisputable fact, although ironically he was the oldest new King of France for over a hundred and fifty years as his grandfather had succeeded at the age of five, Louis XIV had succeeded at four and Louis XIII had come to the throne at the age of eight in 1610. That the new King had reached his majority and could thus dispense with a regent was considered a huge point in his favour but to those who more closely knew him it was, again, the cause of some alarm for unlike his predecessors he would be thrust straight into the deep end of statehood rather than spending his boyhood learning statecraft during a long regency before being allowed to take up the reins of government. However, his refusal to appoint the Duc de Choiseul as his Minister of

State had at least quietened some worries that Marie Antoinette would become the power behind the throne, as it gave a clear signal that the new King, in other ways considered so weak and malleable, was determined not to become the cat's paw of his wife and was in fact actively keeping her at a distance from his government.

As for Maria Theresa, who was being kept closely informed about events by Mercy, she too felt disquiet about the fact that her daughter and son-in-law had been called upon to reign too soon, being all too aware of how terribly unprepared they both were. She instructed the faithful Mercy to immediately report Louis' every action to her so that she could judge whether he was following her own interests and also added that her daughter, who wrote to say that she could not '*help but admire the disposition of Providence which chose me, the youngest of your daughters, for the finest kingdom in Europe. I am more than ever aware of how much I owe to the love of my august mother, who took such care and effort to get me such a good settlement*', should '*never for a minute lose sight of all the possible ways of ensuring her complete and exclusive control over her husband's mind*'. Clearly, as far as Maria Theresa was concerned, they should make the best of the situation and set to work reaping the full benefits of the marriage they had brokered four years earlier. However, she now looked set to be unexpectedly confounded and thwarted by Louis, allegedly so irresolute and meek, having the hitherto unimagined backbone to stand up to his wife and make it clear that he was not going to be the puppet of either her or her Austrian relatives, which led the exasperated Empress to eventually reluctantly conclude that '*some of his behavioural traits make me… doubt that he will be very compliant and easy to control*'.

When smallpox followed the royal party to Choisy they unwillingly left its delights behind and moved on to La Muette on the edge of the Bois de Boulogne, where Marie Antoinette had spent the night before her wedding and which was a favourite summer residence of the young couple. The gates to the Bois de Boulogne were usually locked to maintain their privacy whenever the royal family were in residence but this time, to signal perhaps the new informal direction that they wanted their reign to take, Louis and Marie Antoinette ordered that they be left open so that the people could enter and walk about the shady avenues between the trees as usual. The Parisians were astonished and delighted to regularly see their new King and Queen having picnics in the glade with their friends or simply walking amongst them, arm in arm and giving every appearance of being devoted to each other. There were cheers and applause on one occasion when the Queen, out riding on her stallion, came across the King on one of his walks and immediately dismounted and ran to greet him, whereupon he picked her up in his arms and kissed her in front of everyone. It made a pleasing contrast to their shy diffidence just four years earlier and everyone was enchanted by it. Even Maria Theresa wrote from Vienna to compliment her daughter, saying: '*Everyone is ecstatic, everyone is mad about you; there are expectations of great happiness; you bring new life to a nation which was in desperate straits and sustained only by its attachment to its princes.*'

Louis XV's death was so gruesomely horrible that it was not entirely surprising when Louis XVI and his brothers announced their intention of getting inoculated against smallpox, encouraged by Marie Antoinette who had seen for herself how much devastation the disease could wreak. Smallpox inoculation in the eighteenth century was still a relatively risky business though and there was a great deal of panic when the King's intention was announced as it was feared that he might die too. Marie Antoinette, still erroneously believed to be the power behind the throne, was blamed for the whole thing and even accused of deliberately putting her husband's life at risk with this foolhardy procedure. Luckily for everyone, however, the inoculation was a success and after a brief convalescence, Louis was fully restored to his usual rude health. From now on, every member of the royal family would be routinely inoculated and there would be no more premature deaths from smallpox in the French royal family.

The youthful fledgling court of Louis XVI and Marie Antoinette would be a pleasure seeking one but for now, as they were still in mourning for the previous King, they delighted in the gentle pastimes of horse riding, picnics, quiet family parties and private concerts. On one occasion at La Muette, Marie Antoinette suddenly announced that she had never seen the sun rise and so a small party was arranged to climb one of the nearby hills at three in the morning and watch the day begin. Louis refused to go as he liked his sleep too much but the others gamely trotted up the hill at the appointed time and watched as the sun rose over Paris, while Marie Antoinette, the Comte d'Artois and their friends exclaimed and sighed like true acolytes of Rousseau about the majestic wonder of nature.

Drawn together by their very natural apprehension about the future, the young royal couple had never been so close and as further proof of his great affection for his wife and knowing how much she disliked the stifling formality of court life, Louis presented her with the domain of the Petit Trianon, the delightful little pleasure pavilion in the grounds of Versailles where his grandfather had been taken ill not all that long before. This sad recent event didn't seem to weigh too much on their minds though and indeed there wasn't really much scope for such sentimentality at a court where almost every single room had its sad little ghosts from the past. Marie Antoinette was clearly delighted by her present and immediately began to plan renovations to the main building, an exquisite little château just big enough for herself and only a few trusted companions, and the surrounding gardens, which she envisioned transforming into a true paradise on earth where she could escape the scrutiny and endless rules and regulations of the court and truly be herself. Of course, people couldn't help but notice that the Petit Trianon had previously always been the preserve of the old King's mistresses, having originally been built for Madame de Pompadour and then passed on to Madame du Barry, and so for it now to given to the Queen was taken as another clear signal that they were living under different times and that Louis was obviously going to be a very different type of Bourbon King to his predecessors

The court stayed away from Versailles for almost six months, a halcyon honeymoon period for the new reign which they spent travelling between Compiègne, Marly and Fontainebleau as well as Choisy and La Muette. The summer and autumn of 1774 were delightfully sunny and warm, perfect honeymoon weather, which seemed to make the new reign seem even more enchanted and blessed. In keeping with the relaxed, optimistic mood, the new King and Queen took the opportunity to set a more informal tone at their court, surrounding themselves with people of their own age and making as many changes as they dared to the rigid ceremonial etiquette that had dominated court life for decades, for instance abolishing the custom of dining in public every day and also ending the custom whereby Marie Antoinette, as Queen, needed to be accompanied by two ladies in waiting at all times, which she often found unnecessarily irksome. Instead, she now made do with a valet and two footmen, who were naturally chosen for their good looks and impressive height and bearing. Another change was to allow the ladies of the royal family to dine with men who were not related to them, which meant that the King and Queen could now hold merry little twice weekly supper parties in their apartments to which they invited people whom they most particularly wanted to honour. Naturally, the competition for invitations was intensely fierce but as guests were occasionally rewarded with the edifying spectacle of the royal couple flicking rolled up bread crumbs at each other across the table and the King and his brothers playing silly pranks on each other they clearly thought it well worth the trouble.

However, this new informality could also go too far. Not long after his succession to the throne and after their period of mourning had ended, Louis decided at the very last minute to attend a court ball being held in the Salon of Hercules, arriving without his usual entourage and a total lack of any fanfare so that no one noticed that he was actually present until, failing to push his way through the crowds to where his wife was holding court, he asked an absolutely astonished lady of the court if he could share her stool. Marie Antoinette found this immensely amusing but the rest of the court was scandalised by such un-majestic behaviour. It seemed extraordinary that a King should not even be noticed in his own ballroom. No one could imagine something like this happening to Louis XIV or even Louis XV and Maurepas was forced to warn his abashed royal master that 'we are not accustomed to seeing our King count for so little in public.'

This diffidence and lack of presence on the part of the King would in time become increasingly problematic for both his ministers and his wife and nowadays it might even be wondered if Louis was on the autistic spectrum[1], although such a thing was unheard of in the eighteenth century. Certainly, his total lack of interest in anything that bored him, his scruffy appearance, strange shambling manner, inability to hold eye contact, intense and often unusual interests, impressively retentive memory, difficulties with facial recognition[2], social awkwardness and often inappropriate sense of humour might all suggest such a thing. Either way, whether it was simply his personality or due to a more complex cause, what could be considered mere eccentricity in a normal man, was absolutely intolerable in a King.

However, it wasn't just the King's manners that were beginning to raise eyebrows at court. At the age of eighteen, Marie Antoinette hadn't really grown up at all and wasn't all that different to the quick tempered, petulant, fun loving and yet essentially very eager to please girl that had left Vienna over four years earlier. Although her powers of concentration had improved along with her French, she was still incapable of hiding her boredom while sitting through the interminable court ceremonies that now became her lot[3] and caused much offence by openly yawning, rolling her eyes, fidgeting and giggling behind her diamond encrusted fan during presentations. Louis was also bored by royal ceremonies but hid it much better than his wife, although he could often be abrupt to the point of rudeness with people, even his ministers if he wasn't interested in what they were saying. Many of the older courtiers now began to pessimistically wonder if their impetuous little Queen was ever going to grow up and it was certainly beginning to look as though her lack of a properly fulfilling marriage and by extension continued childlessness were artificially prolonging her own childhood and were in danger of eventually trapping her in an extended adolescence.

She was also exceedingly rude to the older ladies of the court, a grave mistake when so many of them were actually extremely influential and could have done much to smooth her way at court and make life easier. In alienating them, she was also alienating some of the grandest families in France and forcing more people to lend an ear to the malicious little tales and songs that were starting to circulate about her, most of which came from the apartments of Madame Adélaïde, the grandest older lady of all. 'I don't know why women over the age of thirty bother showing their faces at court,' Marie Antoinette said on one occasion with the blissful lack of foresight of youth, causing a furore and making many women declare that if that was how she felt then they wouldn't come back again. Others, however, wondered if she would feel the same way when she herself turned thirty[4].

There was also an unfortunate incident at La Muette after the death of Louis XV, when all the ladies of court came in their mourning clothes to pay homage to the new Queen, some of them looking really quite macabre in their black weeds and elaborately veiled headdresses. One of Marie Antoinette's younger ladies, the Marquise de Clermont-Tonnerre, was so amused by this weird spectacle that she sat down on the floor behind the other ladies in waiting and began to quietly mock them mercilessly to Marie Antoinette who, despite also being perturbed by the strange sight, tried her best but naturally completely failed to hide her laughter, completely affronting the visiting ladies.

Perhaps unsurprisingly then, one of her first moves after becoming Queen was to appoint her dearest friend the Princesse de Lamballe to the position of *Surintendante de la maison de la reine*, an old and extremely highly paid position which had been dissolved several years earlier but was now revived specially for her. The Princesse now outranked the haughty Madame de Noailles, who was already very offended by her royal mistress' impolite behaviour towards the older members of the court and immediately tendered her resignation as Mistress of the Household, doubtless to Marie Antoinette's great relief. The position of *Surintendante* was one that required great tact and social aplomb, neither of which were skills that the Princesse was exactly replete with. A silly little affected mouse of a woman, she was so nervous and highly strung that she once fainted clean away at the sight of a painting of a lobster.

Although she had all the enormous personal wealth and polished, well-dressed veneer of a great court lady, Madame de Lamballe was, like Marie Antoinette, completely out of her depth and in no way suitable for such an important court job. Also, although she gave all the appearance of being a wispy, ethereal, special little snowflake, Madame la Princesse was at heart also extremely proud and just as ambitious and grasping as anyone else who entered Marie Antoinette's circle at this time and worked tirelessly to promote the interests of her family while at the same time neglecting her own post. She very quickly insulted the other court ladies by refusing to invite them to balls and supper in her apartments, which was one of the traditional duties of the *Surintendante*, claiming that her ill health and royal status made it impossible and wilfully ignoring the fact that her enormous salary was intended as recompense for hosting such gatherings. The ladies began to stay away from Versailles in protest and Marie Antoinette was reluctantly forced to intervene and demand that her friend perform her duties properly.

As *Surintendante* it was the Princesse de Lamballe's duty to supervise Marie Antoinette's daily routine at Versailles and the royal family's other residences: Fontainebleau, Marly, La Muette and Compiègne as well as, later on, Saint Cloud, Rambouillet and the Tuileries. Whereas the King's routine, laid out so precisely by Louis XIV that you could set your clock by it, was dynamic and busy, the Queen's, in contrast, was languid and involved many empty hours which had to be filled. In the early years of her queenship, Marie Antoinette was a late riser who liked to have a lie in after coming back from the delights of Paris in the early hours of the morning and would lounge in bed with her breakfast of hot chocolate infused with cinnamon and coffee and Austrian pastries for quite a while, dreamily sticking pins in her Gazette des Autours[5], to select the day's clothes and chattering about the previous evening's exploits, before finally rolling out of bed and heading off to have her daily bath. Her official *toilette*, attended by the Princesse de Lamballe, a lady in waiting, the First Woman of the Bedchamber and two ladies, would then follow. Madame de Lamballe had the honour of helping Marie Antoinette into her lace edged petticoat before the lady in waiting poured the lavender scented water that she used to wash her hands then handed her a fine lawn chemise, although this honour would be given to any ladies of the royal blood that happened to be present.

The rest of the Queen's elaborate dressing ritual would then follow as she was laced into her morning gown and had her hair dressed and powdered by the highly fashionable hairdresser Léonard, who came from Paris every morning for this purpose, his apparently endless store of juicy gossip adding an extra layer of fun to his ministrations. When she was ready, Marie Antoinette would then go down to Mass in the royal chapel, either accompanied by her ladies or with the King, who would come to collect her on Sundays, when the official weekly court was held at Versailles. The royal party would progress down the Hall of Mirrors and Marie Antoinette would make a point of nodding and smiling at anyone that she wished to show favour to or pointedly blanking those whom she did not want to notice.

Mass took place at midday and Louis, Marie Antoinette and the royal princesses would observe from a gallery above the rest of the congregation, while the Queen's ladies threw their trains over their panniers and rushed to find spots close by. Each lady was attended by a page boy carrying her missal in a large red velvet bag, trimmed with gold fringe but as Madame de la Tour du Pin would later recall rather ruefully, the ladies would hardly ever get to read it for the scramble to find a pew took so long that the priest would already have moved on to the Gospel before they had found the right place.

When Mass was over, the Queen would curtsey to her husband and then return to her apartments, again making a point of stopping to talk to favoured people on the way. Once back in her rooms, she would amuse herself with her friends, play cards with her ladies or withdraw into her private rooms in the ever growing maze that lay behind her state apartments to play her harp, listen to the Abbé de Vermond read or, more thrillingly, consult with her favourite dressmakers Rose Bertin and Madame Éloffe who came out from Paris at least once a week to show off their latest designs or discuss ideas for new gowns and pieces of millinery. All of which was a reasonably pleasant way to pass several hours before it was time to go off to dinner, which on Sunday was eaten publicly in the Antechamber of the *Grand Couvert* in the Queen's apartments.

Marie Antoinette and Louis would sit in front of the fire on two large green armchairs placed behind a small table laid with just two places and covered with a white tablecloth that came down to the ground, on top of which was an array of dishes. A semi-circle of stools was placed about ten feet in front of them where the grand ladies who had the privilege of being permitted to sit on a stool in the royal presence could observe them eat, while everyone else arranged themselves behind. As Madame de la Tour du Pin[6] would later recall: '*The King ate heartily, but the Queen neither removed her gloves nor unfolded her napkin, which was a very big mistake. As soon as the King had drunk his wine, everyone curtseyed and left.*' The abstemious dining habits drilled into Marie Antoinette as a child remained with her for the rest of her life as she would always eat very sparingly and would never touch alcohol, despite the rumours that floated about her dissipated social life. The fact that she was expected to take meals while being stared at by curious bystanders can't have helped matters very much either.

On Sundays, the courtiers would then head off to pay their respects to the rest of the royal family in their apartments, with Madame de la Tour du Pin later recalling that everyone loved calling on the Comte d'Artois, who was '*young and had that charming appearance which he was never to lose. Great efforts were made to please him, for to succeed was a guarantee of fame.*' That he had an eye for the ladies of the court didn't hurt either. Everyone then returned to the Queen's apartments for seven, when the Queen would play cards in public until, yawning behind her fan, she either headed off to bed or to Paris for more congenial entertainment. On other days of the week, Marie Antoinette and her ladies would be left to their own devices until the early evening when there were either the usual court entertainments such as the weekly balls, supper parties, card games or concerts or she was free to go off to the capital to amuse herself at the opera, theatre or at a ball before coming back in the early hours and falling back into bed again.

Louis' coronation took place at Rheims on 11 June 1775 with the entire court in attendance. There had been suggestions that the ceremony should take place at Notre Dame in Paris, which would be both more economical and also appeal to the good nature of the Parisians, who had so loathed the old King. However, Louis was adamant that tradition must be upheld and so they all trooped off to Rheims as usual. Marie Antoinette took no active part in the coronation itself, a half-hearted attempt by Mercy to have her crowned alongside her husband having been firmly rebuffed with it being pointed out to him that Queens had traditionally always been accorded separate coronations in France and that the position of this one, who still remained childless five years after her marriage, was by no means secure even if her husband seemed so fond of her. To add further insult to this undoubted injury, the Comtesse d'Artois, wife of Louis' youngest brother, had recently announced her pregnancy, which only served to further highlight the fact that the Queen herself had failed to conceive.

Marie Antoinette gave every appearance of being entirely unconcerned by her exclusion from the ceremony, although it must have rankled at some level, and consoled herself by ordering a magnificent new dress and an exceedingly high feathered headdress from Rose Bertin for the event, which she no doubted regretted when the coronation day turned out to be swelteringly, headdress droopingly, hot. Although she was not herself to be crowned, Marie Antoinette sat in a place of honour close to her husband and was seen to be visibly moved by the coronation ceremony, even having to withdraw for a few moments when she was completely overcome by tears. Afterwards, she appeared on her newly crowned husband's arm and the couple promenaded around Rheims, receiving the applause and acclamations of their people. Later she would write to her mother that: '*The sacred ceremony was perfect in every way. Everyone is delighted with the King, and rightly so. From the grandest to the humblest of his subjects all were equally enthusiastic. There was even a moment during the coronation when the ceremony was interrupted by an outburst of spontaneous acclamations. It was so touching that however much I tried I was unable to restrain my tears.*'

Although Marie Antoinette remained on outwardly good terms with her brothers-in-law and their wives, their relationship had soured a great deal after the succession of her husband. His brother Provence, always so resentful of Louis' pre-eminence, was deeply jealous of him but still clever enough to treat both him and Marie Antoinette with the greatest respect. In fact, it was rumoured at court that he had a bit of a crush on his sister-in-law, which, if true, would have added to the secret hatred that he harboured for his brother. His wife, Marie Josephine and her sister Marie Thérèse both disliked Marie Antoinette though and took very little trouble to hide the fact, doubtless emboldened by Marie Thérèse succeeding where Marie Antoinette most clearly had not when she became pregnant. They now openly aligned themselves with the aunts and everyone knew that most of the jealous, nasty tittle tattle about the Queen almost certainly originated with them. Artois, the King's handsome, charming youngest brother, was the only one whom Marie Antoinette counted as a friend as their tastes and personalities accorded so well and he was not spiteful or jealous like the others. However, his cheerful over familiarity and total lack of outward respect for both the King and Queen raised eyebrows at court and, in the case of the latter, kicked off several rumours that their relationship, which was entirely innocent, was rather more intimate than that of just brother and sister-in-law.

Although Louis and Marie Antoinette had become much closer in the immediate wake of his grandfather's death and the prolonged honeymoon period of their early reign, they soon began to slide even further apart as Louis became caught up in the seemingly never-ending work of government. Encouraged by Maurepas, he was also becoming increasingly suspicious of his wife's allegiance to Austria, only too well aware of the constant stream of letters that passed between the Empress, Emperor Joseph II, Mercy and Marie Antoinette, who was still being encouraged by her mother to seek total dominance over her husband and bend him to her will. There were practical issues too – now that Louis was living in the King's apartments at Versailles, he was even further away from his wife than before and going to her rooms had become a mortifyingly public event requiring passage through the busy Bull's Eye Chamber, which always seemed full of loitering courtiers who watched his every move with malicious amusement. To Marie Antoinette's chagrin, he had installed Maurepas in the rooms formerly inhabited by Madame du Barry, which were linked directly to the King's rooms by a private staircase, which was handy if he needed late night political advice but far less useful when it came to the important task of conceiving an heir to the throne. In the end, a passage way was built between their two apartments but still Louis' conjugal visits were becoming increasingly infrequent and once again Marie Antoinette found herself back in the same frustrating position of a few years ago – more or less ignored by her husband, harangued by her disappointed mother and beset with worries about her vulnerable position at court, while all the while her enemies seemed to be massing against her.

Thanks to the influence of her brother-in-law and her extravagant, foolish new friends, the Princesse de Lamballe, the Princesse de Guéméné and Lucie Dillon[7], all of whom were habitués of the Duc de Chartres' incredibly wild Parisian set, Marie Antoinette began to spend more time at the Duc's Parisian residence the Palais Royal where the balls were licentious, the gambling stakes were high, the parties were extraordinarily opulent and the champagne apparently never stopped flowing. Frustrated and distressed by the King's apparent lack of interest in her and also her mother's endless stream of complaints about her continuing childlessness, Marie Antoinette saw no reason not to throw herself headlong into this new, enticing and extremely glamorous world, where all that mattered were the latest fashions, the most up to date gossip, the throw of the dice and the turn of a card. The Duc de Chartres threw a splendid fancy dress ball for her at the Palais Royal, which she attended without the King, who did not at all approve of his handsome cousin's dissipated lifestyle but at the same time did not stand in the way of his wife joining in. There were also sleigh rides during the winter and visits to the races, where Marie Antoinette caused a stir by travelling alone in her brother-in-law Artois' open carriage, this being considered quite shocking behaviour. Again, Louis was absent and it was not long before people began to notice that the royal couple were rarely seen together and that the King clearly preferred to stay behind at Versailles while Marie Antoinette went off to Paris every night to be amused.

'I am so terrified of being bored,' she told Mercy when he tried to talk to her about the dangerous effect that her extravagant and increasingly erratic lifestyle was having on her already precarious marriage. She found life at Versailles stagnant, dull and hostile and whereas once upon a time she had felt like she could count on Louis for support, he seemed to be becoming increasingly distant to her. She couldn't remember the last time he came to her bedchamber and their sex life, never particularly fulfilling or all that amazing to start off with, was even worse than before as these days he was too tired by his duties of state to do more than make a desultory attempt to have sex before rolling over to his side of the great bed and starting to snore, which just incensed her even more. For his part, Louis was well aware of his limitations and how miserable his wife was but felt too overwhelmed by work and his own natural diffidence and awkwardness to do very much about it. Encouraged by the wily Maurepas, who was keen to see Marie Antoinette kept well away from any meddling in politics and believed her to be an agent of Austria at heart, he urged his increasingly capricious wife to enjoy her chaotic social life and spend as much money as she liked, hoping in this way to both distract her from her troubles and also, in some way, make amends for his own shortcomings.

Their interests also continued to be completely different and very rarely overlapped. While Marie Antoinette escaped the tedium and frustrations of her life by indulging in sartorial extravagances, gambling and other expensive and meaningless frivolities, her husband escaped the pressures of his own new, restrictive and bewildering role by retreating to his private forge, where he tinkered about happily with his tools and made locks and other small articles which he would shyly present to his family as gifts. He also enlarged the royal libraries for his personal use, whereas nowadays Marie

Antoinette, as the Abbé de Vermond sadly noted, never so much as glanced at a book any more. Like his grandfather, Louis had always been fascinated by astronomy and he installed a comfortable armchair and telescope high up on the roof on Versailles so that he could both look at the stars and also spy on his courtiers, the latter rather surprisingly mischievous activity perhaps being more to Marie Antoinette's taste than the rest. However, although she could never bring herself to take even the slightest bit of interest in his forge, Louis did on occasion scrub up, put on a splendid suit and accompany her to the balls that she loved so much. On one occasion he attended a costume ball dressed as Henri IV, one of his most popular ancestors (notably Marie Antoinette appeared dressed as Henri's mistress Gabrielle d'Estrées rather than one of his two wives, Marguerite de Valois and Marie de' Medici) and he made very rare appearances at the court balls that Marie Antoinette held twice a week in her rooms, although it was rumoured that his wife and brother, Artois liked to put the clock forward so that he left an hour earlier than usual.

The star that was the Princesse de Lamballe was also beginning to wane as Marie Antoinette began to tire of her timidity and silly, pretentious affectations, although she still referred to her as her 'dearest heart' and fussed over her as much as ever. Instead she found herself drawn more towards the delightfully pretty Comtesse de Polignac, a niece of the Comte de Maurepas, who was newly arrived at court and was just the sort of charmingly frivolous and playful companion that Marie Antoinette most yearned for at this time in her life. The Comtesse shared the exact same birthday as the Princesse de Lamballe, which no doubt gave Marie Antoinette an excuse to throw an annual wildly extravagant party, but was a very different character. On the surface she was all huge soulful blue eyes, artlessly tumbling dark curls and languid charm yet she was also extremely amusing, excellent company and could always be relied upon to say exactly the right thing to placate Marie Antoinette, whose always erratic mood swings had recently become much worse, and distract her thoughts towards a more cheerful direction. However, like the Princesse de Lamballe, although on the surface Gabrielle de Polignac[8] was all about sighing over clouds and flowers and enjoying innocent frivolities, she was at heart as rapacious as any royal favourite and managed to amass an enormous amount of wealth and favours for her large and grasping family over the course of the next decade.

Marie Antoinette didn't care though. She had felt desperately lonely at court until Gabrielle came along and now gratefully showered her with affection, keeping her with her at all times and whole heartedly transferring the rather schoolgirl crushes that she had once had on the Princesse de Lamballe and then Lucie Dillon to her new friend, who to her great delight gave every appearance of reciprocating. Although the malign gossips of the court obviously whispered that there was something 'unnatural' about the Queen's love for her friend, who was being accorded the sort of attention and honour that had always in the past been given to a King's *maîtresse de titre*, it was almost certainly nothing more than another example of the fashion for intense friendships that flourished between women at this time, which often took on a performative romantic appearance. Although malicious court gossip hinted that the Queen and her favourite were engaged in lesbian orgies in the relative privacy of the Petit Trianon, where even the King had to wait to be invited and everything was done 'by order of the Queen', there was almost certainly nothing more scandalous than an innocent and sentimental girl crush going on, albeit one that was very likely one sided on Marie Antoinette's part.

In fact, relieved that his wife had made a close friend at court and almost certainly entirely deceived by Gabrielle de Polignac's deceptively sweet and innocent demeanour to the extent that it began to be rumoured that he also had a massive crush on his wife's best friend, Louis encouraged this friendship to blossom, although he baulked somewhat when he learned what sort of company the new favourite was keeping in her new and extremely lovely apartment at Versailles, where she entertained her lover, the Comte de Vaudreuil, apparently with the full complacency of her husband, Monsieur le Comte. She was also, while claiming that it was all part of her duty to keep the mercurial Queen amused, encouraging Marie Antoinette to squander even greater sums in her pursuit of distraction so that by the late 1770s her extravagances were becoming worrying even to her indulgent spouse and, more troublingly still, her public popularity began to wane as word about the Queen's spending sprees began to spread.

This fall in Marie Antoinette's popularity was also fanned by the stories about the Queen's behaviour that were beginning to leak out from Versailles and be whispered around Paris where her critics tutted over tales of the Queen's distinctly un-royal behaviour, including one about her carriage breaking down on the way to a ball upon which she had been forced to hail a common hackney carriage to take her to her destination. Marie Antoinette, so desperate for novelty, had considered this an enormous adventure and told everyone she met about it the next day – without realising that her escapade would be very much frowned upon outside her own rather rakish and cocky circle. There was also general condemnation over the fact that she still visited the masked balls at the Opéra with her brothers-in-law and friends, especially after an incident when Provence, who had a foul temper, had caused an immense stir by punching the face of a total stranger who had the misfortune to accidentally jostle him. It wouldn't have been so bad if the King had accompanied her every now and again, after all the sentimental Parisians loved to see the royal couple mooning over each other in public, but he was always left behind at Versailles and would often rarely see his wife for days on end as she rushed off to balls in the evening, arriving back at Versailles in time for Mass before going off to bed for the rest of the day so as to refresh herself for another round of dissipation later on.

'*For more than a year now, I have heard no more about your reading or music; instead, I only hear about horse rides, hunts, all without the King and with many ill-chosen young people, which worries me greatly because I love you so dearly*,' Maria Theresa wrote reprovingly to her youngest daughter in May 1776. '*Your sisters-in-law are behaving very differently, and I must tell you that all these noisy pleasures which the King doesn't share are not proper. You will tell me that, 'He knows all about them and approves of them.' I will answer that he is kind and that you must therefore be all the more careful and share your amusements with him. In the long run you can only be happy if you two are linked by a loving and sincere union and friendship*.'

Clearly, something urgently needed to be done before the situation spiralled completely out of control. But what?

Chapter 7

Queen of Fashion 1776–1778

'Indiscreet pleasures.'

In November 1776, Marie Antoinette turned twenty one and to celebrate there were several fetes, balls and parties arranged at Fontainebleau where the court was enjoying its traditional autumn sojourn. By this time, the heedless little Queen was completely obsessed with gambling and as a birthday present entreated her husband to allow some proper Parisian gambling bankers to come to the palace for a special game of Faro, a much more exciting game that was played for far higher stakes than the polite *cavagnole* enjoyed by the older members of the royal family. Louis agreed to her request but stipulated that they could remain in the palace for one game only. The bankers duly arrived and the game was played in the apartments of the Princesse de Lamballe with all of Marie Antoinette's circle, including Gabrielle de Polignac and the handsome Duc de Lauzun, who was said to be madly in love with the Queen, in attendance. The gamers paused in the early hours of the morning then resumed again in the evening, eventually lasting for thirty-six hours. When Louis gently remonstrated with his wife, she laughingly reminded him that he although he had agreed to a single game he had not, however, stipulated how long it should last. 'You are all a worthless bunch!' Louis replied, joining in her laughter.

At the end of her life, Marie Antoinette's cosmetics were reduced to a tarnished mirror, a swansdown puff with some powder and a vial of scented water. As she patted the powder onto her already pallid cheeks, she must have reflected with some wonder and sadness about the fact that not too long ago, her *toilette* had been one of the high points of the court day, attended by dozens of courtiers, all vying for attention and dictated by an arcane and complex etiquette that had been handed down for generations. Ironic then that Marie Antoinette's own tastes inclined towards the discreet and modest. To the ordinary people, she was a haughty, spoiled, pampered creature who delighted in extravagance and ceremony whereas those who were closest to her, knew that on the contrary she preferred simplicity and a total lack of pomp and fuss.

She had an unerring and exquisite taste and the beautiful objects owned and worn by Marie Antoinette still exert a tremendous fascination today. Sadly, the ravages of the Revolution resulted in the destruction of Marie Antoinette's fabulous wardrobe and most of her belongings were either looted, sold abroad or lost forever but enough remains for us to have a very good idea of the tasteful luxury that she liked to surround herself with. The Queen's clothes collection was vast, with three whole rooms put aside at Versailles just to store it. The rooms were open to public so it was possible to visit the Queen's clothes, just as you could go and watch her have dinner or walk past on her way to Mass in the morning and it's likely that for the fashion mad ladies of Paris and Versailles a trip to the Queen's wardrobe, where her amazing gowns were laid out on special shelves to prevent them from creasing, was viewed with as much reverence as seeing her in person.

Marie Antoinette was given a fixed allowance of 120,000 livres a year for clothes and accessories, a vast sum that was somehow still never quite enough (she spent 258,000 livres in one year), probably because at some point along the line etiquette had decreed that eighteen pairs of pastel coloured gloves scented with violet, hyacinth or carnation and four new pairs of shoes had to be ordered for her on a weekly basis along with several other such items that seemed like small fry but amounted to vast sums when added together. Her weakness for the designs of Rose Bertin was also a problem as each of her gorgeous dresses, which had swooning, irresistibly romantic names like 'Indiscreet Pleasures', 'Heart's Agitation' and 'Stifled Sighs', cost around 1,000 livres, sometimes even 6,000 livres each, which quickly mounted up when you were ordering dozens at a time along with matching shoes, perfumed fans, feathers and extravagant hair decorations.

Strictly speaking, Marie Antoinette's wardrobe purchases were supposed to be restricted to orders of thirty-six dresses for the summer and thirty-six for the winter but the Queen adored fashion and so ordered far more, bypassing the usual court dressmakers and even on occasion her Mistress of the Wardrobe[1] who was supposed to deal with sartorial matters on her behalf and instead directly consulting with the fashionable couturiers of Paris. According to etiquette she was only supposed to wear dresses once and had to change three times a day but clearly seventy-two dresses a year wasn't going to cut much of a dash at Versailles and so she ordered more. Once worn, favourite dresses were kept and carefully looked after, and perhaps cleverly altered, so that they never looked anything less than brand new but others were given away to her ladies in waiting, who saw this as being one of the most valuable perks of what could be a very arduous and tiresome job.

When the Queen's gorgeous bedchamber was renovated in the last century, several pins were discovered wedged between the wooden floorboards, a remnant of the elaborate daily ceremonial that surrounded the dressing of the Queen. Every morning before she got out of bed, Marie Antoinette would be presented with the *gazette des atours*, a huge book full of fabric swatches from each of her gowns and she would place a pin in the dresses that she wanted to wear that day, which would then be brought down from the wardrobe in vast green taffeta covered baskets. Marie Antoinette would change three times in the course of the day: first of all there would be a formal silk or velvet gown to be worn to Mass, followed by a lighter, more informal muslin, lawn or cotton dress for the rest of the day and then finally a gorgeously elaborate evening dress to be worn to dinner, concerts, balls or the theatre in Paris, where Marie Antoinette had private boxes at the Opéra House, Comédie Française and Comédie Italienne. The young Queen's preference was for light fabrics and pale, pastel colours such as a soft lemon yellow, dove grey, pale green and lilac. Again, Madame Bertin was inventive, taking an almost poetic pleasure in thinking up names for different shades – '*Incendie de l'Opera*' was a vivid orange red; '*Cheveux de la Reine*' a soft gold inspired by her strawberry blonde hair and, most poetically, '*Caca Dauphin*' was a pale brown inspired by the 'caca' of her infant son.

Marie Antoinette took as much care of her person as she did her clothes and her beauty regime was extensive. At night she would sleep wearing gloves lined with wax, rose water and sweet almond oil and she probably treated her hair with a wash of saffron, turmeric, sandalwood and rhubarb in order to accentuate its strawberry blondness. Before she applied her make-up, she would carefully cleanse her skin with *Eau Cosmetique de Pigeon*, followed by *Eau des Charmes* astringent and then *Eau d'Ange*, a gentle whitener that maintained her famously luminous complexion. After this, the young Queen's face would be lightly powdered, her eyebrows would be subtly darkened with kohl or a lead comb and finally a small amount of rouge was applied to her cheeks and lips. Although heavy make up had long been considered *de rigeur* at Versailles[2], Marie Antoinette's exquisite complexion needed no such assistance, especially in her youth, and like most young women today she chose to accentuate her best features rather than conceal her appearance behind a mask of cosmetics. Sticks of pomade scented with rose, carnation or vanilla were used to gloss her lips, eyebrows and eyelashes. Marie Antoinette had survived her childhood bout of small pox relatively unscathed bar a few unnoticeable scars but it is likely that she still enjoyed the fashion for black velvet beauty patches – perhaps applying one to the corner of her mouth, which signalled her wish to be kissed or one on the forehead, which suggested that the wearer was haughty and definitely *not* to be kissed.

However, although Marie Antoinette preferred only the lightest touch of make-up, her hair was a very different matter. Then, as now, the beauty standard was for luxuriantly thick and healthy hair and women used more or less the same means to achieve this, such as regularly using special treatments, regularly pomading and powdering, which worked as well as washing and conditioning, and, when all else failed, using wigs and hair pieces. Marie Antoinette's hair was dressed every day by one of her favourite hairdressers, most usually Léonard Autié, who would first wet her hair with a conditioning pomatum made from rendered animal fats mixed with essential oils such as clove, lavender or neroli, which not only smelt good but also kept lice and other pests at bay, and then coat it with a powder made from wheat starch and orris root, which was also scented with essential oils and occasionally also dyed pink, blue or yellow. Much like the dry shampoos available today, the hair powders used by Marie Antoinette kept her hair clean and fresh and also had a flattering thickening effect. After this, hair was arranged over a hair cushion in order to create the often incredibly towering high hairstyles that were fashionable at the French court and beyond from the second half of the 1770s onwards.

There was a definite emphasis on the senses in Marie Antoinette's *toilette* – Versailles at this time, particularly in the summer, could smell rather unpleasant[3] and the courtiers did everything they could to keep bad odours at bay. Marie Antoinette's rooms were scented with a profusion of fresh flowers, fragrant pastilles which were melted over burners, pot pourri, oils and perfumed sachets. She particularly loved the fresh scents of orange blossom, lemon, rose, lavender and violet and her rooms would have smelled deliciously sweet as you entered them. The Queen loved to douse herself with *eau de fleur d'oranger* (orange blossom water); simple violet, rose and jonquil scents or more complex perfumes made with vanilla, musk, lavender, iris, jasmine and lily or lemon, cinnamon, angelica, cloves and coriander. It seems that everywhere she went, she wanted to be surrounded by gorgeous fragrances.

Always keen to stay as fresh as possible, which was not unusual in an era when the connection between hygiene and health was fully understood and everyone was keen to avoid infectious diseases, Marie Antoinette insisted on daily baths and her bathroom at Versailles still exists with simple dove grey walls and a sloping tiled floor so that the water could drain away. Her perfumer Fargeon devised a *bain de modéstie* for her, which involved bathing in a flannel chemise so that her body would not be exposed even to the gaze of her ladies in waiting. Once in the bath she would sit on a large pad filled with sweet almonds, pine nuts, linseed, marshmallow root and lily bulb while she washed herself with muslin pads filled with gentle and exfoliating bran and soaps scented with herbs, amber and bergamot, before settling back in the scented water to daydream about what the future might hold.

Glimpses of this world of beautiful lace trimmed dresses, rose and violet scented powdered hair and delicately applied cosmetics can be gleaned from the portraits of Marie Antoinette during this time. She was perhaps the most painted Queen of France and portraits exist from every period of her life, charting her development from wide eyed Austrian *ingénue* to dignified Queen, dressed in elaborate silks and with a glittering crown on the table beside her. However, her famously luminous complexion was difficult to accurately capture and as she grew older and her features developed, artists seem to have difficulty reconciling her strong and not conventionally attractive Habsburg looks with the annoyingly intangible qualities of charm and charisma that the vivacious little Queen exuded in real life. Certainly her mother would frequently complain about the likenesses that made their way to Vienna and Marie Antoinette would be forced to explain that none of the available artists were quite up to scratch.

The famous 1775 portrait by Jean-Baptiste Gautier-Dagoty, which depicts the young Queen in an extraordinarily elaborate swagged and embellished state gown with the robes of state falling elegantly from her shoulders and one small hand resting lightly on a prominently positioned globe is considered very pleasing to modern eyes but failed to impress anyone at Versailles, where it was roundly denounced as a hideous and amateurish daubing. It was actually intended as a present for Marie Antoinette's mother but she decided that she was too scared to send it to Vienna and so instead presented it to a friend. Gautier-Dagoty's 1776 goache painting of the Queen sitting in her beautifully flounced dressing gown in her exquisite bedroom at Versailles surrounded by friends, her milliner, musicians, hairdressers and poor Gautier-Dagoty himself, shown hard at work on his earlier portrait, was much more successful, as were his portraits of her sisters-in-law, whom he managed to make look rather prettier than they were in real life.

On 6 August 1775, the Comtesse d'Artois, wife of Louis' youngest brother went into labour at Versailles and gave birth to a son, Louis-Antoine, who was given the title of Duc d'Angoulême. Although the new *régime* had gone some way towards abolishing the outmoded ceremonials of the past it had not yet managed to do away with the tradition whereby ladies of the immediate royal family gave birth in public, a most humiliating ritual designed to ensure that no tiny interlopers could be smuggled into the royal bedchamber to take the place of still births or unwelcome baby girls. Not that the Comtesse, thoroughly enjoying her new and unprecedented prominence at court as the first of the trio of wives to give birth, cared about this and indeed she probably relished having as many people as possible there to witness her triumph. Etiquette decreed that

Marie Antoinette should be present at the birth along with her husband and although she found this to be an intensely painful experience, fully aware that the censorious eyes of the court were trained as much on her as on the labouring Comtesse, she bore it as gracefully as she could and even managed to smile and compliment the overjoyed new parents when their son was born. However, on her way back to her apartments, she was rudely harangued by a crowd of market women, the traditionally self-appointed voice of the Parisian people, who demanded to know when she would give the nation a Dauphin and shouted crude advice about what she should be doing with the King to make it happen. Overwhelmed, humiliated and devastated, Marie Antoinette broke down as soon as she reached the relative safety of her magnificent bedchamber and according to her First Lady of the Bedchamber, the sympathetic Madame Campan, cried for a long time.

Encouraged by her friends, Marie Antoinette now became even more extravagant and reckless than ever, seeking to forget her personal troubles with an endless round of parties, gambling and self-indulgence. Her innocent flirtations with those handsome, sophisticated womanisers the Duc de Lauzun (who was said to be the secret illegitimate son of the Duc de Choiseul, who was married to his aunt and had also been his mother's lover), the Prince de Ligne and the Duc de Coigny, the latter the acknowledged lover of her friend, the Princesse de Guéméné, caused much comment at this time, even though they were almost certainly just meaningless and entirely understandable distractions from her dissatisfactory marriage. While Marie Antoinette loved to flirt and to be admired as the most beautiful lady at her court, she was not by nature a very sensual woman and the thought of taking these brief little infatuations any further would have horrified her, although on the other hand there was talk at court that she had told her friends that she wished the King would take a mistress and that she would be 'neither grieved nor very annoyed' if it happened as he 'might thereby acquire more vitality and energy'. Perhaps more troublingly in the long term, she also developed a fascination with jewels, particularly diamonds, encouraged by the Princesse de Guéméné, who had extremely expensive tastes herself and persuaded the Queen to buy a pair of beautiful diamond earrings from the Swiss jeweller, Boehmer for the amazing sum of 600,000 livres and on another later occasion, a pair of diamond bracelets for 250,000 livres, which led to a scolding from her mother. Huge sums were also spent on the continued beautification of the Petit Trianon which now became her refuge against the mounting disapproval of the court and Count Mercy's endless boring lectures about her mounting debts which Louis, with typical generosity, still insisted upon paying off.

Like many other young people at court, Marie Antoinette was also gripped by a passion for all things English, particularly horse racing and country dances, which she loved to dance with young British gentlemen visiting the court. Like all the other fashionable women at court, she ordered her specially tailored riding habits from London and smattered her conversation with a few choice English phrases, although it must be assumed that she stopped short of reading the translations of Shakespeare's plays that were popular at the time and such a favourite with her husband. She also delighted in making friends with English visitors, in particular striking up a very close friendship with Georgiana, Duchess of Devonshire who visited Versailles in 1775. The two young women had met before but it was during this visit that they really hit it off, perhaps because they realised that they had a lot in common – both had been married at a young age to men that they didn't love, had difficult relationships with overbearing and highly critical mothers and had a tendency to form extremely close and passionate friendships with other women. Most significantly, however, both were experiencing difficulties conceiving a child[4] and were hiding their frustration and deep unhappiness beneath the same brittle veneer of fashionable frivolity, which meant that Georgiana and Marie Antoinette probably had much to talk about over the hot chocolate and cakes that were served when they got together at the Petit Trianon.

Another, perhaps more surprising friendship was the one that developed over the years between Marie Antoinette and her British counterpart Queen Charlotte, who was eleven years her senior. It had long been the custom for the British and French rulers to write polite letters acknowledging the various happy and sad events in each other's life, maintaining at least a pretence of friendship even when hostilities raged between the two nations as they so often did. However, a true friendship sprang up over the years between Charlotte and Marie Antoinette, who had both been in their teens when they were sent away from their own countries to be married and had become queens before they were out of their twenties. Although their personalities were markedly different and Charlotte, obviously, had never had any problems conceiving children (by May 1774, when Marie Antoinette became Queen of France, Charlotte already had ten children and would go on to have five more) they were still drawn together by the things that they did have in common which included a typically Germanic lack of pretension and a certain wry sense of humour. Later on, when things turned sour for Marie Antoinette, Charlotte would urge her to escape to England and even had apartments made ready for the French royal family should they make it to London. Sadly, they were never used.

Rather touchingly, Marie Antoinette also at this time fostered a five year old peasant boy called François Michel Gagné, known to his family as 'Jacques', who had the bad luck to very nearly be knocked down by her carriage while she was travelling past Louveciennes. The impetuous Queen immediately jumped down to make sure that the boy was unhurt and then, upon learning that he was an orphan and, along with four other siblings, being raised by his grandmother, whisked him away to a new and doubtless bewildering life in the lap of luxury at Versailles, where he would henceforth be known by the rather more elegant name of Armand. Her mother did not at all approve of this escapade, especially as little Armand himself made it very clear that he did not want to be there and wanted to be returned to his grandmother, but Marie Antoinette did not care and for a time was fully absorbed in her new role as 'mother' to Armand, who was treated like her own child and even breakfasted with her every morning. She lost some interest in the boy after the birth of her daughter in 1778, but continued to care for him, supervise his education and also send a generous allowance to his family[5].

Increasingly troubled by the reports of Mercy and the Abbé de Vermond, who at one point was exasperated enough to hand in his notice, which the Queen refused to accept, Maria Theresa redoubled her efforts to force her daughter to live in a more restrained and sensible way, foreseeing that her current hedonistic lifestyle could only end in ruin. She was also profoundly shocked by Marie Antoinette's dismissive, almost contemptuous way of speaking about the King, even referring to him as '*the poor man*' which to Maria Theresa's mind suggested that there had been a severe diminishment in her respect towards him – certainly she would never have *dreamed* to refer to her own husband in such a disrespectful way. The continued lack of a royal baby, which she blamed on the fact that Marie Antoinette and Louis did not share a room every night rather than the fact that very little happened between them when they *did*, also weighed heavily on the Empress' mind and she never ceased to lecture her daughter about how best to accomplish this while at the same time apparently completely failing to grasp that Marie Antoinette's marriage and, indeed, husband were *very* different to her own.

In the end, she decided that the best course of action was to send Marie Antoinette's eldest brother, Emperor Joseph II, to Paris to speak to the hapless pair and find out what was happening – or rather, *not* happening. A previous visit to Versailles from Marie Antoinette's younger brother, Archduke Maximilian had ended badly due to a tiresome argument over precedence as the young Archduke was travelling incognito as a lowly count, as was the fashion at the time, but still demanded that proper reverence be paid to him as the brother of the Queen which several gentlemen at court, including the King's brothers and the irascible Duc de Chartres, unsurprisingly, refused to do. It was determined that *this* visit would go much more smoothly and, unlike the last one, cause the Queen of France, already in such a precarious position, no residual embarrassment.

The Emperor Joseph II, travelling incognito as Count von Falkenstein, arrived at Versailles on the morning of 18 April 1777. Unlike his youngest brother, he had no wish to insist upon the full honours that were due to his rank but instead rather relished being treated as a lowly count just as his sister Marie Antoinette loved to play at being an 'ordinary' woman at the Petit Trianon. The always faithful Abbé de Vermond was waiting to discreetly escort the Emperor through the secret back staircases and passages of the palace to where his sister, dressed in a simple black mourning gown (her godfather, the King of Portugal had recently died) and with her hair loosely pinned up and lightly powdered as she had been so impatient to see him that she'd rushed away from her morning *toilette* before it was finished, was waiting for him in the warren of intimate private rooms that lay behind her opulent bedchamber.

Marie Antoinette had not seen her eldest brother, whom she had hero worshipped as a child, for seven years and wept with joy as she threw herself into his arms and embraced him, delighted beyond measure to be reunited with one of her favourite siblings and furthermore, one who had always seemed so capable and supportive. Surely, she felt, if anyone could sort out the mess that she had made in France, it would be Joseph? She took him into one of her private sitting rooms and for the next few hours poured all of her troubles and woes into his apparently sympathetic ears, sparing no detail about her unfulfilling marriage, desperate wish to have a child and sad attempts to distract herself and at the end, to her immense relief, Joseph did not tell her off but instead promised to do all that he could to help. She then took him to meet her husband for the first time and found that, rather touchingly, Louis had made a great deal of effort to look presentable for his brother-in-law which made a good first impression and probably confounded Joseph's preconceived ideas about the King of France being a scruffy, badly dressed clown. They then took luncheon together at a table placed at the end of Marie Antoinette's bed and everything looked set for a very cordial visit.

Joseph stayed in Paris for over three weeks, having a whale of a time exploring the city and its environs and spending lots of time with his beloved sister who introduced him to all of her friends, very few of whom he liked, and spent most of her afternoons alone with him, talking about her life and its problems to this apparently most sympathetic and kindly of listeners. However, after listening for hours to the shy yet astonishingly frank confidences of both the King and Queen about their sex life and relationship, Joseph suddenly went on the offensive and started to lay down the law. First of all, he told Marie Antoinette that he didn't approve of her friends and considered them at best frivolous and stupid and at worst downright iniquitous. Secondly, he informed her at an evening *soirée* that they were attending without the King, that she ought to pay her husband more attention and made her go off and fetch Louis, who no doubt protested strenuously to be dragged away from his books, telescope and forge, to the party.

Most crucially though, he took a great interest in the young couple's sexual issues, writing with astonishing frankness to his brother Archduke Leopold that '*in his conjugal bed, he has normal erections; he introduces his member, stays there without moving for about two minutes, then withdraws without ejaculating, and still erect, bids good night. This is incomprehensible because he sometimes has nocturnal emissions, but while inside and in the process, never; yet he is content, and says quite frankly that he is doing it purely from a sense of duty and without any enjoyment. Oh, if I could only have been present once, I would have taken care of him; he should be whipped so that he would discharge sperm like a donkey. My sister, moreover, has very little temperament and together they are two complete fumblers.*' Ouch.

He further commented that Louis was '*badly brought up; his appearance works against him, but he is honest… The man is weak but no fool.*' About his sister Marie Antoinette, he was far more harsh, saying that she was '*fulfilling neither her duties as a wife nor her duties as a Queen in satisfactory fashion… She is empty headed and driven to run all day from dissipation to dissipation. She thinks only of having fun. She feels nothing for the King. She is a likeable and honest woman, a bit young, unreflective, but deep down honest and virtuous.*' All of this would form the basis of the instructions that Joseph left with Marie Antoinette upon his departure, which he hoped would go some way towards rectifying her poor attitude towards both her marriage and her husband.

'*Look into yourself. Do you put all your efforts into pleasing him? Do you study his desires and his character and try to conform to them? Do you try to make him enjoy your company – beyond all other objects or amusements – and the pleasures you can grant him, where, without you, he would find only a void? Do you make yourself essential to him? Have you persuaded him that no one loves him more sincerely than you, or takes his glory and happiness more to heart? Does he see your affection focused exclusively on him?*' Although Joseph could totally understand why Louis, so lacklustre and shambling beside the debonair Duc de Lauzun and other highly polished gallants of Marie Antoinette's circle, had failed to capture either her attention or affection, he was still very clear that it was her absolute duty to make the King love her no matter what.

He also strongly criticised the '*dreadful fecklessness*' of her current lifestyle, addressing poor Marie Antoinette in the strongest terms because he had come to the conclusion that shaming her was perhaps the only way to make the reckless young Queen, of whom he was actually genuinely extremely fond, see sense. '*What is it that you want? To be unknown and play the role of a person different to yourself? Why the need for adventures and naughtiness? Why mingle with a crowd of libertines, girls, strangers, listening to their conversation and replying in kind? What indecency! The King left alone for a whole night at Versailles and you mixing with the Paris riffraff!*

Marie Antoinette was exceedingly distressed by her brother's blunt advice, which she saw as a personal attack not just upon herself but also her dearest friends, with not even the delightful Comtesse de Polignac escaping his scorn. However, she was also forced to admit the truth of his words and consequently did her best to comply with his advice by toning down her whirlwind of a social life and trying to spend more time with the King and less with her friends. In October she proudly wrote to her mother that, '*I hardly ever stay up late at night any more, and I hardly went out all summer, both for my health and because I know a little better how to spend my time at home than in the past. I read, I embroider, I have two music masters, one for voice, the other for the harp; I have started drawing again – all that keeps me busy and entertains me.*' She also told her mother that she was gambling much less but pointed out that etiquette decreed that she still play in public three times a week. These public card games took place on Wednesdays, Saturdays and Sundays and occurred at a large round table set up in the Salon of Peace that lay between Marie Antoinette's rooms and the Hall of Mirrors. However, unlike the gambling that went on at the Palais Royal or apartments of the Princesse de Guéméné, the stakes at the royal table at Versailles were relatively small.

As for Louis, nothing remains of the advice that Joseph left for him but we can be sure that it was expressed in equally blisteringly forceful terms and doubtless reminded the young King that it was his duty towards his wife and his nation for him to man up and do the deed properly, whether he liked it or not. Like Marie Antoinette he was doubtless exceedingly stung and humiliated by whatever the forthright Joseph said to him but similarly was forced to concede that his brother-in-law was in the right and so do his best to comply. Although the young couple would never fully regain the honeymoon atmosphere of the beginning of their reign, they now made a great deal of effort to increase the intimacy and affection in their marriage by once again walking about arm in arm in public and taking the signal step of spending two hours every day closeted alone together in their rooms – Joseph having advised his sister to '*get him to bed with you in the afternoon as there's no use waiting until after supper, when he is already sunk in a state of apathy*'. Finally, on the morning of 18 August, not all that long after Joseph's departure, the King shyly came to see his wife after she'd had her bath and they fully consummated their marriage for the first time. '*I am now enjoying the most essential happiness of my entire life,*' Marie Antoinette wrote to her mother. '*It has already been more than eight days since my marriage was perfectly consummated; the event has been repeated and again yesterday more completely than the first time.... I do not think I am pregnant yet, but at least I have the hope of being so any day.*'

In fact, Marie Antoinette was not to become pregnant until the following spring. She wrote to her mother on 19 April 1778 that: '*Already eight days ago I wanted to tell you something of my hopes but did not dare to do so, for fear of how upset you would be if they failed to materialise.*' Luckily, her hopes turned out to be reality and the royal pregnancy was announced the following month, causing enormous excitement at a court where quite a few people had long given up all hope of the Queen ever conceiving a child. As might be expected, Louis was pleased as punch about the great news and his approaching fatherhood gave him a new swagger and confidence while his wife renounced her former chaotic life and instead took up more gentle pursuits, preferring to spend her time in solitude at the Petit Trianon, supervising the planting of her new gardens, than staying up until all hours gambling and dancing with the Polignac and Chartres sets.

Marie Antoinette's first and much longed for pregnancy should have been a peaceful and halcyon time but was instead marred by the eruption of hostilities between Prussia and Austria after her brother, emboldened by the death of the Elector of Bavaria, laid claim to territories in southern Bavaria which were immediately contested by the King of Prussia, who had no wish to see his Austrian enemies grab more land. To the annoyance of Marie Antoinette, the French came down firmly on the side of the Prussians and she soon found herself caught between a rock and a hard place, beset on one side by passive aggressive recriminations from her family who ordered her to secure French support and kept at arm's length on the other by her husband who informed her, not unsympathetically, that 'the ambitions of your family are going to upset everything. They started with Poland and now it is Bavaria. I am annoyed on your account.'

As might be expected, Marie Antoinette completely lacked the political acumen to be able to navigate the pitfalls of such a delicate situation and, unsurprisingly, ended up pleasing nobody. Although her natural instincts were now to be loyal to her adopted country France, she had still tried her best to placate her family by promising them as much assistance as she was able to procure, which when it failed to materialise ended up leaving them disappointed and angry with her. Worse still, the situation aroused the old feelings of distrust in her husband and his advisors, especially Maurepas, which left her feeling isolated and unhappy. On the other hand, when it came to the fledgling war between America and England, in which the French had thrown their support behind the American republicans, Marie Antoinette had no qualms about wholeheartedly supporting the French in what looked set to develop into a war with England itself, even though she had friends in England, including the charming Georgiana, Duchess of Devonshire and Queen Charlotte herself.

However, all these political contretemps could not entirely diminish the joy that Marie Antoinette found in her pregnancy. The proud expectant mother sent regular reports about her health to her mother and was often to be found measuring her waist as if to reassure herself that, after all those years of longing, a child was indeed growing inside her. When she felt the baby's first movements she immediately hastened to Louis' apartments and announced: 'Your Majesty, I have come to complain about one of your subjects, who has had the audacity to kick me in the stomach.' Louis was thrilled and immediately lifted her up into his arms and kissed her in front of everyone.

Although there were still weekly card parties, balls and suppers at Versailles, the overall atmosphere was altogether more muted and low key as everyone waited for the royal baby to be born. Marie Antoinette no longer travelled by carriage for fear that this might bring on early labour and so the usual summer excursions to Compiègne and Marly were cancelled. Instead, the Queen fled the stifling apartments of Versailles for the Petit Trianon, which she had transformed into a sumptuous jewellery box of a house since Louis presented it to her with the words: '*Vous aimez les fleurs. J'ai un bouquet à vous offrir*'. It's easy to see why Marie Antoinette lost her heart to the Petit Trianon though – built along the lines of a small and compact chateau and exquisitely decorated in light, fresh colours, it was the perfect size for a tiny court with only enough bedrooms to house the Queen, a couple of her closest companions, which included her sister in law Madame Élisabeth, Madame de Polignac and the Princesse de Lamballe and, later, her children. As with all the royal palaces, there was a special Trianon Livery – scarlet and white, which was worn by all visiting gentlemen and would have looked striking against the delicate gilded panelling.

The rooms of the Petit Trianon remain one of the most perfect examples of late eighteenth century design and mark the moment when the rococo frivolity of the mid part of the century began to give way to the more austere beauty of the neo-classical. Keen to stamp her own personal taste on the building, Marie Antoinette very deliberately eschewed the grandeur of nearby Versailles and instead filled her rooms with pale greens, blues and pinks and hung soft muslin drapes at the windows and around her bed. The paintings too were a mixture of romantic classical scenes and portraits of her brothers and sisters, most of whom she would never see again, which were sent at her request from Vienna. Rumours gradually spread across France that the Petit Trianon was a temple to excess with diamond encrusted panelling and all manner of lavishness to frame the orgies of the woman they were beginning to regard as a Courtesan Queen. The truth was actually very different, as although her renovation of the house and gardens were indeed extremely and indeed eye-wateringly costly, the little estate was furnished with quiet elegance and quite unlike the extravagant bordello that Marie Antoinette's detractors, none of whom could ever hope to be invited there, claimed it to be.

As if to underline the difference between Versailles and the Petit Trianon, Marie Antoinette also dressed completely differently there – eschewing the powdered coiffures, stiff panniered gowns and jewels that formed her court attire and instead favouring softly flowing silks and her favourite muslins, un-powdered loosely dressed hair and straw hats. Obsessed as she was with theatre, it would have seemed natural and perhaps even comforting to Marie Antoinette to don different costumes for what she must increasingly have seen as her two completely different lives – one as the elegant and sparkling Queen of France dressed in silk and sparkling with jewels and the other as a private individual, quietly tending her flowers and drinking orange blossom tea in a muslin dress and straw hat at the Petit Trianon.

There was a new arrival to Marie Antoinette's close circle of friends that year when the handsome Swedish nobleman Axel von Fersen arrived back in France after an unsuccessful attempt to woo an heiress in England. The young Axel loved Parisian high society and was also hopeful of securing a commission in the French army in the war against England. Although the Queen had certainly not been pining for him during the four years that had passed since they first met and briefly chatted at the Opéra ball, she was glad to have him back at Versailles, where his good looks and charming manner won hearts everywhere. However, it didn't take long for jealous whispers about Marie Antoinette's obvious admiration of this good looking and rather dashing young man to start doing the rounds, even though the flirtation between them was almost certainly entirely innocent, not least because of the Queen's pregnancy.

There were also, predictably, all the usual malicious rumours about the paternity of the royal baby, probably fanned by Louis' disgruntled younger brother the Comte de Provence who saw his position as heir to the throne slipping away from him. It was whispered around the louche salons of Paris that the baby had actually been fathered by either the Duc de Lauzun or Duc de Coigny, both of whom who had the much prized *entrée* to the Petit Trianon and were known to be particular favourites of the Queen. It was all nonsense of course but had the effect of making Marie Antoinette retreat still further away from the court, hurt that her much longed for happiness was being tarnished so cruelly – which made her cling even more onto the few people that she felt she could really trust.

Like many other expectant mothers, Marie Antoinette took a great deal of interest in her appearance, turning to the redoubtable Rose Bertin to provide her with lovely, flowing new gowns to make her feel more comfortable and attractive. Mademoiselle Bertin started to make wonderful breezy silk gowns, known as *lévites* for her royal mistress, which were designed to accommodate the growing royal bump, which the royal physicians thought was measuring very large for her dates, and also keep her cool during what turned out to be a scorching hot summer, when it was so hot that the Queen had to spend all day indoors and could only venture out in the evening when it was cooler and the royal musicians were asked to play on the terraces while she took the air beneath the stars. There were also concerns about Marie Antoinette's hair, which had a habit of thinning whenever she was under emotional strain and which now began to fall out in clumps, a common enough problem in pregnancy, which her hairdresser Léonard had to conceal with artful use of hair pieces, feathers and *poufs* of muslin.

The long-awaited royal labour began in the early hours of 19 December 1778, when Marie Antoinette began to feel ominous pains shortly after midnight and realised that her time had come. The Princesse de Lamballe was immediately summoned to preside over the event and word was sent to everyone who had the right to be present with the King arriving at three in morning, full of excitement and also not a little fear for childbirth in the eighteenth century was still a very risky business indeed. Marie Antoinette had chosen Charles-Toussaint de Vermond, the brother of Abbé de Vermond, to act as her *accoucheur* and under his watchful eye she paced her chamber until eight in the morning when, overwhelmed by the pain, she took to the little delivery bed that had been placed beside the ornate main bed in her chamber.

As Marie Antoinette laboured, she was attended by Vermond, physicians and midwives and surrounded by the royal family, the princes and princesses of the blood and her closest friends while beyond in the cabinet next door there was crammed the rest of the royal household and everyone else who had the right to be present at such an auspicious event, which numbered several hundred people. The rest of the court, their numbers swollen by nobles who had travelled to Versailles just for the day, found whatever space they could in the outer rooms of the Queen's apartments and the Hall of Mirrors, where they lounged against the walls as they waited for news of the royal delivery to spread. The whole situation must have been absolutely intolerable for a woman so fastidious and concerned with her privacy but it's likely that, at least once the pains of labour had begun in earnest, Marie Antoinette probably didn't care who was there to see it although she was no doubt glad to have the steadfast, practically minded Louis keeping vigil at her side.

The baby, a little girl, was born at around 11.30am. At first she did not make a sound and there was panic when it was thought that she had been born dead but then the first cries were heard and all was well. Enthralled by his daughter, Louis went off with the rest of the royal family to watch the child being washed and swaddled in the next room leaving Marie Antoinette, who had not yet been informed of the child's sex, to the ministrations of the physicians. However, within moments of the King leaving the room, the Queen had a convulsive fit and lost consciousness, no doubt overcome by exhaustion and the sweltering heat of the room, exacerbated by the fact that the windows had been sealed up to prevent even the slightest wintry breeze touching the precious newborn. Seeing that the Queen had collapsed, her husband and some of the gentlemen jumped up and tore the windows open, which revived her from her faint.

Shortly after this Marie Antoinette was allowed to hold her daughter for the first time. Naturally both Marie Antoinette and Louis had hoped that their first child would be a Dauphin, as girls were barred by Salic Law from succeeding to the throne, but they hid any disappointment well. For now, they were both just truly delighted to finally be parents at last. 'Poor little girl, you are not what was desired, but you are no less dear to me on that account,' Marie Antoinette, visibly moved, reportedly said to her daughter. 'A son would have been the property of the state. You shall be mine; you shall have my undivided care; you will share all my happinesses and you will alleviate my sufferings.'

Marie Antoinette spent the next eighteen days recuperating from the birth of her daughter. As was the custom she remained in bed and received her friends Gabrielle de Polignac and the Princesse de Lamballe there, propped up against lace edged pillows and dressed in a charming lace and ribbon trimmed *peignoir* and a delightful cap which hid the fact that her hairdresser Léonard had finally given up trying to make her hair stop falling out and persuaded her to have it cropped so that it would grow back stronger. She was extremely proud of her baby, who had been christened Marie Thérèse Charlotte (the first two names were in honour of her mother, while Charlotte was almost certainly for her favourite sister Maria Carolina, the Queen of Naples), and kept her beside her as much as she could. She even tried to breastfeed for a time, even though it was far more usual for women of her status to exclusively employ wet nurses as her own mother had done. Naturally, this deviation from tradition caused some consternation in Vienna, with Maria Theresa making her displeasure known.

Everything changed for Marie Antoinette when she finally became a mother. Reared since early childhood to believe that one of her primary functions was to bear children for some unknown prince, she had regarded the lack of a child as a shameful failure and a total betrayal by her own body. She had done her best to distract herself from this great lack in her life and had in the process lost some of her husband's affection and the respect of her people. Now, however, Louis loved her more than ever but could she also regain the love of their people? Only time would tell but for now the future looked promising as the young couple celebrated the birth of their baby by distributing money to their favourite charities and attending a celebratory Mass at Notre Dame. Naturally, there was some disappointment that the baby had turned out to be a girl rather than the hoped for Dauphin but they were both still only in their early twenties and now that they had defied all expectation and had one child, surely more would follow?

Chapter 8

Mother
1778–1785

'This ill-starred princess.'

Although Marie Antoinette, who had spent so many years longing for motherhood, would obviously have loved to look after her daughter by herself, the main care of the little princess, who was to be known as Madame Royale at court, fell to the charge of the royal governess, the Princesse de Guéméné, whose rather rakish lifestyle makes her seem like a most unsuitable person for such an important charge. However, this was typical of Versailles where all the most plum jobs had been passed down through families for generations, regardless of the suitability of the latest incumbent. In this instance, Madame la Princesse was the niece of the former royal governess Madame de Marsan, who had been in charge of Louis XVI and all of his siblings until her retirement, upon which the Princesse had taken over the post.

The Princesse de Guéméné had been born Victoire Armande de Rohan at the beautiful Hôtel de Soubise in the Marais district of Paris, the daughter of Charles de Rohan, Prince de Soubise and his second wife, Anne Thérèse de Savoie, which made her a relative of the Princesse de Lamballe as well as the Comtesse de Provence and Comtesse d'Artois. Clever, lively and extravagant, the Princesse was known to be something of an eccentric, who claimed to be able to communicate with the dead via the several tiny pet dogs that surrounded her wherever she went. She had also, more seriously, been accused several times of cheating at cards, not that this discouraged Marie Antoinette from attending her card parties in her apartments which the Emperor Joseph, who thoroughly disapproved of the sophisticated Princesse, described as nothing better than a 'gaming hell'. However, for all her faults, Victoire, who had five children of her own, seems to have had an affectionate, fun loving nature that young people really responded to. Even Madame Élisabeth, Louis' pious youngest sister (her elder sister Madame Clotilde had been married to the Prince of Piedmont, the brother of the Comtesse de Provence and Comtesse d'Artois, in August 1775), who had entered her charge after the departure of Madame de Marsan, was very fond of the Princesse de Guéméné although, unlike Marie Antoinette, she managed to resist the lady's attempts to make her attend her rather *risqué* parties.

The low key atmosphere that had prevailed during the Queen's pregnancy continued for quite some time to come as Marie Antoinette devoted herself as much as possible to her daughter and allowed herself to delight in the entirely novel but thoroughly delightful joys of new motherhood. Duty compelled her to continue to attend the weekly card parties, suppers and balls that had always formed an important part of her routine but she took much less joy in the rakish soirées, masked balls and clandestine excursions that had once delighted her so much.

In the spring of 1779, Marie Antoinette was struck down by a bad case of measles which left her so debilitated that she was encouraged by her physicians to completely retire from court life for three weeks and recuperate in the peace and quiet of the Petit Trianon. Up until now she had only been there during the day and although there was a pretty bedroom set aside for her use, had never actually stayed the night so naturally she was delighted to be packed off to her favourite little bolthole, which she had transformed into a house entirely to her own taste. There was only room for her most favourite ladies to stay with her though, while the rest of the household stayed at the nearby Grand Trianon. Unfortunately, Madame de Polignac had also fallen ill with measles and was unable to join her.

Although Marie Antoinette felt genuinely poorly at first, she still managed to have the most delightful time as she spent her days eating strawberries in her lovely new gardens and lazily drifting across the Grand Canal on a boat. The evenings were spent in the new salon where she was attended by her favourites: the always loyal Duc de Coigny, Baron de Besenval, Count Esterhazy and the Duc de Guines (whose influence over the Queen was considered especially harmful by Count Mercy although as he was twenty years older than her and also extremely overweight[1] while she had a preference for elegant young men like the Swedish count Fersen, it's unlikely that she had any romantic interest in him), who took turns to amuse her with light conversation and the occasional musical interlude as Monsieur de Guines was an extremely talented musician and patron of Mozart. It was all completely harmless but as usual the malicious tongues of the court gossips had plenty to say about the whole thing, especially as the King, who had never had measles and so was kept away for fear of contagion, was not present although he visited on one occasion and stood out in the courtyard, calling up to the Queen who leaned out of her bedroom window like Juliet to his unlikely Romeo.

It was around this time that Marie Antoinette was painted for the first time by Madame Vigée Le Brun, whose portraits of the Queen remain amongst her most iconic representations. Their association began when Marie Theresa requested two full length portraits of Marie Antoinette for her personal collection of full-length family portraits. Forgoing the usual court painters, Marie Antoinette chose someone new for this important commission: a rising star in art, the Parisian portraitist Élisabeth Vigée Le Brun, who had already painted Marie Antoinette's brother-in-law the Comte de Provence and was a great favourite of her cousins, the Duc and Duchesse de Chartres. It was to be the first painting in a series spanning a decade that would immortalise both sitter and artist in the eyes of posterity: when one thinks of Marie Antoinette, it is the vision of her as painted by Madame Vigée Le Brun that one usually sees, either dressed in shimmering white silk with plumes in her powdered hair, radiant in blue silk and holding a rose in the gardens of the Petit Trianon, shyly smiling in soft white muslin or holding her precious children close while surrounded by the splendours of Versailles.

'*She was then in the heyday of her youth and beauty,*' Madame Vigée Le Brun later wrote in her lively memoirs. '*Marie Antoinette was tall and admirably built, being somewhat stout, but not excessively so. Her arms were superb, her hands small and perfectly formed, and her feet charming. She had the best walk of any woman in France, carrying her head erect with a dignity that stamped her queen in the midst of her whole court, her majestic mien, however, not in the least diminishing the sweetness and amiability of her face. To any one who has not seen the Queen it is difficult to get an idea of all the graces and all the nobility combined in her person. Her features were not regular; she had inherited that long and narrow oval peculiar to the Austrian nation. Her eyes were not large; in colour they were almost blue, and they were at the same time merry and kind. Her nose was slender and pretty, and her mouth not too large, though her lips were rather thick. But the most remarkable thing about her face was the splendour of her complexion. I never have seen one so brilliant, and brilliant is the word, for her skin was so transparent that it bore no umber in the painting. Neither could I render the real effect of it as I wished. I had no colours to paint such freshness, such delicate tints, which were hers alone, and which I had never seen in any other woman.'*

The first of the paintings, a full-length work depicting the twenty-three-year-old Queen in white silk, was sent off to Vienna in January 1779 and the Empress immediately fired off a letter saying how delighted she was with it while Marie Antoinette liked it so much that she ordered another copy to be hung in her apartment at Versailles. Marie Antoinette was painted several times during this period by a wide variety of different artists but none managed to capture her essential charm and freshness as well as Vigée-Lebrun, who managed the hitherto apparently impossible feat of managing to capture a likeness while at the same time hinting at the elusive charm that made Marie Antoinette so irresistible in person and softened her rather heavy Habsburg features.

The period of convalescence at Petit Trianon was just the beginning of Marie Antoinette's gradual withdrawal from court life as she pursued a more informal and private existence. Whereas before she had become a mother the Queen had perhaps been a little too visible thanks to her hectic Parisian social life, now everyone complained that she was not seen enough as she often spent weeks on end at the Petit Trianon surrounded only by the congenial company of her closest friends and sister-in-law Élisabeth. After 1780, this select little coterie were able to enjoy the new theatre, where she and her friends put on amateur theatricals for a very small audience and, tellingly, the Queen made a point of always playing simple village maidens, milk maids and servant girls – women who were free of expectation and responsibility in a way that the Queen of France could never be.

When Marie Antoinette entered a room at the Petit Trianon no one was expected to stop what they were doing and rise, as they were at the royal palaces, but instead could continue playing the piano, reading or sketching without doing anything more than politely acknowledging her arrival, just as they would do for anyone else. She was also keen to introduce a less formal tone at Versailles but naturally faced a lot of opposition from most of her husband's courtiers, who had no desire to lose any of the privileges and status that their families had been able to acquire over the decades. Nonetheless, with her husband's support, Marie Antoinette was still able to make some changes and as, rather cleverly, they made life a bit more comfortable for everyone and did little to diminish anyone's prestige, there were very few complaints. One of her targets was the outmoded 'obsolete and unbearable' court dress worn by the ladies on important occasions, which Marie Antoinette successfully petitioned to be made much less cumbersome by reducing the width of the panniers and length of the train. In 1783, it was officially decreed that, with the exception of young women who were being presented for the first time, court ladies could wear the much less constrictive *robe à la Française,* which was much more becoming and far less unwieldy as well as being much more fashionable.

Meanwhile, behind the scenes, Marie Antoinette was copying her husband by creating a veritable warren of stairs, corridors, mezzanines and exquisite little rooms behind her apartments at Versailles, where she could escape from the prying eyes of the courtiers and be entirely herself with only a few of her most favoured companions. Here there was to be found a library, some pretty little sitting rooms and a billiards room as well as rooms for her maids. It was all very cosy but again added to the general feeling that the Queen was gradually vanishing from public life, which naturally gave rise to rumours that she clearly had something to hide – after all, Louis XV's well known passion for privacy was popularly supposed to have derived from his dissolute and sexually promiscuous lifestyle which he naturally wished to keep a secret from both his courtiers and the general public so why should it not be the same case with Marie Antoinette?

In the spring of 1780, her childhood friends, Princess Charlotte of Hesse-Darmstadt and her younger sister Princess Louise, along with several other family members, came to visit Paris and Marie Antoinette was delighted to be reunited with them after so many years apart and be able to show them around her world. They were immediately honoured with invitations to the hallowed precincts of the Petit Trianon with Marie Antoinette writing that: '*It's looking so beautiful that I should be charmed to show it to you… I shall be quite alone so don't dress up; country clothes and the men in frock coats.*' The young Queen truly relished what she fondly imagined to be a simple bucolic country existence and considered it to be a much needed respite from what she increasingly regarded as the relentless and tiresome drudgery of court life.

However, although 1780 began brightly for Marie Antoinette it would end with tragedy. Her mother Maria Theresa had been ailing for quite some time after her bout with smallpox but had struggled on, her indomitable spirit refusing to accept that it was time to slow down. On 3 November she wrote to her daughter: '*Yesterday, I spent the time more in France than Austria, and I remembered all the happy times in the past, which is indeed gone. Just the memory consoles me.*' It was to be her last letter to Marie Antoinette as just a couple of days later the Empress caught a chill while praying in the family vault beneath the Capuchin church. The chill turned into pneumonia and after two terrible weeks the Empress died in the arms of the distraught and sobbing Joseph.

It took eight days for the terrible news to reach Versailles and when it eventually did, Louis insisted that the Abbé de Vermond should be the one to tell Marie Antoinette that her mother, who had been the mainstay of her life, was gone. '*Crushed by most dreadful misfortune, I cannot stop crying as I write to you,*' she wrote to Joseph. '*Oh, my brother, oh, my friend! You alone are left to me in a country which is, which will always be, dear to me! Take care of yourself, watch over yourself; you owe it to all… Adieu, I no longer see what I write. Remember that we are friends and allies. Love me.*'

Marie Antoinette was completely devastated by her mother's death, perhaps sensing that without Maria Theresa's overbearing care and admittedly often entirely unwelcome advice, she would from now on be adrift in the world without a proper anchor to keep her from harm. Her mother may have been prophesying doom and all manner of woe ever since the giddy, thoughtless Marie Antoinette first arrived in France over ten years earlier but at least she had been reasonably confident that should any disaster actually happen, Maria Theresa would be there to pick up the pieces, dust her down and put everything right again. Could she trust Joseph, now Emperor in fact as well as name, to do the same for her?

Inconsolable, Marie Antoinette retreated for several weeks to the peace of the Petit Trianon where she remained sequestered alone but for her closest friends Madame de Polignac and the Princesse de Lamballe. She gave herself up completely to grief, reminiscing for hours about her childhood and berating herself for not paying proper attention to her mother's well-meaning advice while she still had the chance to prove her obedience and loyalty. It was only now that she had lost her forever that Marie Antoinette finally came to realise just how much her mother had loved her and, equally, how much she had lost.

Louis, it seems, was one of those clumsy, awkward men who have the gift of being able to truly step up to the mark when called upon to do so and he was a rock now for Marie Antoinette. He sat for hours with her, listening to her outpourings of grief and regret and always seemed to know exactly what to do and say to make her feel better. The couple were drawn together by Marie Antoinette's sorrow and within a couple of months were surprised and delighted to find that she was pregnant once again. Intimidating though she may have been in latter years, Maria Theresa had always retained a certain dry sense of humour and she would no doubt have appreciated this unlooked for result of her passing, especially as she had spent the two years since Madame Royale's birth haranguing her daughter constantly about the necessity of having another baby.

Marie Antoinette's second labour began on the morning of 22 October 1781 with, as before, the Princesse de Lamballe summoning the King and other dignitaries to the royal bedchamber where the Queen was pacing back and forth in order to alleviate her pain. However, keen to avoid the terrible and mortifying press of people that had attended the Queen's last lying in, this time Louis restricted the audience to just those who absolutely had to be there with the Comte d'Artois, aunts and Princesse de Lamballe representing the royal family. Also present were Marie Antoinette's favourite ladies: the Comtesse de Mailly, Comtesse d'Ossun, Princesse de Chimay and Comtesse de Tavannes as well as her daughter's governess, the Princesse de Guéméné, who was waiting to take the baby to the royal nurseries. Everyone else was banished to the outer rooms of the Queen's apartments to wait for news.

As is common with second labours, this one was much quicker than the first and was over in around an hour and fifteen minutes when the Queen gave birth to a healthy child. The baby, as was the custom, was immediately whisked away to be washed and swaddled before the King, weeping and his voice trembling with emotion, brought the child back to Marie Antoinette saying, 'Madame, Monsieur le Dauphin asks for permission to enter.'

The wonderful news was announced to the crowds of courtiers waiting outside and spread like wildfire through the palace so that by the time the Princesse de Guéméné, looking as proud as if she had given birth to the heir to the throne herself, appeared with the baby in her arms and seated in a bath chair so there would be no risk of dropping the precious heir on his way down to the chapel to be baptised, there were enormous crowds thronging the Hall of Mirrors to see her go by. King Louis hurried in the wake of his son, unable to take his eyes off this most miraculous and longed for child, and

Emperor Francis Stephen and Empress Maria Theresa, parents of Marie Antoinette, painted by Bencini in the year of her birth, 1755. (*Royal Collection Trust/His Majesty King Charles III*)

Empress Maria Theresa at around the time that Marie Antoinette was born, painted by an unknown Swiss artist. (*Royal Collection Trust/His Majesty King Charles III*)

Empress Maria Theresa in mourning for her husband, painted by Ducreux in around 1777. (*Royal Collection Trust/His Majesty King Charles III*)

Maria Theresa and Emperor Francis Stephen with their thirteen surviving children, including Maria Antonia, engraved by Johann Probst. (*Royal Collection Trust/His Majesty King Charles III*)

Maria Carolina of Austria, Queen of Naples and favourite sister of Marie Antoinette, engraved in 1777 by Raphael Morghen. (*Royal Collection Trust/His Majesty King Charles III*)

Emperor Joseph II, eldest brother of Marie Antoinette, engraved by Schultze after a 1777 portrait by Kymli. (*Royal Collection Trust/His Majesty King Charles III*)

Louis XV of France, engraved by Cathelin. (*Royal Collection Trust/His Majesty King Charles III*)

Louis XV with his three grandsons, the Dauphin, Comte de Provence and Comte d'Artois and their wives, etched by Claude Briceau. (*Royal Collection Trust/His Majesty King Charles III*)

The Comte d'Artois and his sister Madame Clotilde, two of Louis XVI's younger siblings engraved in 1767 by Beauvarlet after a painting by Drouais. (*Royal Collection Trust/His Majesty King Charles III*)

Jeanne Bécu, Madame du Barry, painted in around 1770 by Drouais. (*Courtesy National Gallery of Art, Washington*)

Madame Adélaïde, the oldest and most formidable of Louis XVI's aunts, engraved by Beauvarlet after a youthful portrait by Nattier. (*Royal Collection Trust/His Majesty King Charles III*)

Marie Antoinette as Archduchess of Austria before her marriage in 1770, engraved by Guillaume Benoist. (*Courtesy Metropolitan Museum of Art, New York*)

Louis Auguste, Dauphin of France, engraved by Richard Brookshaw in 1774, the year of his succession as Louis XVI. (*Royal Collection Trust/His Majesty King Charles III*)

Madame Clotilde, Queen of Sardinia, sister of Louis XVI, engraved by Nicolas Voyez. (*Royal Collection Trust/His Majesty King Charles III*)

Madame Élisabeth, youngest sister of Louis XVI, engraved by Le Beau. (*Royal Collection Trust/His Majesty King Charles III*)

Marie Antoinette as Dauphine of France, engraved by Johannes Nilson. (*Royal Collection Trust/ His Majesty King Charles III*)

Louis Stanislas, Comte de Provence, eldest brother of Louis XVI, drawn by Madame Vigée Le Brun in 1777. (*Royal Collection Trust/His Majesty King Charles III*)

Marie Joséphine, Comtesse de Provence, sister-in-law of Louis XVI, drawn by Madame Vigée Le Brun in 1777. (*Royal Collection Trust/His Majesty King Charles III*)

Charles Philippe, Comte d'Artois, youngest brother of Louis XVI, etched by Jeanne Deny. (*Royal Collection Trust/His Majesty King Charles III*)

Marie Thérèse, Comtesse d'Artois, sister-in-law of Louis XVI, engraved by Jacques Cathelin. (*Royal Collection Trust/His Majesty King Charles III*)

Louis, Duc d'Orléans and his wife Louise Marie Adélaïde de Bourbon with their sons, the future King Louis Philippe of the French and the Duc de Montpensier, engraved in 1779 by Helman after a painting by Lepeintre. (*Royal Collection Trust/His Majesty King Charles III*)

Marie Louise, Princesse de Lamballe, engraved by Pierre Grevedon. (*Royal Collection Trust/His Majesty King Charles III*)

Marie Antoinette in 1775, the year after her husband succeeded to the throne. (*Royal Collection Trust/His Majesty King Charles III*)

Marie Antoinette in 1778, a copy after her first portrait by Madame Vigée Le Brun. (*Royal Collection Trust/His Majesty King Charles III*)

Louis XVI in around 1775, a copy after Duplessis. (*Royal Collection Trust/His Majesty King Charles III*)

Marie Antoinette in 1783, a copy after a portrait by Madame Vigée Le Brun. (*Courtesy National Gallery of Art, Washington*)

The Dauphin Louis Joseph and his sister Marie Thérèse, eldest children of Louis XVI and Marie Antoinette, engraved by Maurice Blot after a painting by Madame Vigée Le Brun. (*Royal Collection Trust/His Majesty King Charles III*)

Marie Antoinette walking in a park in 1780, drawn by Madame Vigée Le Brun. (*Courtesy Metropolitan Museum of Art, New York*)

Marie Antoinette engraved in 1783 by Jean-Baptiste Isabey. (*Courtesy Metropolitan Museum of Art, New York*)

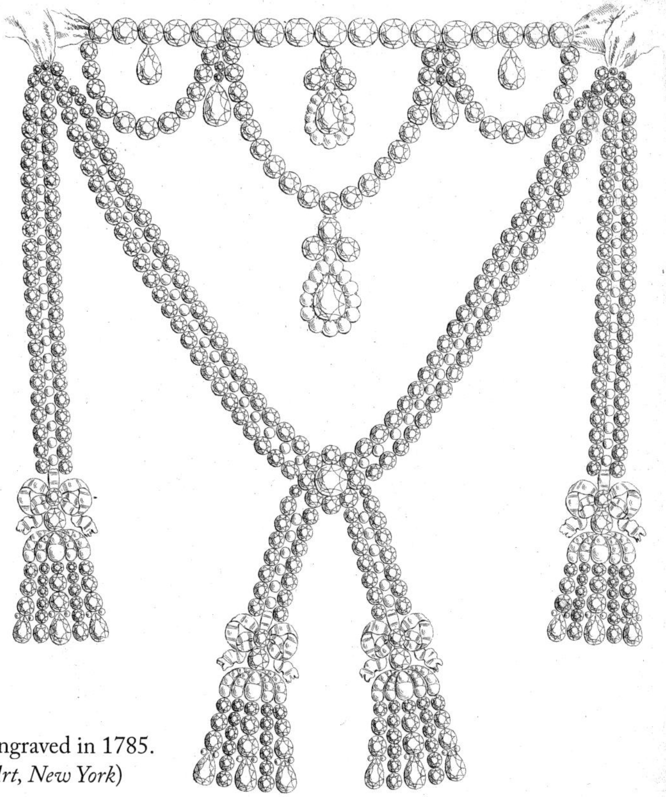

The infamous diamond necklace, engraved in 1785. (*Courtesy Metropolitan Museum of Art, New York*)

Marie Antoinette with her children, Marie Thérèse, Louis Joseph and Louis Charles, engraved by Nargeot after the painting by Madame Vigée Le Brun. (*Royal Collection Trust/His Majesty King Charles III*)

Madame Élisabeth, painted in 1787 by Adélaïde Labille-Guiard. (*Courtesy Metropolitan Museum of Art, New York*)

Caricature of Marie Antoinette as a dragon. (*Courtesy Metropolitan Museum of Art, New York*)

Caricature of Marie Antoinette as a leopard, an example of the scurrilous drawings of her that circulated at court and beyond. (*Courtesy Metropolitan Museum of Art, New York*)

Cameo miniature of Louis XVI, Marie Antoinette and their son Louis Charles, painted in around 1790 by a follower of Louis-Bertin Parant. (*Royal Collection Trust/His Majesty King Charles III*)

Slippers allegedly lost by Marie Antoinette during the royal family's ignominious return to Paris after their failed escape attempt in 1791. (*Courtesy Metropolitan Museum of Art, New York*)

Dauphin Louis Charles dressed in armour and bearing a shield with portraits of his parents, engraved during the family's imprisonment in around 1792. (*Royal Collection Trust/His Majesty King Charles III*)

Marie Thérèse, Madame Royale, sole survivor of the royal family, painted in 1795 by Jacques Joseph de Gault. (*Courtesy Metropolitan Museum of Art, New York*)

Marie Antoinette dressed in mourning for her husband after his execution in 1793. Mezzotint by John Murphy after a painting by the Marquise de Brehan. (*Royal Collection Trust/His Majesty King Charles III*)

Madame Royale being treated by Doctor Brunier in the Temple, three days after the execution of Louis XVI in January 1793, painted that year by Jean-Baptiste Mallet. (*Courtesy Metropolitan Museum of Art, New York*)

LETTRE
Ecrite par la
Reine de France Marie
Antoinette, à la sœur de Louis XVI,
Madame Elisabeth, le 6 Octobre, à 4 heures ½ du matin.
C'est à vous ma sœur que j'écris, pour la dernière fois.
Je viens d'être condamnée, non pas à une mort honteuse, elle
ne l'est que pour les criminels, Mais à aller rejoindre votre
Frère; comme lui innocente; j'espère montrer la même fermeté
que lui dans ces derniers moments. Je suis calme comme on l'est
quand la conscience ne nous reproche rien, j'ai un profond regret d'-
abandonner mes pauvres enfants; vous savez que je n'existais que
pour eux et vous, ma bonne et tendre sœur; vous qui avez par votre
amitié tout sacrifié pour être avec nous; dans quelle position je vous
laisse! J'ai appris par le plaidoyer même du procès que ma chère fille était
séparée de vous, hélas. la pauvre enfant, je n'ose pas lui écrire, elle ne re-
cevrait pas ma lettre. Je ne sais même pas si celle-ci vous parviendra, re-
cevez pour eux deux ici, ma bénédiction. J'espère qu'un jour, lorsqu'ils
seront plus grands, ils pourront se réunir avec vous et jouir en entier de
vos tendres soins. qu'ils pensent tous deux à ce que je n'ai cessé de leur inspirer; que les principes et l'exécution exacte de ses devoirs, sont la première
base de la vie; que leur amitié et leur confiance mutuelle, en feront le bonheur; que ma fille sente qu'à l'âge qu'elle a, elle doit toujours aider son
frère par les conseils que l'expérience qu'elle aura de plus que lui et son amitié
pourront lui inspirer. Que mon fils, à son tour, rende à sa chère sœur
tous les soins, les services, que l'amitié peut inspirer; Qu'ils sentent enfin tous
deux que, dans quelque position où ils pourront se trouver, ils ne seront vraiment
heureux que par leur union. Qu'ils prennent exemple de nous. Combien dans
nos malheurs, notre amitié nous a donné de consolations, et dans le bonheur on
jouit doublement, quand on peut le partager avec un ami; et où en trouver de
plus tendre, de plus cher que dans sa propre famille? Que mon fils n'oublie
jamais les derniers mots de son père, que je lui répète expressément: qu'il
ne cherche jamais à venger notre mort. J'ai à vous parler d'une chose
bien pénible à mon cœur. Je sais combien cet enfant doit vous avoir fait
de la peine; pardonnez-lui, ma chère sœur, pensez à l'âge qu'il a, et combien il est facile de faire dire à un enfant ce qu'on veut, et même ce qu'il ne
comprend pas. Un jour viendra, j'espère, où il ne sentira que mieux tout le
prix de vos bontés et de votre tendresse pour tous deux. Il me reste à vous con-
fier encore mes dernières pensées. J'aurais voulu les écrire dès le commence-
ment du procès; mais, outre qu'on ne me laissait pas écrire, La marche
en a été si rapide, que je n'en aurais réellement pas jamais eu le temps.
Je meurs dans la religion Catholique, Apostolique et Romaine, dans celle
de mes pères, dans celle où j'ai été élevée, et que j'ai toujours professée
n'ayant aucune consolation spirituelle à attendre, ne sachant pas
s'il existe encore ici des prêtres de cette religion et même le lieu
où je suis les exposerait trop, si ils y entraient une fois. Je demande sincèrement pardon à Dieu, de toutes les fautes que j'ai pu
commettre depuis que j'existe. J'espère que dans sa bonté et sa miséricorde, il voudra bien recevoir mes derniers vœux, ainsi que ceux
que je fais depuis longtems, pour qu'il veuille bien recevoir mon
âme dans sa miséricorde et son inépuisable bonté. Je demande pardon à tous ceux que je connais, et à vous ma sœur, en particulier.
de toutes les peines que sans le vouloir, j'aurais pu vous causer.
je pardonne à tous mes ennemis, quels qu'ils soient, le mal qu'ils
m'ont fait. Je dis ici adieu à mes Tantes et à tous mes Frères
et sœurs. J'avais des amis, l'idée d'en être séparée pour jamais
et leurs peines, sont un des plus grands regrets que j'emporte
en mourant, qu'ils sachent, du moins, que jusqu'à mon dernier
moment, je n'ai cessé de penser à eux. Adieu ma bonne
et tendre sœur, puisse cette lettre vous arriver! puisse
t'elle parvenir jusqu'à vous sans obstacles. Pensez
toujours à moi, comme je pense à vous. Je
vous embrasse de tout mon cœur; ainsi que
mes pauvres et chers Enfants. Mon Dieu
qu'il est cruel, qu'il est déchirant de les quit-
ter pour toujours. Adieu, Adieu! je ne vais plus
m'occuper que de mes devoirs spirituels. Comme
je ne suis pas libre dans ma volonté et dans mes
actions. On m'amenera peut-être
un Prêtre, Mais je proteste ici
de toutes mes forces, que je ne
lui dirai pas un mot, et que
je le traiterai comme un
être absolument étranger.
A la Conciergerie, le six
Octobre Mil sept cent
quatre vingt treize.
à 4 heures ½ du matin.
MARIE ANTOINETTE

The last letter of Marie Antoinette, etched as a portrait by Pelicier in around 1794. (*Courtesy Metropolitan Museum of Art, New York*) grinning affably at the shouts of congratulations. Finally, he felt that he had done his duty and furthermore proved himself to be a man like any other.

The baby, whose healthy weight and size was a source of great relief to his parents, was baptised Louis Joseph Xavier François in the glorious chapel at Versailles before being taken off to the royal nursery to meet his sister Madame Royale and be placed into the care of his wet nurse, the wonderfully named Madame Poitrine (Madame Breast). Meanwhile, Marie Antoinette, completely worn out, rested in her bedchamber where shortly she would receive the homage of the Parisian market women, who regaled the happy royal couple with some salacious couplets about Louis' sexual prowess before trooping off to enjoy a splendid supper in the royal apartments.

Shortly after the Dauphin's birth, on 21 November 1781, the wily old Maurepas, Louis' chief advisor and Chief Minister and uncle of Madame de Polignac, passed away. There was immediate debate about who would be his successor as Chief Minister but Louis surprised everyone by rejecting Loménie de Brienne, who was the choice of the Queen's party and making it known that from now on he would be ruling alone, with his Foreign Minister, the Comte de Vergennes as advisor. This news was greeted with delight by Mercy and the Emperor Joseph, who had taken up Maria Theresa's mantle when it came to persuading Marie Antoinette to make herself the power behind her husband's throne. However, to their disappointment and despite their urgings, Marie Antoinette had very little taste for politics and her few attempts at persuading King to take her advice had mixed results. She had failed when it came to restoring Choiseul but then again had undoubtedly had a hand in the disastrous appointment of the Comte de Ségur as Minister of War and also the fall of Turgot in 1776 after he had attempted to put through plans for a more egalitarian tax system that no longer disproportionately favoured the aristocracy. The principal danger here though, as Louis knew all too well, was that Marie Antoinette had no real grasp of politics and based her political opinions on personal likes and dislikes and, worse, whatever her friends, specifically the ambitious and grasping Polignac *cotérie*, and family chose to tell her. Her advice could therefore never be trusted as she was usually acting as the mouthpiece of other people.

'*This ill starred princess either did not know how to consider people's feelings or was not prepared to do so*,' Madame de la Tour du Pin would later recall. '*When she was displeased she allowed it to be evident, regardless of the consequences. And this did great harm to the King's cause. She was gifted with a very great courage, but very little intelligence, absolutely no tact and worst of all a mistrust always misplaced in those who were most willing to serve her*.' However, even if her political use was severely limited by her own deficiencies, Marie Antoinette could still be useful in other ways. When her brother and Empress Catherine II of Russia were in cahoots and planning to partition the Ottoman Empire, Joseph asked Marie Antoinette to lend a hand and royally entertain the Empress' son and heir Tsarevitch Paul and his wife Archduchess Maria Feodorovna when, travelling incognito as the Comte and Comtesse du Nord, they visited Paris in May 1782. Their visit was not altogether popular with Louis and Vergennes, who did not at all approve of the Austrian alliance with Russia or their plans for the Ottoman Empire and were well aware that although the Tsarevitch was keen to make his visit look like simple tourism, he had actually been sent by his mother to try and gain some French support. When Marie Antoinette, following her brother's instructions, asked to be allowed to entertain them, Louis was grateful to hand the baton over to her, relieved to have nothing to do with it.

Marie Antoinette spared no expense when it came to entertaining their Russian guests, who were treated to a concert in the Peace Room, a splendid supper party, a trip to Trianon, several magnificent galas and a fancy dress ball in the royal opéra where Marie Antoinette again appeared dressed as Gabrielle d'Estrées, the mistress of her ancestor Henri IV, with the Pitt diamond, valued at 2 million francs, attached to her plumed hat. The whole visit was extraordinarily expensive, with the Queen and her ladies spending a fortune on dresses from Rose Bertin and Madame Éloffe and the Russian party, who appeared to have limitless funds, spending even more in order to compete with the famously fashionable French courtiers. There was also a visit to the famous porcelain factory at Sèvres, which had long enjoyed the particular patronage of the royal family – once a year, the company's new wares would be laid out on display at Versailles so that the court could make purchases. The Russian visitors spent over 300,000 francs at the Sèvres factory, with the additional treat of discovering that a particularly lovely lapis blue toilette set which the Grand Duchess had particularly admired was to be a personal present from Marie Antoinette and had already been thoughtfully decorated with her monogram.

The visit ended with a formal court ball in the Hall of Mirrors where the Queen danced with the Tsarevitch and Louis partnered Maria Feodorovna. However, although the Russian party left Versailles completely overawed and delighted by the reception they had enjoyed, Marie Antoinette was pleased to see them go, having taken one of her sudden dislikes to the Tsarevitch after he had asked her some very impertinent questions about her falling out with Madame du Barry, who was still banished from the court.

Once her awkward guests had gone, Marie Antoinette took herself off to the Petit Trianon for a few weeks, doubtless congratulating herself on the success of her hostessing even if she winced a bit at how much it had cost. However, the true costs were yet to be counted as the people grumbled about such extravagance at a time when the nation's coffers were known to depleted almost to the point of bankruptcy by the wars in America. Worse still was to come later on in the year when the Prince de Guéméné, husband of the Royal Governess, declared himself to be bankrupt with astonishing debts of over 33 million livres. This catastrophe caused an enormous scandal at court with wider repercussions elsewhere as the fall of the powerful Guéméné family also ruined countless tradesmen and others who were owed vast sums of money and would now never be paid. The ripples caused by the Prince's bankruptcy were to be widespread and devastating, not least for his wife who was now in awkward position when the full extent of the disaster became known, as it was considered utterly unthinkable for the wife of someone so completely ruined to continue as governess to the royal children.

Marie Antoinette, who was very fond of Madame de Guéméné, did everything she could to help even though Mercy counselled her to keep her distance so that she wasn't tainted by association, but had to accept the Princesse's resignation of her post in October 1782, exactly a year after the birth of the Dauphin. She managed to secure a large pension for the couple though and encouraged the King to buy the Princesse's country estate at Montreuil, near Versailles, for his sister Élisabeth who had fallen in love with the spot during her numerous visits there when she was under the charge of the disgraced governess.

The whole dismal affair was talked about everywhere and although Marie Antoinette had had nothing to do with the Guéméné's debts, it still had a parlous effect on her already dwindling popularity, which had revived a little after the birth of the Dauphin but then plummeted sharply when word of the extravagance that attended the Russian visit started doing the rounds in Paris. With the country teetering on the verge of financial disaster, the excessive spending of the royal family and those close to them was being held up to scrutiny and this very public disgrace of two key members of the royal household was considered a justification of the criticisms that were beginning to be directed at the frivolity and wastefulness of the court in general and the Queen in particular.

The not entirely unexpected appointment of Madame de Polignac (who had recently become a Duchesse when her husband succeeded to his father's title) to the post of Royal Governess also caused murmuring at court as the position had been passed down through the Rohan family for years and to bestow it elsewhere and, furthermore, on someone who was not from one of the most prominent blue-blooded families at court, was considered extremely controversial, if not provocative on the part of the Queen. Here again, Marie Antoinette's personal feelings had got the better of her – she had never quite liked the numerous Rohan family since hearing that their scion Prince Louis de Rohan (now Cardinal de Rohan), who had performed Mass before her in Strasbourg when she first arrived in France, had been going about the place saying insulting things about her mother. She knew that Madame de Polignac's appointment to such a prestigious court position was not entirely appropriate but she didn't care and in this she was unexpectedly supported by Louis[2], who would have preferred to place his children in the care of his aunt Adélaïde but knew better than to oppose Marie Antoinette in a matter of such personal interest to her.

Madame de Polignac didn't have any complaints though. The post of governess came with a splendid thirteen room apartment next door to the rooms of the royal children, right on the palace terrace and overlooking the famous Orangerie. The enterprising Duchesse proceeded to build an elaborate wooden conservatory at one end of her rooms so that she would have more space to throw lavish parties three times a week, which were attended by the entire court as well as the Queen, who astounded everyone by behaving like a guest rather than the mistress of the palace.

In early 1783, Marie Antoinette posed again for Madame Vigée Le Brun, this time choosing not to appear in a splendidly ornate court dress but rather a simple muslin gown of the sort that she liked to wear while frolicking with her children and pet dogs at the Petit Trianon. Although she still liked a good party, the twenty-seven-year-old Queen was now almost entirely engrossed by her domestic life, preferring to spend her time at her own private residence rather than showing herself off amidst the splendours of Versailles. This portrait was intended to reveal to the world what Marie Antoinette was increasingly seeing as her true self; the real woman behind the glittering façade of the Queen of France.

As anticipated, the painting caused a sensation when it was displayed at the prestigious Paris Salon of 1783 – but if the artist and her subject were hoping to be heaped with praise and admiration, they were to be sorely disappointed. Marie Antoinette and

Madame Vigée Le Brun, young women of exactly the same age with minds full of all sorts of romantic and idealistic ideas about the simplicity and virtue of private life were entranced by the lack of etiquette in the painting, by the lack of heavy court gowns and jewels, by its essential charm and honesty. The critics and visitors to the Salon, however, were rather less charmed and saw in the lack of queenly decoration and etiquette a quite deplorable *lesé majesté* that acted as a metaphor for the gradual erosion of the dignity of both France and its royal family. It was also whispered that the Queen had posed in her shift, which of course was not at all the case and, worse, that the painting was deliberately intended to ruin the silk industry at Lyons, which formed an important part of the country's revenues. The painting was intended for Versailles but Marie Antoinette was so upset by the reaction that she sent it to her friend, the Princess of Hesse-Darmstadt instead. Interestingly a very similar portrait by Vigée Le Brun of the Comtesse de Provence dressed in a muslin gown with a pale blue sash was displayed at the same time and received no way near so much opprobrium as the one of Marie Antoinette.

A second portrait, painted in the same year, was far more popular as it depicted the young Queen in much the same pose, holding a pink rose, but this time dressed in shimmering pale blue silk, trimmed with costly lace and ribbons and with priceless pearls around her white throat. *This* was apparently more like how a Queen of France should look and indeed this painting remains the most iconic portrayal of Marie Antoinette even now, probably because it delivers the most perfect balance of majesty and coquetry, both of which are qualities associated with the doomed Queen.

Certainly, Marie Antoinette's alleged coquetry was giving rise to plenty of talk that year as the handsome Swedish nobleman Axel von Fersen, whose chiselled high cheeks, steely blue eyes and pouting lips rather belied the fact that he was actually rather boring, had arrived back in Paris and been immediately accepted into the heart of the Queen's circle yet again. It was rumoured that he was her lover but this seems very unlikely to have been the case. Marie Antoinette may have been capricious, rather shallow and essentially frivolous but she was also extremely personally modest and above all deeply devoted and loyal to her family. She may never have been madly in love with Louis, her '*poor man*', but she respected him and furthermore knew that she owed him her loyalty.

However, that's not to say that she wasn't partial to the odd bit of harmless flirtation, as several other gentlemen of the court, such as the dashing Duc de Lauzun, could (and sadly *would*) testify to. That she, as we would say today, fancied Axel von Fersen cannot be doubted and that he, deeply flattered to have been singled out by the Queen of France, reciprocated her attraction is also very likely but it is very unlikely that this was ever acted upon or at least went further than perhaps the odd kiss if it even went as far as that. That Marie Antoinette, raised by her mother to be a dutiful spouse and bred for the very highest position, should compromise the French royal succession for the sake of a pair of fine eyes and a tumble in bed is unthinkable, while for Axel von Fersen it was her very untouchability, her unattainability that made her so irresistible. One gets the sense from his letters that if Marie Antoinette had capitulated and welcomed him to her bed then his image of her would have been forever tarnished as his adoration was fuelled as much by her aloofness as by her gentle charm and obvious favouritism.

Marie Antoinette became pregnant again during the summer of 1783 but despite taking all of her usual precautions she suffered a miscarriage on her birthday in November.

It was to have a devastating effect on her health and she did not fully recover for several months, which were naturally mostly spent in the seclusion and safety of the Petit Trianon. There were other worries too as the two-year-old Dauphin's health began to give concern, whereas his sister Madame Royale continued to be a boisterous butterball of a child, all pink cheeked good looks and bouncing blonde curls, just as her mother had been in her youth. The Dauphin was wan and sickly though and it was becoming unpleasantly clear to his doting parents that it might be prudent to have another son to secure the succession should the worst happen.

In the meantime, Marie Antoinette lavished attention on her children, who took up residence with their households in the Grand Trianon so that she could keep them close to hand when she was living at the Petit Trianon. Sadly, for the Queen though, the closeness that she had anticipated with Madame Royale failed to materialise as the child made it plain that she much preferred her father, probably because he was far less strict than her mother, who was fond of making her play with peasant children in order to curb her snobbish tendencies (even fostering Ernestine Lambriquet[3], the daughter of a pair of palace servants, to be her constant playmate) and on one occasion gave all of her toys away to the poor. While such egalitarian sentiments are obviously admirable, they don't seem to have pleased the haughty little Madame Royale very much and when the Abbé de Vermond told her that her mother had almost died after suffering a fall from her horse, the little princess replied that she wouldn't have minded not seeing her mother ever again because then she could do as she pleased.

Although the princess only turned five at the end of 1783, her future marriage was already a topic of considerable importance with several glittering matches, ranging from the heir of the King of Sweden to various Habsburg cousins on Marie Antoinette's side, being considered. Closer to home there was her first cousin, the Duc d'Angoulême, the eldest son of the Comte d'Artois and also the Duc de Valois[4], the eldest son of the Duc de Chartres, who would be Duc d'Orléans one day. Although Marie Antoinette was naturally hoping for a match that would keep her daughter in France, she could not bring herself to approve of a marriage into the Orléans family now that her early friendship with the Duc de Chartres, who had acted as her host at the Palais Royal on more than one occasion, had soured into an icy feud thanks to her not entirely unfounded suspicions that he and his racy social set were responsible for some of the nasty rumours circulating about her. When the Duc de Chartres formally requested the hand of the princess for his son at the start of 1784, he was turned down flat by her parents which had the effect of increasing his enmity towards Marie Antoinette, whom he regarded as entirely responsible for this humiliation. In hindsight it was probably not the wisest course of action to offend the Duc and turn down this opportunity to ally themselves with the powerful and, above all, very popular house of Orléans[5] but the events of 1789 were five long years away and no one could ever have predicted what terrible calamities lay ahead.

By the summer of 1784, Marie Antoinette had recovered from her miscarriage and was beginning to feel much more cheerful and optimistic about the future. It was during this period that she oversaw the building of her pretty little hamlet at Petit Trianon, a masterpiece of elaborate set design which the Queen fondly imagined looked just like a real peasant village, although it had more in common with the progressive model farms that were becoming popular with the English gentry. Here, she could oversee the milking of specially imported pure white Swiss cows, feed her hens and help her children pet the rabbits. The sight of Marie Antoinette harmlessly frolicking in her white frock and straw hat (both of which cost a fortune), was utterly charming to be sure, but not everyone was a fan. '*Perhaps by spending a little more, Her Majesty would have been able to erase the look of misery worn by our real hamlets within a radius of thirty leagues and improve the dwellings that are the homes of so many decent citizens, instead of representing them in their hideous decay*,' the Marquis de Bombelles wrote, admittedly with some justification.

The Queen's new theatre at the Petit Trianon was also in constant use, either with the plays that she and her friends rehearsed and performed for a select audience or a programme of concerts, operas and plays. It was here that the incredibly talented violinist and composer Joseph Bologne, Chevalier de Saint Georges[6], who was much favoured at court despite being a friend and protege of the now much disliked Duc de Chartres, performed before Marie Antoinette and her friends and even on occasion played with the Queen herself accompanying him on her pianoforte.

In June 1784, Louis and Marie Antoinette were astounded by the news that the eccentric King Gustav III of Sweden had suddenly arrived, fashionably incognito of course, at Versailles to pay a surprise visit. That he had brought the dashing Axel von Fersen with him in his train was probably of small consolation to the doubtless exasperated French royal couple as they hastened to greet their unexpected guest with all the necessary pomp. In fact, so hasty were their preparations that Louis, who had been hunting in the forests at Rambouillet when the news of Gustav's arrival came, appeared in odd shoes, which earned him a gentle rebuke from his famously *soignée* wife, who naturally looked as immaculate as ever.

King Gustav stayed for six weeks and despite his unexpected arrival, Louis and Marie Antoinette put on an astonishing and most gratifying parade of entertainments for his amusement, culminating in a wonderful party at the Petit Trianon on 27 June, where the guests were requested to conform to a white dress code and were treated to ballets and music by Grétry as they wandered freely about the pavilions, hamlet and new English gardens, all of which were illuminated by thousands of coloured lanterns for the occasion. Marie Antoinette also found time during the visit to whisk off to Paris for the gala performance of Beaumarchais' *Le Mariage de Figaro*, which had been previously banned by the King due to its seditious nature, and was reportedly very much amused by this tale of aristocratic iniquity, assignations and mistaken identity. Her husband, only too aware of the calumnies that were being spread about his wife and her friends, thought that Beaumarchais' play, which sharply criticised the upper classes, would do them all untold harm but Marie Antoinette, who loved to be at the forefront of all that was fashionable even if it was at the cost of her own dignity, believed that it was all just a piece of harmless fun and no worse than the Shakespeare plays that Louis was so fond of.

Marie Antoinette, who had become so large during pregnancy that it was thought that she was expecting twins, gave birth to her third child, another son, at half past seven in the morning of 27 March 1785. As was now the custom[7], the baby was immediately whisked away to the royal chapel to be baptised Louis Charles and was given the title

Duc de Normandie by his overjoyed father before Madame de Polignac took him off to the royal nursery on the ground floor, where he joined Madame Royale and the Dauphin. As with his elder sister, Marie Thérèse Charlotte, his last name was given in honour of his godmother, Marie Antoinette's favourite sister, Maria Carolina, Queen of Naples, who was represented by his aunt Madame Élisabeth during the ceremony.

However, whereas the births of her two eldest children had been greeted with universal acclamation, Marie Antoinette was astounded to be greeted by silent, resentful crowds when she drove into Paris for the formal thanksgiving ceremony at Notre Dame after the birth of Louis Charles, whom she referred to as her '*chou d'amour*'. Until that moment she had had no real idea just how unpopular she actually was and was completely shocked and bewildered by the experience. 'Why do they hate me so much?' she asked her husband upon her return to Versailles. 'What have I ever done to them?' Her unpopularity was further increased when the King, who in his usual clumsy way was seeking only to show his gratitude and affection to his wife, purchased the Orléans family's grand country seat, Saint Cloud on the outskirts of Paris for 6 million livres (with the assistance of his brilliant Director General of Finance, Calonne who had temporarily abated the pressure on the royal coffers by borrowing large sums of money) and, in an unprecedented act, presented it to Marie Antoinette as her own personal property rather than that of the crown as was more usual.

The main impetus for this rather expensive and foolish purchase was the ongoing major renovation work going on at Versailles (Louis and Marie Antoinette had actually considered rebuilding large parts of the palace, which was badly in need of repair, until they fortunately realised that this plan was financially unfeasible) which made it advisable to have another large residence near Paris. It was thought that the air at Saint Cloud, which was built on a hill overlooking the city and had famously beautiful gardens that swept down towards the Seine, was far healthier than that at Versailles, which after all had been built on a swamp, and would therefore be better for the royal children, in particular the ailing Dauphin. The purchase of Saint Cloud was still an act of folly though and the fact that it now belonged to Marie Antoinette just made the situation far worse as people were absolutely astounded that a foreign Queen of France would now own property in her own right and therefore have the right to dispose of it as she pleased, perhaps even bequeathing it to one of her Austrian family. That she had already made it absolutely clear that upon her death the property would be inherited by one of her younger children did not matter – people were worried that it would somehow become the property of the hated Austria and that the Emperor would therefore have a foothold in France, as if it wasn't already bad enough having his sister on the throne with the King popularly and totally falsely supposed to be completely under her thumb.

As always, Marie Antoinette grandly ignored all of the murmurings and threw herself wholeheartedly into the refurbishment of Saint Cloud, which hadn't been visited by the Orléans family for quite some time and was in serious need of an overhaul, which the Queen enthusiastically delivered, installing her favourite beautiful pastel coloured panelling everywhere and filling the rooms with exquisite furniture and costly decorations, including the famous Nocret painting of the young Louis XIV and his family which now hangs at Versailles but took pride of place at Saint Cloud during Marie Antoinette's residence. She took great delight in posting rules there '*by order of the Queen*' and insisted that all of the servants wore her own personal red livery[8] and if she knew that this was causing opprobrium in certain quarters, she didn't seem to care one little bit.

In the wake of the Duc de Normandie's birth and the purchase of Saint Cloud, rumours about the Queen's private life began to multiply at an alarming rate. There had always been ill-natured whispers about the paternity of the royal children, but never on quite the same scale as now when all of Paris was talking about the fact that the latest royal baby had obviously been conceived during the Swedish royal visit when King Gustav had had the dashing Axel von Fersen, whom the Queen was known to have a liking for, amongst his entourage of handsome young men[9]. Pamphlets, leaflets, ribald songs and erotic novels about the Queen's alleged sexual exploits with a variety of partners that included her brother-in-law Artois and friends Gabrielle de Polignac and the Princesse de Lamballe began to appear in such great numbers that the Parisian police could barely keep tabs on the situation, although they seized and destroyed as many as they could. However, countless more were being openly sold in the arcades of the Palais Royal and many even made their way to Versailles where they were left on chairs in the royal salons and even on occasion surreptitiously placed where the Queen herself would see them.

Marie Antoinette did her best to laugh all of this off but the real danger lay in the fact that although the pamphlets and rhymes were generally seen as amusing little pieces of nonsense in the glittering and sophisticated salons of Paris and Versailles there was a serious risk that they were being taken as fact by the less erudite and cosmopolitan citizens of her country and those who lived so far afield that they probably had no real idea what their Queen even *looked* like let alone anything else. The sullen reception that she had received in Paris after the birth of the Duc de Normandie certainly suggested that her star was not so much on the wane but had fallen completely and the rumours of her promiscuity had a lot to do with this. '*How many times have you left the marriage bed and the caresses of your husband to abandon yourself to Bacchantes or satyrs and to join yourself with them through their brutal joys?*' one pamphlet demanded of the Queen. The message was clear – Marie Antoinette was a bad woman, a bad wife, a bad mother and a bad Queen.

Not that the rumours were entirely restricted to the gutter press of Paris, however. There had been all sorts of lurid little tales floating around the candlelit rooms of the royal palaces for years: whispers about the Queen's flirtations with various gentlemen of the court and raised eyebrows over her close friendships with Madame de Polignac and Madame de Lamballe, which were obviously completely innocent but, then as now, malicious tongues will find fodder wherever they can and can twist even the most innocuous things to make them appear far more sinister than they actually are. There was also plenty of talk about Marie Antoinette's secretive behaviour at Versailles and the other palaces where she insisted upon locking herself away in her private cabinets and even the King would often find himself left out in the cold on the other side of the door. There had been much laughter, for example, over the occasion at Fontainebleau when poor Louis had traipsed past several amused courtiers to visit his wife's bedchamber at night only to find the door firmly locked against him. The unfortunate and extremely embarrassed King had then had to perform the very worst sort of walk of shame past a crowd of sniggering courtiers, who hid their smiles behind the painted fans and wondered just what the Queen was trying to hide from her husband and everyone else.

Chapter 9

Madame Deficit 1785–1788

'My fate is to bring bad luck.'

However, despite things seeming as bad as they could possibly be in the first six months of 1785, things were about to take a turn for the even worse for Marie Antoinette. On 12 July 1785, while the Queen was excitedly preparing for the court's first period of residence at the newly refurbished Saint Cloud and painstakingly learning her lines for the role of Rosine in a private performance of Beaumarchais' *The Barber of Seville*, the Parisian jeweller Charles Auguste Boehmer, who worked in partnership with Paul Bassenge, sent her a very strange and perplexing note.

> '*Madame,*
> *We are filled with happiness and venture to think that the last arrangements proposed to us, which we have performed with zeal and respect, are a further proof of our submission and devotion to Your Majesty's order, and we have genuine satisfaction in thinking that the most beautiful set of diamonds now existing will belong to the greatest and best of Queens.*'

Amused by what she believed must be an unfortunate misunderstanding, Marie Antoinette read the note out to her First Lady of the Bedchamber, Madame Campan then set fire to it with a candle, remarking that it was so mad that it would be a kindness not to keep it. Clearly she had forgotten that Boehmer and Bassange had visited her a number of times over the years to beg her to buy an extravagant and now extremely outmoded looped necklace that had originally been made for Madame du Barry when she was at the height of her relationship with Louis XV and had her royal lover so completely wrapped around her little finger that he would have bought it for her without a single qualm. Marie Antoinette had never got over her adolescent loathing of Madame du Barry, who was still banned from ever returning to Versailles and currently living a relatively blameless life on her country estate at Louveciennes, and this association with the hated former royal mistress would have been more than enough to put her off buying the necklace if it hadn't also been utterly hideous and ruinously expensive at an eye watering 1.8 million livres. Always eager to please his wife, Louis had initially offered to buy the piece for her but Marie Antoinette, who hated it and had, besides, begun to economise where diamonds were concerned, turned him down, saying that the country had more need of war ships than diamonds and besides she had more than enough of the latter anyway.

However, the cryptic note apparently brought none of this to mind and instead Marie Antoinette thought that it must simply be a rather stupid ploy to persuade her into buying some other extravagant and doubtless ugly piece of jewellery. She instructed

Madame Campan to let Boehmer know that she would no longer be buying her jewels from him and then would almost certainly have thought no more of the matter if it hadn't been forced upon her attention once again and in rather more alarming terms after the utterly devastated Boehmer visited Madame Campan later that same day and poured a tale of woe into her increasingly horrified and shocked ears. It seemed that long after he had given up all hope of the Queen relenting and taking the now infamous necklace off his hands, Boehmer had been delighted and highly relieved to be contacted by the Cardinal de Rohan who informed him that he had been instructed to buy the necklace on behalf of Marie Antoinette, who wished the transaction to be kept completely secret. Convinced by notes that had allegedly been signed by the Queen herself, the jeweller had delivered the necklace to the Cardinal, who in return informed him that the Queen would make the first payment of 400,000 livres on 1 August and would make a glittering *début* in her purchase in the next few weeks.

A few days later Boehmer and Bassenge were summoned to Versailles in order to repeat their tale in front of Marie Antoinette, Vermond and the Minister of the King's Household, the Baron de Breteuil, all of whom were appalled by the implications of what they were being told. Marie Antoinette was particularly incensed – she had hated the Cardinal de Rohan for years ever since he'd been extremely rude about her mother, and had subsequently snubbed several attempts on his part to get into her good books. It seemed absolutely incredible to her that, knowing full well how much she disliked him for she never learned to hide her feelings about anyone, he could *ever* have believed that she would put such a delicate commission into his hands or, perhaps even worse, that she would even for a second have considered plotting with him behind the back of the King.

However, Baron de Breteuil's investigations were to uncover even worse revelations when further questioning of the unfortunate Boehmer and Bassenge brought the name of Madame de la Motte-Valois, a well-known adventuress who claimed to be descended from the Valois kings and had for a long time embarrassed herself by being obviously desperate to get accepted into the Queen's inner circle, into the mix. Madame de la Motte-Valois had been going about Paris boasting of her friendship with Marie Antoinette and popularity at court where, she said, she was received everywhere as a cousin of the King and Queen and was privy to all of their secrets. It was all lies, of course, but the desperate jewellers had fallen for it hook, line and sinker and asked her if she would have a word in Marie Antoinette's ear about the diamond necklace. After taking a look at the piece in question, Madame de la Motte-Valois had promised to do her best and at the start of 1785 had returned to inform them that she had succeeded in her quest and managed to persuade the Queen to buy the jewels. According to Madame de la Motte-Valois, Marie Antoinette had been secretly hankering after them all along but had not dared to openly buy them for fear of displeasing the King and drawing further adverse comment about her extravagance.

At the same time as she was enmeshing the unfortunate Boehmer and Bassenge in her web of lies, Madame de la Motte-Valois was also spinning a fairytale for her lover Cardinal de Rohan, who was also well known to be desperate for the Queen's favour and a chance to ingratiate himself out of her bad books. The Cardinal, who was clearly a very credulous and rather stupid man, was only too willing to believe that Madame de la Motte-Valois was friends with the Queen, despite the lack of any concrete evidence to support this, and after she appeared to set up a secret midnight meeting between him and Marie Antoinette in one of the secluded groves at Versailles, he was like putty in her hands. He grandly agreed to act as go between with the jewellers in the purchase of the fabulous necklace, with his haughty aristocratic authority dispelling any lingering concerns that they might have had about the veracity of Madame de la Motte-Valois' claims to be on intimate terms with the Queen. It was the Cardinal who took charge of the necklace after the jewellers brought it to the Hôtel de Rohan at the start of February and he who made the arrangements for payment before it was passed on to the very grateful Madame de la Motte-Valois, who had allegedly been instructed to take it straight to the Queen at Versailles.

However, when Marie Antoinette failed to appear in public wearing the fabulous necklace, Monsieur Boehmer began to get rather nervous about the whole transaction. Reports that Madame de la Motte-Valois had gone on a massive shopping spree then departed Paris in order to take up residence in her new and extremely lavishly furnished château were also very worrying and in the end the anxious jewellers had decided to break their promise to maintain a discreet silence about the transaction and approach Madame de Campan, in order to find out what had happened.

At first the Baron de Breteuil advised keeping the whole affair from the King until more was known about the Cardinal's involvement. However, on 14 August he decided that the time had come to come clean and laid the whole sorry affair in front of his master, who in turn discussed it with his advisor Vergennes and then the Keeper of the Seals, Armand de Miromesnil. Breteuil, who was wholeheartedly the Queen's man, was all in favour of publicly humiliating the Cardinal for this act of *lèse majesté* but the cannier Vergennes and Miromesnil were mindful of the terrible scandal that this might provoke and instead hastened to advise the King to tread carefully and instead privately question the Cardinal about the affair before he made any rash decisions.

The Cardinal was ordered into the presence of the King, Queen and three ministers the very next day, 15 August 1785. It was the Feast of the Assumption and Marie Antoinette's name day and the whole of Versailles had turned out *en masse* to watch the procession and attend that morning's Mass in the Queen's honour. Having been out of royal favour for several years, Cardinal de Rohan was extremely surprised to be informed that he had been summoned to the King's presence but hopeful that his secret assignment for the Queen had finally marked a significant turn in his fortunes at court, he obediently made his way through the huge crowds in the Hall of Mirrors to the Council Room. However, if he expected to find the King wreathed with grateful smiles he was sorely mistaken as instead he found himself being interrogated by Louis and his ministers, all under the cold and distinctly unfriendly gaze of Marie Antoinette who spoke only once to insist that the notes that the Cardinal claimed he had received from her via Madame de la Motte-Valois must obviously have been forgeries. She was absolutely livid when the Cardinal produced one of these missives, which he had fortuitously kept on his person, and upon examination it was quickly spotted that it had been signed by 'Marie Antoinette de France' which as Queen, she would *never* have done – members of the royal family were obviously so grand and well known that signing off with just 'Marie Antoinette' was enough.

When the crestfallen Cardinal had left, Vergennes and Miromesnil counselled the King to tread cautiously and keep the whole sorry affair completely quiet, no doubt already fearing that there were further sordid revelations in the pipeline and all too well aware how much damage such a scandal, touching as it did upon the Queen's alleged extravagance as well as her much whispered about personal relations with the courtiers, would do to Marie Antoinette's already beleaguered reputation. However, Breteuil and the Queen, who had burst into tears as soon as Rohan left, were determined to see the Cardinal fully punished for his actions and urged Louis to have him arrested and properly questioned. Never able to resist his wife's tears, Louis duly gave the order to have the Cardinal arrested and Breteuil, who looked absolutely delighted, stepped out of the Council Room and loudly gave the order to have Rohan apprehended at once. It would have been more usual for such a high-profile arrest to take place in private so to have the Cardinal arrested so publicly and within the walls of Versailles itself was extremely shocking and had the effect of causing an immense scandal before anything was even known about the whole affair.

Madame de la Motte-Valois was arrested shortly afterwards and of course denied everything, painting herself as the innocent patsy in the Cardinal's schemes and claiming to have nothing to do with the necklace which had, *quelle surprise*, now completely vanished from sight. The official investigations continued well into the summer until Louis called another meeting and, despite the continued reservations of Miromesnil and Vergennes, ordered that the Cardinal be put on trial so that his wife's name could be completely cleared of any involvement in the matter. Marie Antoinette was horrified that the Cardinal, a man whom everyone knew she absolutely loathed, could have been so stupid as to think for so much as a second that she would not only pass him secret notes but, far worse still, arrange private little assignations with him in the middle of the night. That a public airing of the whole sordid affair would not do her any favours did not apparently weigh on her mind, which was now entirely focused on getting revenge on the arrogant Cardinal. It would have been a kindness on the part of Vergennes to point out at this juncture that her own reputation was by now so blackened that a public trial of this nature could only do harm no matter what the outcome was, but he remained silent and the whole miserable process continued.

Meanwhile, Marie Antoinette continued to distract herself with her performance as Rosine in *The Barber of Seville* which was put on at the Petit Trianon theatre in front of a very select audience made up of members of the royal family and the Queen's own close little circle of friends. She also thoroughly enjoyed her first proper stay at her new acquisition Saint Cloud, which lived up to expectations and quickly became a favourite residence of the royal family. Marie Antoinette even opened up the gardens to the public and the curious Parisians turned up in their droves to see the royal family disporting themselves in their country idyll and even managed to politely applaud when the Queen appeared on the flower filled parterres holding the Dauphin in her arms and with Madame Royale trotting at her side in a pretty dress. However, if Marie Antoinette thought that this applause was indicative of a softening of the public mood towards her, she was to be sorely disappointed as the rumours were worse than ever thanks to the ongoing inquiry into the affair of the diamond necklace, the juicy details of which were, as had been gloomily predicted by Vergennes, being talked about all over Europe.

At the start of October, Marie Antoinette travelled by boat to Fontainebleau for the court's customary autumn visit to the palace, where the King was looking forward to some excellent hunting. The boat was a new purchase – a pleasure yacht in the English style, complete with a beautifully appointed salon, which had cost 100,000 livres. However, despite the glory of her arrival, looking like Cleopatra aboard her splendid new ship, the normally vivacious Queen was unusually downcast during her stay at Fontainebleau, with events in Paris clearly weighing heavily on her mind as the former lovers La Motte-Valois and the Cardinal did their best to incriminate each other in their testimonies. However, in the minds of the people the only person who was really incriminated by the whole sorry affair was the Queen herself. Although she had been shocked beyond measure to hear that the Cardinal had absolutely believed her to be the woman he met in the moonlight glade at Versailles, it seemed that no one else found it all that hard to believe that she would indulge in a secret night time assignation, so thoroughly had Marie Antoinette's reputation been tarnished over the years. When it was further revealed that the woman in question had in fact been a Palais Royal prostitute who traded off her spurious resemblance to the Queen, this made the whole scenario all the more appalling as people chuckled over the mental image of the proud Cardinal falling to his knees in reverence before a common whore dressed, ironically enough, in one of the fashionable white dresses that Marie Antoinette was so fond of. There were plenty of people who muttered that Queen or whore, there was no difference either way and therein lay the danger of the whole enterprise as the Queen's unpopularity was laid bare for all to see.

On 2 November, Marie Antoinette turned thirty and like plenty of other women she had some trouble reconciling herself to the inexorable onward march of time and became obsessed with her weight and appearance, declaring to Rose Bertin that she would be dressing more maturely from now on and renouncing the ostentatious fashions of her youth. Possibly she also regretted her foolish words as an arrogant nineteen-year-old Queen, when she had wondered why women over the age of thirty still bothered showing their faces at court. Although very pretty by anyone's standards as a young girl, by her thirties Marie Antoinette had filled out and become rather more Rubenesque and was, in modern parlance, more a woman who made an effort to make the best of herself than a natural beauty. Although never naturally blessed with great natural beauty she had, thanks to the artifice of wonderful clothes, elegant coiffures, make up, jewels, exquisite bearing and a winsomely charming demeanour, long been used to hearing herself described as the most beautiful woman at court – now, however, her new young ladies in waiting, freshly married girls in their late teens and early twenties, were instructed by the older and wiser ladies of the court to stay out of direct sunlight so the fresh radiance of their complexions wouldn't remind the Queen of the youthful good looks that she now feared that she was losing.

Marie Antoinette's rejection of the pretty, frothy, beribboned gowns of her youth can be charted in the portraits of Madame Vigée-Lebrun who painted the Queen's favourite portrait of herself in late 1785, depicting Marie Antoinette in a lace and fur trimmed gown of rich crimson velvet that opens over a petticoat of saffron yellow silk. Her fichu is trimmed with exquisite lace and on her head there is balanced one of Mademoiselle Bertin's famous *poufs* of white muslin trimmed with pearls. The Queen's gaze is steady and somewhat amused and in her hands, neatly arranged on a green velvet cushion, she holds a book with her fingers marking the place – presumably to signify her renunciation of the frivolities of youth. It's a delightful portrait and one of the very few that properly manages to convey Marie Antoinette's famous charm, despite being more obviously sober in both palette and composition than her previous depictions.

Also captivating is another portrait that Vigée-Lebrun painted in the same year for the Comte d'Artois' exquisite Paris residence the Château de Bagatelle[1], which was built in the Bois de Boulogne after Marie Antoinette, who loved a wager, bet her brother-in-law that he couldn't build a château in less than three months. In the end it took sixty-three months to complete and a grand full-length portrait of Marie Antoinette, who was often entertained there, was commissioned for one of the salons. In this work, which bears some aesthetic resemblances to the later more famous painting of Marie Antoinette with her children, Madame Vigée-Lebrun painted the Queen against splendid surroundings, dressed in a sumptuous gown of rich blue velvet, trimmed with lace and fur and this time opening over a cream silk petticoat. Once again she holds a book in her lap, her fingers marking the place, while her gaze is dignified with just a touch of amusement. This time though the overall effect is undoubtedly majestic thanks to the combination of that splendidly restrained yet still magnificent gown, the rich swags of crimson velvet falling from the table and the opulent beauty of the sitter herself, who presides over her palatial surroundings with that famously rare combination of both grandeur and grace.

One of her pages, Alexandre Tilly, described her at this time as having '*eyes which were not beautiful but which were expressive of every disposition: benevolence or aversion were displayed on her countenance in a manner which was entirely her own… Her skin was admirable; her neck and shoulders also; the bust a little too full and the figure lacking in elegance; I have never seen such beautiful arms and hands. She had two ways of walking: one firm and a little hurried, but always noble; the other less vigorous, more poised.*' He added that: '*In a word, she was the sort of woman to whom one would instinctively have offered not a chair but a throne.*'

With great insight into the character of the Queen that he served, Tilly also wrote that: '*She treated us all with a singular sweetness and we all adored her. Her most destructive fault, and one which did a lot of harm, was her dislike of all pomp and formality, the formality which is more necessary in France than anywhere else. She was childish and inconsequential, with no definite ideas except to free herself of the burdensome ties imposed by her rank. When she wanted to, no one could be more royal and dignified. One has never seen anyone curtsey so gracefully, singling out ten persons in one curtsey and giving to each in turn the regard which was their due.*'

Marie Antoinette's charitable and philanthropic instinct never abated and each significant event in her court life, such as the births of her children, was marked with generous financial gifts to favourite charities, such as those set up for orphans or indigent wet nurses, while Louis also regularly emptied his coffers to assist the less fortunate. During the winter of 1784, he distributed three million francs of his own money and also ordered that much of the royal forest should be cut down to provide firewood for those who could not afford it. Madame de la Tour du Pin, one of Marie Antoinette's ladies in waiting, wrote in her memoirs that the Queen would regularly walk around the games room at Versailles with a small bag in order to collect donations from the courtiers playing at the cards tables. Men were expected to give a gold louis, while women were asked for six francs – a mere pittance compared to the fortunes that were won and lost at cards at court on a daily basis, and yet this strategy '*aroused considerable resentment among the younger courtiers*'.

The Cardinal's trial came to a dramatic conclusion on 31 May 1786, when Madame de la Motte-Valois and her accomplices were found guilty and the gullible Cardinal, whose family, the powerful Rohan clan had turned up to the court room all dramatically decked out in full mourning dress, acquitted. Marie Antoinette was incensed by this result and not at all pacified by the sentencing of the others, who were small fry in comparison to the hated Cardinal. She burst into tears when she heard the verdict, furious and deeply hurt that the judges had appeared to believe the Cardinal's defence that he had totally believed the web of lies created by La Motte-Valois and therefore had no reason to doubt that the woman he met in the arbour at Versailles was not in fact the Queen. Others would go further and express their belief that the Cardinal had been the puppet of not one but two faithless, untrustworthy women: La Motte-Valois and Marie Antoinette, who had no doubt colluded together to try and bring about his downfall. Either that or the entire blame lay at the door of Marie Antoinette who had engineered the whole thing in order to grab the diamonds without paying for them and also bring down the Cardinal at the same time. Either way, although the Cardinal had been acquitted and the trial was at an end, Marie Antoinette felt as though she herself had been condemned by the judge's verdict which had, as Vergennes had feared, only served to underline the fact that she was now so unpopular that the French people would believe her guilty of almost any calumny.

The news at the start of 1786, that Marie Antoinette was expecting another baby did nothing to cheer the depressed Queen up but rather made her feel even more pressured and put upon as she had considered her family complete and had no wish to undergo the rigours of pregnancy and childbirth once again. The King left her at Versailles for the last few weeks of her pregnancy while he went off to Normandy on a rare trip to the provinces, which lasted for eight days and involved fascinating visits to harbours and coastal fortifications – which was exactly the sort of thing that Louis most enjoyed. Astonishingly, it was the first time that the King, who had only once in all his life left the environs of Paris and the Ile de France when he travelled to Rheims for his coronation, had ever beheld the sea. Marie Antoinette, however, would never see it and would instead have to content herself with her husband's excited reports about his visit when he returned to Versailles to be greeted by herself and their three children, who shouted 'Papa! Papa!' when they saw the King approach from their vantage point on the balcony overlooking the marble courtyard of the palace.

Just over a week later on 9 July, Marie Antoinette's labour began. Keen to put off the inevitable and also rather alarmed as the baby was not due for a few more weeks, she at first claimed that all was well and the pains were due to indigestion before finally having to concede defeat at around half past four in the afternoon when the ministers were summoned to attend the royal birth. Sophie Hélène Béatrice was born three hours later and from the start it was clear that like her eldest brother the Dauphin, this new baby was far from robust, which just added to Marie Antoinette's feelings of dejected lassitude. She was also physically ailing and suffering from unexplained pains in her legs, terrible headaches and feelings of breathlessness which were probably all due to anxiety and depression. When her sister Maria Christina visited Paris for a month in the summer of 1786, Marie Antoinette made very little effort to see her and caused great offence by not inviting her to the Petit Trianon. More surprisingly, a few months later she turned down an opportunity to visit her brother Joseph in Brussels, claiming that her fragile health and that of the Dauphin and baby Sophie would not allow it.

Later on in the year the royal family went to Fontainebleau for the customary autumn visit, not realising that this would be their last stay in the splendid old Renaissance palace. Marie Antoinette inhabited rooms as opulent as those at Versailles, including a pretty boudoir decorated in shimmering mother of pearl which had only just been completed for her that year and which she would barely have a chance to enjoy. Madame Vigée-Lebrun, the Queen's favourite portrait painter saw her there that year and later recalled in her memoirs that: '*When the Queen went for the last time to Fontainebleau, where the court, according to custom, was to appear in full gala, I repaired there to enjoy that spectacle. I saw the Queen in her grandest dress; she was covered with diamonds, and as the brilliant sunshine fell upon her she seemed to me nothing short of dazzling. Her head, erect on her beautiful Greek neck, lent her as she walked such an imposing, such a majestic air, that one seemed to see a goddess in the midst of her nymphs. During the first sitting I had with Her Majesty after this occasion I took the liberty of mentioning the impression she had made upon me, and of saying to the Queen how the carriage of her head added to the nobility of her bearing. She answered in a jesting tone, "If I were not Queen they would say I looked insolent, would they not?"*'

Things went from bad to worse in 1787, which started with the death of Louis' friend and advisor Vergennes in February, just when the King needed his support and level headed advice more than ever in the face of a financial crisis that threatened to tip the country over the edge of bankruptcy. The distraught Louis cried when he heard the news and lamented that 'I have lost the only friend that I could rely on, the only minister who never betrayed me' and his distress deepened when rumours began to spread that his wife had poisoned Vergennes in order to put a stop to his consistently anti-Austrian policies.

Without Vergennes at his elbow, Louis floundered hopelessly when confronted with the facts about his country's financial situation which involved a deficit of 112 million francs and appalling debts, many of which were due to French involvement in the American Revolution. Calonne, whose clever juggling of loans had enabled the purchase not just of Saint Cloud but also that of the château of Rambouillet for Louis, came up with a plan for a radical tax overhaul that would free up some extra cash but as it involved taxing the property of the nobility, who had been living it up tax free up until then, this was bitterly opposed at Versailles and led to the ignominious fall from grace of Calonne. There were calls for the return of his predecessor Jacques Necker, whose resignation in 1781 had been blamed on Marie Antoinette, who was said to have been displeased by the attention he drew to the enormous expenses of the court and in particular the extravagant financial favours being showered on her friends, especially Madame de Polignac. It would be another year before Necker was recalled to office and optimistically hailed as the saviour of France but in the meantime things would only get worse for the beleaguered Queen of France as she was harangued by Count Mercy and her brother about the appointment of replacements for both Vergennes and Calonne. It was her duty, they told her, to ensure that both posts were filled by people sympathetic to the Austrian alliance. However, Marie Antoinette had very much had enough of playing piggy in the middle between the interests of Austria and those of France and curtly informed Mercy that: 'It is not right for the Viennese court to appoint ministers to the court of Versailles.' However, it was nonetheless her choice Loménie de Brienne who was appointed to the position of Director General of Finance in the end.

The atmosphere at court was becoming increasingly gloomy. As Madame de la Tour du Pin wrote in her memoirs: '*It was the fashion to complain of everything. One was bored being in attendance at court. The officers of the Garde de Corps, who were lodged in the château when on duty, bemoaned having to wear uniform all day; the ladies of the household could not bear to miss going to supper in Paris during the eight days of their attendance at Versailles. It was the height of bon ton to complain of their duties at court, profiting from them nonetheless. All the ties were being loosened, and alas it was the upper classes which led the way.*' Attendance at court was extremely poor (the royal couple held 'court' on Sundays and for religious festivals and occasionally on Tuesdays, when the ambassadors would come to pay their respects) and even the Queen's balls were very scantily attended, which led to a lack of partners and general disgruntlement all round.

In response to all of this, the royal couple were becoming increasingly elusive. Louis had sunk into a depression after the death of Vergennes and spent all of his time either hunting, eating, sleeping or crying, while Marie Antoinette hid herself away either at the Petit Trianon or in the warren of tiny rooms behind her state apartments and saw very few people. Even Madame de Polignac was kept at arm's length as the Queen began belatedly to realise that it was the favours that she had showered upon Gabrielle and her set that had, in part at least, contributed to the terrible mess that she had found herself in. However, with Louis wallowing in a state of depressed apathy, it fell to Marie Antoinette, encouraged by Loménie de Brienne, to take up a more active role in the government. She had taken no interest in politics in the past and still had very little wish to get involved now but the circumstances demanded that she do her best to support the weakened King – which of course played straight into the hands of her enemies who could now say that they had been right all along about the fact that she was meddling in politics and therefore entirely to blame for everything that had gone wrong.

She was even beginning to feel alienated from people who had always been wholeheartedly on her side, such as the Duc de Coigny, who had always been one of her greatest admirers but had fallen out with the King and Queen when their financial reforms at court had forced him to lose one of his most prestigious and fiscally rewarding positions. The Comte de Vaudreuil and Duc de Polignac also lost positions and income and became noticeably icy around the Queen and her husband as did many others who also found themselves bereft of valuable favours and offices as a result of the royal economy drive. Marie Antoinette had always counted upon her little faithful *cotérie* of friends to boost her ego and offer a sweetened antidote to the unpopularity and censure that she faced elsewhere but it seemed as though even they were beginning to desert her now that she had cut off their supply of favours. It must have made the already downcast Queen wonder if she had ever truly had any friends at all.

There were some consolations though. The Princesse de Lamballe was as faithful as ever and Marie Antoinette was also beginning to spend more time with her Mistress of the Robes the Comtesse d'Ossun[2], who was an altogether more steady character than Gabrielle de Polignac and her rakish set and did her best to cheer the disconsolate Marie Antoinette up with quiet supper parties and low-key balls in her apartments. The Queen, who had once danced until dawn, rarely danced nowadays but she obliged the kindly Comtesse by politely taking part in a few dances before sitting out the rest.

Marie Antoinette also did her best to foster a friendship with her young sister-in-law Madame Élisabeth, who turned twenty three in 1787. Élisabeth was a sweet natured and extremely devout girl, very similar in appearance to her eldest brother Louis and passionately devoted to both him and her youngest brother the Comte d'Artois, who could do absolutely no wrong in her eyes. On her sixteenth birthday in May 1780, the princess had left the nursery behind for good and moved into her own apartment at Versailles which Marie Antoinette, with typical generosity, arranged to have freshly and most sumptuously decorated. There were constant rumours that the princess, who never actually publicly expressed a desire to take holy orders, would one day become a nun like her aunt Louise and as the years went by without any sign of a suitable husband (the princess told Madame d'Oberkirch that '*I could only marry a King's son, and a king's son must reign in his father's states so that I would no longer be a Frenchwoman. Better to stay here at the foot of my brother's throne, than to ascend another'*) her brother and those who loved her were worried that she too might take flight in the middle of the night and run away to a Carmelite convent.

However, her new rooms overlooking the Orangery were in a complete contrast to the tiny nun's cell that her soul allegedly desired. She had eight rooms to herself: two antechambers, a reception room, a bedroom (hung with green Lyons damask in the summer and crimson silk velvet in the winter), a grand cabinet, a billiard room, a library and then a private boudoir, all of which were furnished with the most exquisite taste and luxury. She also now owned the Princesse de Guéméné's delightful country house at Montreuil and was happily doing it up although her brother had ordered that she would not be allowed to spend the night there until she turned twenty five in May 1789. Always delighted to offer a surprise to someone that she loved, Marie Antoinette had revealed the news of the purchase of Montreuil in a typically playful manner by suggesting to Élisabeth that they drive out to the house together to say goodbye before surprising her with the keys when they arrived.

However, despite this generosity and thoughtfulness, the two young women never really hit it off. Although she would never say so to Marie Antoinette, Madame Élisabeth very much disapproved of her sister-in-law's ramshackle lifestyle, the dissolute company that she insisted upon keeping and, perhaps worst of all, the disrespectful manner with which she occasionally treated and spoke of the King, whom she herself revered both as her brother and her sovereign. Meanwhile, for her part, Marie Antoinette found Élisabeth's gentle manners and rigid piety extremely dull and almost certainly sensed the disapproval that the younger woman tried so hard to conceal, fearing that it would hurt her brother's feelings. However, for now they muddled along well enough and

Marie Antoinette liked her sister-in-law's company enough to have a room prepared for her beneath the eaves of the Petit Trianon so that she could stay there with her, which she frequently did.

However, her main comfort during these dreary last years of the *ancien régime* was the elegant Swede Axel von Fersen, who had returned to France in the summer of 1787 and immediately hastened to the side of Marie Antoinette at Versailles. Although they were almost certainly not lovers in the sexual sense, they were definitely very close with Axel seeing himself as a sort of chivalric knight chastely adoring and defending the honour of his lady while Marie Antoinette, whose life was increasingly becoming overwhelmed with cares and troubles, sought solace in his flattering attentions and the fact that he never seemed to ask anything of her, unlike everyone else. The fact that, like her, Fersen was an outsider and also didn't come with a demanding family and clinging troop of hangers on all clamouring for money and positions can't have hurt either.

Besides her tattered reputation and the ever worsening financial crisis, Marie Antoinette was also desperately worried about the health of her children. The delicate Dauphin was still continuing to give concern and on 14 June 1787 her youngest daughter Sophie, who had been weak and ailing since birth, died at the age of just eleven months old probably as a result of convulsions brought on by teething. Marie Antoinette was devastated to lose one of her children and referred to the baby as her 'little angel' when she took her sister-in-law Madame Élisabeth to the Grand Trianon to view the child lying in state beneath a tiny coronet and a mantle embroidered with gold fleur de lys. According to court etiquette princesses were not officially mourned until they had reached the age of seven so only her immediate family wore mourning in her memory that summer.

Nonetheless, there was a last lingering reminder of Sophie in the painting of the Queen surrounded by her surviving children which was painted by Madame Vigée-Lebrun in 1787, where the Dauphin points towards the baby's blue silk swathed empty cradle, the child herself having been hastily painted out after her death. To modern eyes, Marie Antoinette, dressed in opulent crimson velvet trimmed with exquisite lace, looks careworn and rather older than her thirty-one years and even Vigée-Lebrun's famously flattering brush couldn't conceal the coarsening of the Queen's once radiant complexion, her double chin or the puffiness of eyes that sparkled not with happiness but with tears. Overall though the portrait is a triumph that cleverly draws inspiration from paintings of the holy family to create something both stately and touching. For many though this portrait evokes feelings of sadness, representative as it is of a way of life that was rapidly approaching destruction and a family that was heading for even more tragedy – by the end of 1795, less than a decade away, only one of the sitters, Madame Royale, would still be alive.

The portrait of the Queen and her children, for which Madame Vigée-Lebrun was paid an enormous 18,000 francs, was due to be displayed at that year's Salon in Paris. However, it arrived late and when the empty frame was displayed for a few days before its arrival, someone pinned a placard saying '*Behold the Deficit!*' inside. However, the painting itself was to be a great success, much to the relief of its artist who, well aware of the unpopularity of its chief sitter, had stayed away from the Salon for fear of hearing it insulted. When the exhibition ended it was transferred to Versailles and placed where

Marie Antoinette could see it every day as she passed by on her way to morning Mass, while the King informed the extremely gratified Madame Vigée-Lebrun that '*I know nothing about painting, but you make me like it.*'

Meanwhile, the political situation was worsening by the day as Loménie de Brienne, well-meaning but completely lacking the brilliance of the likes of Calonne and Necker, battled to save them from financial ruin, became increasingly aghast at the ever increasing deficit and struggled to make the King, now completely sunk into apathy, assert himself against his opponents. Louis, never the most prepossessing of figures at the best of times, was cruelly lampooned everywhere and mocked for his corpulence, laziness and lack of vigour, which of course included sexual ability as well as political acumen. The worst insults, however, were as always reserved for Marie Antoinette, the foreign Queen who was now compared to Catherine de' Medici, Isabeau of Bavaria and Messalina, all women who were deemed to have brought disgrace upon their sex by behaving in an 'un-womanly' way. Then as now, women who refused to remain meekly silent and were seen to step out of line and meddle in affairs that were considered best left to their menfolk, were derided as being somehow unnatural and immoral – their 'vices', of course, being traits that their powerful male counterparts were usually congratulated for. That Marie Antoinette was actually nowhere near as politically savvy, intelligent or ruthless as the likes of Catherine de' Medici is perhaps her tragedy but this fact didn't spare her from having a placard saying '*Tremble, tyrants*' placed inside her box at the theatre.

In August 1787, Louis made a rare visit to the *lit de justice* at the parliament, in order to give his support to Loménie de Brienne's extremely unpopular financial reforms. However, when he tried to push the edicts through he was loudly and rather annoyingly opposed by his cousin the Duc d'Orléans who had recently set himself up as a liberal opponent of the royal party and a mouthpiece for the disaffected nobility. Unable to hide his fury, Louis stalked out of the hall then had the recalcitrant Duc exiled to his château at Villers-Cotterets, far away from his rabble-rousing circle of friends and hangers on at the Palais Royal which had become the source of some disturbingly anti-monarchist sentiments, inflamed by Orléans himself who now, to absolutely no one's surprise least of all hers, came out as Marie Antoinette's greatest and most implacable enemy. Nonetheless, despite all of this overt hostility, social politesse still continued between the two politically estranged sides of the royal family with Marie Antoinette and Louis acting as very generous god parents to the Duc's eldest sons at their official baptism in May 1788. This was still Versailles after all.

Added to these public troubles, there were private ones too as the Dauphin's health became increasingly worse and his despairing parents were forced to confront the fact that their sweet natured and handsome little boy was unlikely to live for much longer. In March 1788 he was sent to live at Meudon[3], a magnificent and treasure filled château with a famously beautiful view of Paris from its terrace, that had been a favourite royal residence since Louis XIV's son took possession in 1695. Here he resided in great comfort with the Duchesse de Polignac and his tutor the Duc d'Harcourt in attendance. His parents visited as often as they could, although his mother was extremely distressed by his appearance which was emaciated and twisted by tuberculosis. However, the air at Meudon was said to be extraordinarily good and so she was still hopeful that he would make a miraculous recovery.

Unable to face the court let alone the general populace, Marie Antoinette moved to the Petit Trianon in July but it was a sad shadow of former summers spent there as she held no balls or any sort of galas and instead played games of bowls, read sentimental novels and plucked out melancholy tunes on her harp. She kept her two other children Madame Royale and the Duc de Normandie close by her and even entertained the aunts to a splendid supper, where they were served roast suckling pig, capon in breadcrumbs and German waffles amongst other treats. The King sought distraction from his cares by spending most of his time hunting at Rambouillet but came to Trianon every day to dine quietly with his wife and children when they weren't at Meudon keeping the Dauphin company. The state apartments of Versailles lay silent and empty, deserted by everyone.

Unfortunately, Marie Antoinette's hopes for the nation were not quite so sanguine as those she harboured for her ailing son. The political and financial crisis proved unstoppable and steadily worsened throughout 1788 as Loménie de Brienne and his efforts to resolve matters became increasingly discredited and the King increasingly powerless to do anything to stop the tide rising against him. Finally, on 8 August Louis took the step of announcing a meeting of the Estates General hoping that this would calm his critics and show that he was ready, willing and able to deal with the mounting crisis. The Estates General was a coming together of the three notional estates of France – the nobility, clergy and commons (known as the 'third estate') where voted for representatives met to discuss the issues of the day. However, although it sounds much like a contemporary parliament there had been no meeting of the Estates General for a hundred and seventy five years so this was a bold and significant move on the part of Louis and his council – time would tell if it would also prove to be a reckless one.

There was a small and entertaining respite from all the strife when three ambassadors of Tippoo Sahib, King of Mysore, who was keen to forge an alliance against the British, arrived at Versailles on 12 August after a stay in Paris and took up residence at the Grand Trianon where the delicious aroma of culinary spices, chocolate and exotic perfumes soon began to fill the air. Their formal reception took place at the main palace when they were received by the royal family and rest of the court in the magnificent Hercules Room where the King, looking suitably majestic, was waiting for them on his throne, Marie Antoinette at his side on an armchair. Their daughter, the nine-year-old Madame Royale, who had just recovered from an alarming fever, was sitting amongst the most important ladies on a brocade covered dais to the side.

Everyone was totally fascinated by these exotic and very colourful visitors to the court and the grand reception rooms of the palace were crammed full of courtiers, all dressed in their very finest clothes and eager to catch a glimpse of the three ambassadors and their entourage as they made their way through Versailles. After the formalities had been dispensed with they were taken on a barouche ride around the park and treated to a display by the beautiful fountains before returning to the lofty marble colonnades of the Grand Trianon. Marie Antoinette, always keen to be distracted by novelties, was delighted by them but rather less keen on their curries, although she still gamely managed to try one before deciding that spicy food was not for her. Naturally, the visitors had a tremendous effect on French fashion as everyone sought to emulate their luxurious style and vivid colour palette and of course they did not leave French without being painted by Madame Vigée Le Brun. Sadly, their mission failed and the three men were beheaded upon their return home to India.

However, although apparently it was business as usual at Versailles, behind the scenes the crisis had reached a head and the nation was finally bankrupted while the royal shares plummeted at the Stock Exchange. The desperate Loménie de Brienne announced that the much anticipated Estates General meeting would take place the following May, hoping that this would cause an upswing in confidence and share prices but it was too little, too late. On 16 August, a few days after the glorious reception of the Mysore ambassadors, word spread that he was considering compulsory taxation in order to give the economy a much needed boost. This unpopular measure turned out to be his downfall and after a last-ditch attempt to secure the support of Necker, who disdainfully repudiated him, he was forced to hand Marie Antoinette his resignation just over a week later. She summoned Necker, still commonly believed to be the only hope of turning the situation around, to see her early the next morning and asked him to accept the position of Director General of Finance as well as a position on the Council of State. '*As I am responsible for bringing back Necker and my fate is to bring bad luck, I feel that, should some infernal combinations be once more at work to make him fail, then the King's authority will suffer and I will be even more detested than before*,' the dejected Queen later told Mercy, sadly accepting that as far as the French people were concerned, nothing she ever did would ever be right and she would be damned by them whatever she did. She may never have actually said the words 'Let them eat cake' but as far as the French were concerned, she might as well have done.

Chapter 10

L'Autrichienne 1788–1789

'I am terrified of everything.'

The winter of 1788 was one of the harshest that anyone could remember and as it followed on from the drought and terrible hailstorm of that summer which had decimated much of the country's crops, the poor of France were brought to their knees, crippled by rising bread prices. Meanwhile at Versailles, Louis and Marie Antoinette prepared themselves for the worst as the Dauphin's condition deteriorated by the day. The Queen now spent much of her time at Meudon, watching over her child's sick bed and making stilted small talk with his governess, Madame de Polignac. The two women, once so close that rumours had spread that they were lovers, were now barely on speaking terms. Having finally woken up to the harm that the grasping, gossiping Polignac set was doing to her reputation Marie Antoinette had taken a step back and disassociated herself from them and their antics. She also found herself at odds with the Duchesse over the disgrace of Calonne, who was one of her friends, and the financial cut backs which had resulted in the loss of some pecuniary favours to Madame de Polignac's relatives including her husband and her lover the Comte de Vaudreuil.

The Dauphin, suffering from the final stages of his illness but still as sweet natured and perceptive as ever, was quick to pick up on the fact that the two women had fallen out and now declared that he didn't like the Duchesse's heady floral scent as it gave him headaches and asked for her to be banned from his bedside, which meant that his mother could be alone as she sat beside him during the long cold early months of 1789. The little boy tried to cheer her up by ordering that she be served all of her most favourite meals when she stayed to dine with him but still the silent tears trickled down her cheeks as she looked at her sick child and wondered what the future held.

There had been a great deal of argument about where the much anticipated meeting of the Estates General, the first for 175 years, should take place before the King, who hoped to get plenty of hunting in between the various debates that he would be forced to attend, got his way and the meeting was scheduled to open at Versailles on 4 May 1789. Wracked with worries about her son's health, Marie Antoinette could hardly bear to contemplate what was bound to be a miserable experience and so when she wasn't at Meudon, spent all of her time shut up alone in her private rooms at Versailles where she whiled away the long hours worrying about the Dauphin's health, the forthcoming meeting of the three estates and reports of serious unrest on the streets of Paris, which culminated in an immense riot at the Réveillon wallpaper factory, during which three hundred people were killed before the royal troops could impose order.

'Come, dress my hair, Léonard, I must go like an actress and exhibit myself to people who may hiss at me,' Marie Antoinette said to her hairdresser on the morning of 4 May as she readied herself for the procession through the streets of the town of Versailles that was due to start the meeting of the Estates General. Although her words sound flippant, it was clear that her mood was very far from light hearted as dressed in glittering cloth of silver and with the pale yellow Sancy diamond in her hair, she walked at the side of the King (who also looked splendid in cloth of gold, with the Regent diamond pinned to his plumed hat) at the head of the enormous procession that made its way past huge crowds from the Church of Notre-Dame in Versailles to the Church of Saint Louis, where a celebratory Mass was to be heard. Behind the royal couple there was the rest of the royal family and their attendants, followed by the deputies of the Estates General, with the clergy in their religious dress, the nobility in black silk and white breeches, flourishing plumed hats and with their swords jangling at their hips and the Third Estate in plain black.

To Marie Antoinette's great annoyance, Louis' mutinous cousin the Duc d'Orléans was a deputy for the nobility but in typical showman style opted to walk with the Third Estate instead, towering over the other deputies and making sure that all of the loudest cheers were for him while Louis received only a few muted shouts of approval and the Queen, who stared straight ahead in haughty silence, got nothing at all. It must have been an alarming experience, to find herself on foot and surrounded by hostile crowds but as the true horror of the revolutionary mob had not yet been revealed, it's unlikely that Marie Antoinette felt particularly frightened for her life as she walked by, her face completely impassive until she drew level with the royal stables where the little Dauphin, who had been brought from Meudon for the occasion, was lying on a sofa on one of the balconies, which gave a better view of the procession than the palace windows. Both the King and Queen looked up and smiled at their son as they went past but it was noticed that they had tears in their eyes as they did so.

The meeting officially began a day later when the royal family, court and over a thousand deputies crammed into the huge Salon of the Menus Plaisirs at Versailles to hear the opening speeches, one of which was to be delivered by Necker, who was still being hailed as the man of the moment and the potential saviour of France. Marie Antoinette, this time wearing purple satin spangled with diamonds and with a towering white ostrich feather and delicate *aigrette* of diamonds in her powdered but sadly thinning hair, sat on an armchair placed slightly below her husband (who fell asleep and audibly snored during Necker's admittedly extremely long-winded speech) and fanned herself with a diamond studded fan as she bleakly surveyed the rows of faces in front of her, who all stared back curiously at the Queen of whom they had heard so much and seen so little in recent years.

Versailles was expected to play host to the deputies for quite a few months and with typical generosity Marie Antoinette insisted that the palace gardens and her own Trianon should be open to the delegates, who were then able to assuage their natural curiosity about the extravagance that they had heard so much about. It had been widely and erroneously reported that the Trianon was incredibly opulent with columns inlaid with huge diamonds and cloth of gold hanging at all the windows and all manner of shocking self-indulgent luxuries but the deputies, seeing instead a charming little pavilion decorated with elegant simplicity, were rather disappointed to find that this was not at all the case. What else, they might have wondered, had been exaggerated about the Queen and her reportedly depraved lifestyle, which allegedly involved orgies with both sexes.

However, Marie Antoinette's thoughts were not with the deputies but with her son the seven-year-old Dauphin who was quietly dying at Meudon. Both of the boy's parents spent many long hours at his bedside, doing their best to remain cheerful and trying to distract the ailing child from his sufferings. Like his father he was extremely fond of history so the King read to him from his favourite history books, while the Queen did her best to hide her tears before collapsing and sobbing her heart out on her husband when they left the room. It was said that the little boy was so good natured that he even endured the ministrations of a particularly clumsy valet rather than have the man sent away and one wonders what sort of King he would have made if he had survived. Possibly he was too gentle for the fledgling France that was emerging even as he lay on his deathbed.

The Dauphin died in the arms of his mother in the early hours of 4 June. Both Louis and Marie Antoinette were devastated by their son's death and spent the next day in total seclusion at Versailles while the embalmed body of the dead prince lay in state at Meudon. On 7 June, the entire court turned out to offer their condolences to Marie Antoinette who was going out of her mind with grief and also exhaustion as the result of severe insomnia, while the deputies of the Third Estate gave offence by asking if the King would receive them in the palace to discuss business pertaining to the Estates General. 'Are there no fathers amongst them?' the distraught King asked. Both of the royal couple were stung by the general lack of interest in their son's passing. It seemed inconceivable to them that they had lost the love of their people to such an extent that the death of the Dauphin, whose birth had occasioned such extraordinary joy amongst the populace, gave rise to little more than a polite apathy.

Marie Antoinette's eldest son was laid to rest beside that of his sister Sophie at the royal necropolis at Saint-Denis on 12 June. It was normally decreed that the funeral of a Dauphin, with all the fuss and ceremony that court etiquette demanded, should cost in the region of 350,000 livres but the royal coffers were completely empty and so a rather more modest funeral took place funded by some cash that Louis had managed to find by cutting corners elsewhere. According to custom, the King and Queen did not attend their son's funeral but instead spent the day in prayer at Versailles before going to Marly with their most trusted attendants for what they hoped would be a week of solitude and mourning away from the pressures of the court.

However, their troubles only pursued them from Versailles when on 17 June, after weeks of squabbling between the orders, the Third Estate, who saw themselves as the saviours of France, declared themselves a National Assembly, invited the other orders to join them and announced that they, not the King, would be responsible for drafting a new constitution for the nation. Louis and Marie Antoinette were appalled by what they saw, quite rightly as it happened, as a direct attack on the authority of the monarch. Necker tried in vain to persuade them to seek terms with the fledgling Assembly, which he reminded them was intended to be the mouthpiece of the nation, and even proposed that they modify the current constitution so that it was along the same lines as that in England. However, Marie Antoinette, backed by her two brothers-in-law and most of the aristocracy, urged the King to hold firm and repudiate their insolence, even appearing before him with her remaining two children and falling, weeping prettily, to her knees in order to beg him not to give in to the demands of the Third Estate.

Indecisive as always, Louis wavered between the two sides. On one hand, he had no wish to annoy the Queen, whom he feared rather more than he loved her, but on the other he was terrified of causing offence to Necker and the dour faced men of the Third Estate, whom he knew had ever increasing support throughout the country. Once again he bemoaned the absence of the dead Vergennes, who would have known just what to do and in the end agreed to give a speech, prepared by Necker, to the deputies of all three orders on 23 June. Although Louis promised to introduce reforms and overhaul the current taxation system, Necker was furious to hear the King whom he had counselled to be conciliatory towards the members of the Third Estate, alter the wording of his carefully prepared speech and go on to denounce the merging of the three orders as a National Assembly as illegal and against the constitution of France. For her part, Marie Antoinette was relieved to see him stand firm against the Third Estate but Necker was furious and immediately handed in his resignation.

Angry crowds gathered at the palace when news of Necker's resignation began to spread and Marie Antoinette was forced to go to him and personally beg him to reconsider, even though she had every intention of foiling his attempts to get Louis to accept the National Assembly. In the event, it took just four days for Necker to have his way and Louis to agree that the estates could meet and vote together, by which time most of the clergy and a large chunk of the nobility, including the Duc d'Orléans and the extremely popular Marquis de Lafayette, had already joined with the Third Estate. The news was greeted with acclamation in Paris, but although people were celebrating on the streets about 'their' victory over the old régime, the uneasy atmosphere simmered on and there were increased bouts of violence and rioting amidst the celebrations.

At Versailles, Marie Antoinette appeared with her son in her arms on the balcony above the marble courtyard to receive the cheers of the huge crowd that had gathered there when news of the National Assembly's triumph broke. However, although she was all smiles for the populace, inside she raged against Necker and the King, whose weakness, she believed, looked set to leave them entirely at the mercy of the Third Estate. She urged the King to use his troops to make a show of power and at the same time control the unrest in the capital but as might be expected, the sudden arrival of several thousand soldiers around Paris just made matters much worse as the populace, whipped into terror by the speeches of the rabble rousers of the Palais Royal, many of whom were in the pay of the Duc d'Orléans, believed that the King, hitherto regarded as the apathetic but ultimately benevolent tool of his wicked wife, was planning to massacre them all.

The National Assembly demanded that the troops be withdrawn only to be informed that they were there to control unrest not cause trouble. Urged on by talk of an 'aristocratic plot' masterminded by the Queen and designed to overthrow the Assembly, the deputies, fearing for their lives, proclaimed themselves to be a Constituent Assembly with the power to make their own laws. Urged by Marie Antoinette, Louis reacted by dismissing Necker and most of his ministers on 11 July, replacing them with conservative nobles who could be relied upon to follow the King's line.

The news of Necker's dismissal was greeted with disbelief and then fury in Paris, where the Queen and her cronies were blamed for the former minister's disgrace. There were riots in the capital's streets, which were exacerbated when a regiment led by the Prince de Lambesc, a distant cousin of the Queen, charged into a crowd at the Tuileries in an attempt to disperse protestors who had been pelting them with stones, giving rise to more fears that the King was planning to massacre his own people. On 12 July, a young lawyer called Camille Desmoulins clambered on to a table outside the Café du Foy at the Palais Royal to give a rabble-rousing speech that likened the current situation to the infamous St Bartholomew's Day Massacre of August 1572 and ended by entreating the already panic-stricken populace to arm themselves and don cockades so that they would know each other in the violence that was sure to ensue. Whipped into a frenzy by this the people first adopted a green cockade, green being the colour of liberty, but then when word spread that green was the colour of the Comte d'Artois' livery, red and blue, the traditional colours of the city of Paris were worn instead.

Two days later a huge crowd seized control of the Hôtel des Invalides, where the royal weaponry was stored, and took several thousand guns and a number of cannons which they used to arm themselves against the royal troops. They had no ammunition though and believing that this could be found at the royal fortress of the Bastille, which had been a symbol of royal oppression for over a century thanks to the practice of sending prisoners there by order of a royal *lettre de cachet* which involved no trial and could not be appealed against, they duly marched in their thousands across town to the Faubourg St Antoine where the dark fortress towered over the neighbouring streets. Although more strongly defended than the Invalides, the Bastille fell in a matter of hours and its governor the Marquis de Launay was taken prisoner and crudely decapitated with a flick knife before his head was paraded in grisly triumph through the streets.

At Versailles, the royal family remained in blissful ignorance of events in Paris until the following morning when the Duc de Liancourt woke Louis up at dawn to inform him that the Parisians had rioted and seized control of the Bastille, releasing the seven political prisoners held there. 'Is it a revolt?' Louis asked wearily. 'No, sire,' Liancourt replied. 'It is a revolution.'

Later that morning, Louis paid a visit to the deputies in the Menus Plaisirs, interrupting a rather offensive speech about his wife and Madame de Polignac fraternising with the troops that had recently been stationed at Versailles. For once he had not relied on one of his ministers to prepare his speech but instead improvised his own, in which he informed the deputies that it was never his intention to attack the people of Paris but rather to protect them and that the royal troops stationed there would be immediately ordered to withdraw. In return, the deputies demanded that Necker be reinstated to his former position as this would do much to calm the agitated populace, which the clearly beleaguered King reluctantly agreed to do. Louis was then escorted back to the palace by a great crowd of cheering deputies, relieved that the crisis looked set to end.

However, back at the palace all was in turmoil as Marie Antoinette ordered her trunks to be packed with her jewels and clothes amidst frantic discussions about where the royal family and their associates should flee to. Word had got back to Versailles that the leaders of the mob that had overwhelmed the Bastille and then murdered its governor, had threatened to kill the Queen, Comte d'Artois and Madame de Polignac and so it was decided that the latter two at least should leave France with their families until the situation calmed down. However, there was still some doubt about what

Louis, Marie Antoinette and their own children should do. Louis, hesitant as always, called a meeting of his council and family and suggested that they should withdraw either to Compiègne or to Metz, the fortified town close to the Austrian border where Marie Antoinette had spent her first night on French soil nineteen years earlier. The Queen was in total agreement with the Metz plan, which had the additional bonus of meaning that she would be close to her own country of Austria as well as far away from the dangers of Paris.

However, some members of the council as well as the Comte de Provence argued that the King and his family should remain at Versailles and that it would be ill advised and inflame the situation even further for the royal family to be seen deserting the palace at such a time. They also thought that Metz's proximity to Austria, the very thing that recommended it to Marie Antoinette, would give rise to even more panic if the Parisian rabble rousers got it into their heads that the forces of the Emperor would soon be massing against them in defence of the foreign Queen while their royal family nipped across the border and abandoned the country altogether. There was also the fact that unlike his wife, Louis had not yet been directly threatened by the Parisian mobs and so his safety was not felt to be at immediate risk. Marie Antoinette, however, was a different matter but when it was suggested that she should take the royal children and leave for a place of greater safety, she haughtily refused and reminded everyone present that as both his Queen and his wife it was her duty to remain at Louis' side during this time of crisis even though he himself was urging her to leave.

However, everyone was in agreement that the Comte d'Artois and Madame de Polignac, both of whom were almost as unpopular as Marie Antoinette and held equally to blame for the financial ruin that threatened the stability of the nation, should leave France as soon as possible along with the Abbé de Vermond and some of the more conservative members of the court such as the Prince de Condé. The Comte d'Artois, who remained sanguine that this was just a temporary hiccup and everything would be restored back to its normal state before long, was keen to leave but Madame de Polignac proved harder to persuade and initially refused to go, claiming that her place was beside the Queen, with whom she had recently reconciled, and with her charges, the royal children. In the end, Marie Antoinette and Louis, both of them in tears, had to persuade her to leave, with the Queen telling her that: 'I am terrified of everything; in the name of our friendship go, now is the time for you to escape from the fury of my enemies. Don't be a victim of your attachment to me, and my friendship for you.'

The Artois and Polignac families, as well as several others of the Queen's formerly close little *cotérie* of friends left Versailles at midnight on 16 July. The emotionally shattered Queen, unable to believe the surreal situation that they had found themselves in, could not bring herself to say goodbye in person to her best friend (who had disguised herself as a maid for her escape) but instead sent a purse containing five hundred louis, the last and perhaps most meaningful of the many gifts that she had showered upon Gabrielle over the years, and a tear-stained note that said only: '*Adieu, the most tender of friends. The word is terrible to pronounce but it must be said. Here is the order for the horses. I have no more strength left except to embrace you.*' Although Marie Antoinette had been somewhat estranged in recent years from both Madame de Polignac and her brother-in-law Artois, who had once been the most sympathetic member of her French family, all of this was forgotten in the horrors of the present situation and the terrible sorrow of hearing their carriages rumble out of the palace courtyard at the start of their long journey. It was the end of an era.

The next morning, Louis went off to Paris to show himself to his disordered populace and try his best to restore calm to the situation. Marie Antoinette offered to go with him but, aware of her unpopularity, Louis sadly refused to allow this and instead insisted upon going alone, having taken the precaution of writing his will and receiving what he hoped would not be his final communion before departure. Left behind at Versailles, Marie Antoinette spent the day alone in her apartments with her children, trying her best to distract them while at the same time attempting to hide her apprehension. She had already decided to throw herself on the mercy of the National Assembly should Louis fail to return from Paris and as the day wore on she confided tearfully in the faithful Madame Campan that she believed that he would not be coming back, her faith in the basic humanity of the Parisian mob having been shattered by the hideous and vicious death of the Marquis de Launay.

At six, word came that the King was returning from Paris and several hours later, Louis himself arrived back at Versailles – exhausted, bedraggled but otherwise unharmed and with a tricolour cockade, the new symbol of the French nation, attached to his hat. His wife and children ran down the stairs to greet him and Marie Antoinette, overcome with relief, threw herself into her husband's arms and hugged him as he murmured: 'Thank God there was no more violence.'

The departure of the Polignacs was just the first in what was to be a steady exodus over the next few months as several aristocratic families, fearing the violence and, like the always optimistic Comte d'Artois, believing that this was merely a temporary measure and they would soon be able to return to France, fled Versailles and travelled abroad. The once bustling palace now fell ominously quiet as the cramped apartments, once so prized and hotly sought after, began to empty as their noble inhabitants scurried away like rats fleeing a sinking ship. Marie Antoinette, desperately lonely and fearful of what the future would bring for her family, did her best to keep up appearances but it was obvious to everyone that she was on the verge of a breakdown. The news coming in from the rest of France of rioting in the provincial cities and destruction of dozens of châteaux did nothing to allay her fears but rather underlined that this revolution that was apparently no longer contained in Paris but instead spreading throughout the country, was not a problem that would easily go away.

The beleaguered Queen spent the rest of July isolated in her apartments, seeing hardly anyone other than her family, Count Mercy, who came to deliver bulletins about the latest events in Paris and elsewhere and Axel von Fersen, who had discreetly rented rooms in Versailles and spent as much time with her as he dared to. She spent much of her time writing frantic letters to her sisters and brothers and Madame de Polignac, who had settled in Switzerland with her family. Absence did much to make the heart grow fonder in the case of these two friends and the Queen now poured all of her anxieties and fears out on to the paper, expressing thoughts that she barely dared to speak out loud in this newly silent and sinister Versailles. '*We are surrounded only by distress, misfortune and unhappy people. Everyone is fleeing and at this point I take comfort in thinking that all the people whom I care most about are far away from me. Also I see no one and I spend the whole day alone in my quarters. My children are my sole resource.'* For Marie Antoinette, always so desperate for approval and admiration, the thought that she brought only misfortune to those whom she cared about was a deeply distressing one and the Queen became increasingly withdrawn as the year progressed, while all the while the lampoons and pamphlets denouncing her depravity and cruelty continued to multiply and become ever more vicious.

Outwardly, it seemed as though things had not really changed at Versailles, where the remaining ladies and gentlemen still attended the King and Queen's *levée* and courtiers could still watch as they ate their dinner or played cards in public. But the signs of strain were visible everywhere. It was whispered that the King, like his sister-in-law, the Comtesse de Provence who was suspected by many to be an alcoholic, had taken to drink to ease his worries while the Queen barely ate and was frequently seen to blink away tears or fiddle nervously with her bracelets and rings, which she compulsively twirled around her thin fingers. She seemed utterly bewildered by the new state of affairs and fatally unable to grasp that times had changed and she needed to change with them if she was to survive. On the King's name day in August the state representatives came to Versailles to pay their respects to their monarchs who looked as glittering and remote as ever on their thrones. The new Mayor of Paris, the astronomer Bailly decided to bow to the Queen rather than fall to his knees in abject reverence as etiquette usually decreed and was rewarded with a look of frigid hauteur and an unfriendly nod that broadcast her annoyance at this impudence to everyone present.

It was at this time that an English visitor, Dr Edward Rigby, who was visiting Versailles wrote home that he could not '*behold the face of Marie Antoinette, and not see symptoms of no common anxiety marked on it. The dignity of countenance which, according to various descriptions, formed at an earlier period of her life a most interesting addition to those claims of natural beauty so profusely bestowed on her, might be said, indeed, to remain, but it had assumed more of the character of severity. The forehead was corrugated, the eyebrows thrown forward, and the eyes but little open, and, turning with seeming caution from side to side, discovered, instead of gaiety or even serenity an expression of suspicion and care which necessarily abated much of that beauty for which she had once with truth been celebrated.*'

The one bright ray of hope at this time was the appointment of the widowed Marquise de Tourzel as Governess to the Royal Children, replacing Gabrielle de Polignac who could obviously no longer continue in this role. Sensible, kind hearted, pragmatic and extremely loyal, Louise-Élisabeth de Tourzel[1] was the perfect choice for such an important role in the royal household and gave the Dauphin and Madame Royale some much needed stability at this difficult time. Marie Antoinette personally wrote lengthy instructions for her when she took up the post, describing her children's characters and advising Tourzel about the best way to deal with them, naturally with a particular emphasis on the Dauphin who was, after all, the heir to the throne and therefore obviously the more important of the two. '*My children have always been accustomed to have complete trust in me and when they do something wrong, to tell me so themselves. Which means that when I scold them, I look more hurt and sad about what they did than angry. I have accustomed them to the idea that a yes or no from me is irrevocable; but I always give them a reason befitting their age, so that they do not think it is moodiness on my part. My son does not know how to read and has difficulty learning; but he is too distracted to concentrate. He has no idea of rank in his head and I would like that to continue: our children always find out soon enough who they are. He is very fond of his sister and has a good heart. Every time something makes him happy, a trip somewhere or a gift, his first impulse is to request the same thing for his sister. He was born cheerful; for his health he needs to be outside a great deal, and I think it is best to let him play and work on the terraces rather than have him go any farther.*'

Life at Versailles may have carried on much as it had always done with the inhabitants doing their best to ignore what was happening outside their privileged bubble but events were moving quickly elsewhere. At the end of September, the wife of a labourer who had been assisted by Madame Élisabeth requested a private interview and told her that the people of Paris suspected the King of plotting to escape with his family to Metz and were planning to prevent this. Alarmed, Élisabeth immediately went to tell Marie Antoinette who naturally began to worry about what measures the people might possibly be planning to take. Her thoughts took a more hopeful turn a few weeks later though when the loyal Flanders Regiment arrived at Versailles to act as reinforcements in case there was indeed an incident at the palace. Their arrival at the start of October did much to lighten the mood at court and encouraged the Queen to make the imprudent gesture of taking her family along to visit a banquet that was held in the regiment's honour in the palace theatre, on the very same stage where her own wedding banquet had been held over nineteen years earlier.

The cheers and shouts of 'Long live the Queen!' that greeted her as, dressed in white and blue silk with a beautiful turquoise necklace around her neck, she stepped into the royal balcony went straight to Marie Antoinette's head and smiling radiantly she led her family down to the stage to meet the dashing and no doubt rather drunk officers who now cheered all the more loudly. She carried the Dauphin, who looked most winsome in his sailor suit, in her arms and encouraged by the men, she allowed the boy to walk from one end of the dining table to the other, surrounded on all sides by smiling happy faces as his doting mother, who had not been so acclaimed or felt so popular for a very long time, stood to the side and proudly watched with tears of joy in her eyes.

However, as always, this innocent diversion that had given Versailles' sadly deflated morale such an immense boost, was completely twisted by the Parisian gutter press who described it as an appalling orgy of drunken sedition. They claimed that the soldiers tore their patriotic tricolour cockades from their hats and stamped on them before the Queen and her ladies distributed royalist white cockades. They also claimed that the Queen deliberately intoxicated the soldiers before ordering them to march on the National Assembly and close it down and if they accomplished this, who was going to stop them marching on to the capital as well?

This hysterical reporting of the Versailles banquet unfortunately coincided with a total lack of bread in Paris, where the bakers shops were ominously closed and not a single loaf was to be had in the entire city. Enraged, the market women stormed the Hôtel de Ville on the morning of 4 October and finding no satisfaction there, armed themselves and, no doubt inflamed by the speeches of the Duc d'Orléans' paid rabble rousers who had probably engineered the whole sorry situation, announced their intention of marching on Versailles to demand that the King, who was still regarded as being intrinsically benevolent, provide them with the flour that they needed in order to make bread. However, amidst the shouts demanding bread for their starving families, there were more sinister cries threatening violence towards the Queen, who had for a long time been the focus of all their most bitter hatred and resentment.

It was a beautiful day and, completely unaware of the turmoil in Paris, Marie Antoinette decided to spend it at the Petit Trianon, which was still her favourite refuge. Axel von Fersen was back in the vicinity again and it's likely that he spent at least some of the morning there with her before returning to the palace. Certainly she was alone in her grotto, enjoying the tranquility of a perfect autumn day, when one of her pages raced across the lawn to tell her that an immense mob of women was marching on foot towards Versailles. Alarmed, the Queen scrambled up into the waiting carriage and, perhaps with one last wistful look at the pleasure pavilion where she had spent so many happy hours over the years, hurried back to Versailles where she was reunited with her children and awaited the arrival of the King, who was hunting at Meudon when the news reached him. She was also joined by her sister-in-law Madame Élisabeth who had been at Montreuil but immediately hurried back to Versailles to support her brother and his family.

As the army of women marched inexorably on the palace, the King, Queen and their ministers met to discuss the best response to this new threat. Saint-Priest the Minister of the Royal Household suggested that troops be sent to guard various points along the route in order to either slow the march down or prevent it from passing, while at the same time the Queen and royal children should be taken to Rambouillet where there was a garrison of royal troops willing and able to protect them. The King could then lead the rest of the troops out to meet the mob and either pacify them with promises of assistance or, if they should prove intractable, use force to disperse them. Several of the ministers thoroughly approved of this plan which, it must be said, showed just the right sort of decisiveness and vigour that had hitherto been sadly missing from the royal response to current affairs. However, there was opposition from Necker and also, much more surprisingly, the Queen, who once again grandly declared that she had no wish to desert her husband, whom she guessed could not be counted upon to act with the necessary firmness, in his hour of need. 'I know that they have come from Paris to demand my head,' she said. 'But I learned from my mother not to fear death and I will wait beside my husband for whatever comes.'

Once again an opportunity to escape passed the royal family by thanks to Louis' indecisiveness and Marie Antoinette's poorly judged determination to do her duty and remain at her husband's side and refusal to let their children go without them. Although it was not entirely unheard of for royal families to flee their palaces and live as exiles, it had not happened in France for quite some time (the last time was when the young Louis XIV had been forced to leave Paris in 1648 in the wake of the Fronde uprising) and seemed very much like a last resort option to Louis XVI and Marie Antoinette, who were both of the opinion that leaving Versailles would be a weak gesture that would encourage further revolt and anarchy.

The beautiful sunshine had given way to torrential rain by the time the first straggling groups of women arrived at Versailles at around four in the afternoon with still more arriving over the next few hours until the courtyard before the palace was a great seething mass of people by early evening[2]. The more observant courtiers noticed that several of the new arrivals were either extraordinarily muscular or were actually men disguised as women, which further increased suspicions that the whole thing had been carefully orchestrated by the Duc d'Orléans and his cronies, who would have known that Louis would never allow his troops to fire on women, no matter how much they were provoked.

A delegation of women was received by the King who listened to their lists of grievances, took the petition they carried and gave his assurances that they would be given all possible assistance. His kindly demeanour reduced all of them to tears and one of them even reportedly fainted before they all departed, chanting 'Long live the King', back to their comrades in the courtyard, who were deeply unimpressed by this show of loyalty and had by now apparently conceived a plan to take the King and his family back to Paris with them. When word of this ambitious scheme arrived in the King's council chamber, Saint-Priest ordered that the gates of Versailles, stiff and rusty from lack of use for they had stood open for over a century, should be closed and again urged both the King and Queen to leave for Rambouillet with their children. This time, terrified of the bedraggled mob that she had glimpsed from the palace windows, Marie Antoinette immediately assented and ordered for their luggage to be packed, the royal children to be fetched from their apartments and the carriages prepared. However, as soon as the carriages were brought from the royal stables across the way from the palace, the mob, guessing that the royal family were planning to leave, furiously surrounded them and cut the traces so that they could not move. The royal family were now trapped in the palace.

The mood was desperately tense as the King and Queen, determined as always to behave as normal, sat down for supper in the presence of their attendants. Louis, ravenous as always, ate heartily but Marie Antoinette could barely manage a single bite of food as she sat dazed and shocked at the table. The courtiers gathered at the windows overlooking the main courtyard and peered through the gathering darkness at the dozens of campfires that had been lit in front of the palace. While the King remained with his ministers, Marie Antoinette stayed in her apartments with her sisters-in-law Madame Élisabeth and the Comtesse de Provence, all three of them not quite knowing what to do with themselves as they waited for news. At midnight, General Lafayette, a war hero, liberal aristocrat (his wife Adrienne was the niece of Madame de Noailles) and toasted darling of all Paris, arrived with thirty thousand men to boost the defence of Versailles and offer his support to the King, telling him that 'If my blood must flow, let it be in the service of my King.' Reassured by his confidence, Louis immediately sent a note to his wife, telling her not to worry and to go to bed for all was well.

Believing that Lafayette had managed to restore calm, Marie Antoinette sent away the loyal noblemen who had offered to protect her and told her ladies Madame Thibault and Madame Auguié, the sister of Madame Campan who was known as the Queen's 'tigress' thanks to her great height and fierce loyalty to her mistress, to go to bed and get some much needed sleep. However, clearly not at all reassured by Lafayette's show of bravado, the two ladies decided instead to barricade the doors, remain fully dressed and spend the night keeping watch over their mistress. Their actions almost certainly saved Marie Antoinette's life that night.

In the early hours of the morning, a large group of women who were bored, a bit drunk and understandably sick of trying to sleep on the rain-soaked cobbles, began to prowl around the perimeter of the palace and discovered that one of the small side gates had not been locked overnight, possibly on purpose. In no time at all, the mob had been roused to action again and teemed through the gate and into the courtyard before racing up to the palace itself, shouting curses and threats at the Queen, who was fast asleep in her apartments. The invaders overwhelmed the guards, decapitating at least one of them, before they rushed into the palace and up the marble staircase that led straight to Marie Antoinette's apartments where they slaughtered another guardsman, brutally beheading him with an axe before starting to hack their way through the locked door.

Hearing the terrible shouts and screams and the ominous sound of several dozen pairs of feet, clad in the distinctively noisy wooden clogs commonly worn by the lower classes, rushing up the marble staircase, Madame Auguié ran to the guard room to investigate only to be confronted by the sight of a young guardsman, covered in blood and leaning against the outer door that led to the staircase with all his might to keep the invaders out. 'Save the Queen!' he shouted over his shoulder to the appalled Madame Auguié. 'They have come to murder her!'

Terrified, Auguié and her companion Madame Thibault immediately barred the door and ran to alert their mistress, who was already awake, having been disturbed by a noise on the terrace below her windows. Hastily pulling a petticoat and yellow redingote jacket on over her nightgown and still holding her stockings in her hand, Marie Antoinette pushed open the concealed door beside her bed and ran down the secret corridor that led to the Oeil de Boeuf chamber which acted as the main antechamber of the King's apartments. However, the door turned out to be locked against her and, with the terrible shouts of the mob as they broke into her bedchamber behind her, she had to hammer frantically against the door, screaming for help until one of her husband's valets came to open it with the terrifying news that her husband had gone to her apartments to look for her.

Luckily for Louis, who had taken yet another one of the secret passages that lay behind the splendid walls of the royal apartments, the mob had already been thrown out of Marie Antoinette's now completely trashed and destroyed bedchamber by the time he arrived. After the guards now posted there had reassured that she had come to no harm, he returned to his rooms where he was reunited with his wife, with their children appearing soon after in the care of Madame de Tourzel who had been given strict instructions to take them both straight to the King's apartments if anything untoward happened. Everyone worried now about Madame Élisabeth and the Provences, whose apartments lay in a different wing of the palace but there was nothing that could be done to help them now that the awful shouts and screams of the invading mob could be heard in the Oeil de Boeuf chamber, where they were trying to force the doors open to get to the Queen.

However, just as Louis and Marie Antoinette must have been bracing themselves for disaster and almost certain death, Lafayette arrived on the scene with his troops and dispersed the crowd, forcing them out of the palace and into the courtyard below where they massed in seething fury, shouting threats and insults up at the windows and demanding that the royal family show themselves on the balcony. Marie Antoinette stood beside the window with her daughter and Madame Élisabeth, mercifully unscathed, on either side of her, while the Dauphin stood on a chair in front of her, plaiting his sister's long blonde hair and complaining about being kept waiting for his breakfast. Naturally, no one wanted to step out on to the balcony but somehow Lafayette managed to persuade them to do so and so the windows swung open and after a moment's hesitation, Louis and Marie Antoinette, who carried her son in her arms and held her daughter by the hand, stepped out to confront the hostile gaze of the mob.

Louis tried in vain to speak to the people but his voice was drowned out by the shouts of the crowd. There were a few heartening cries of 'Long live the King!' but they were outnumbered by the calls of 'To Paris! To Paris!' that thundered from every side. Lafayette, who had followed the royal family out on to the balcony, spoke a few words to remind the mob that the King had promised to provide bread, before they all went back inside. However, no sooner had they escaped than the crowd began to chant 'We want the Queen'. Even Lafayette, who had been at some pains to stress that the mob would never actually hurt Marie Antoinette, tried to persuade her to stay indoors but it turned out that the daughter of Maria Theresa was made of far sterner stuff than anyone had hitherto realised and she insisted upon facing the crowd.

Taking her children by the hand, perhaps at the suggestion of Lafayette who hoped that the crowd would be moved to compassion by the sight of the Dauphin and Madame Royale weeping in terror as they clung to their mother, she stepped once more on to the balcony. 'No children! No children!' the crowd bayed and reluctantly she sent them back into the room and turned to stand alone in front of the people. There was a moment of tense silence as they stared up at her and then to the surprise of everyone, including possibly themselves, they began to shout 'Long live the Queen!' Stunned, Marie Antoinette responded with a deep curtsey which just made them cheer all the more wildly. Lafayette, deeply relieved and possibly even rather surprised that the Queen had not been assassinated on the spot, now stepped out and gallantly kissed her hand as the crowd roared their approval and redoubled their shouts of 'To Paris! To Paris!'

'What are your intentions, Madame? Lafayette asked her as they stepped back into the blessed safety of the palace.

'Whatever may be my fate, it is my duty to die at the King's feet with my children in my arms,' Marie Antoinette replied before turning to Madame Necker, the wife of the Finance Minister, and saying: 'They are going to force us to go to Paris, preceded by the heads of our bodyguards on pikes.' To Saint-Priest, who had tried his very best to persuade her to leave the previous day, she could only lament: 'Oh, why did we not leave last night?'

The decision to go to Paris having been made, everyone returned to their apartments to pack and prepare for departure. At one in the afternoon, Louis, Marie Antoinette, their children, Madame Élisabeth and the governess Madame de Tourzel, whose young daughter Pauline[3] followed in another carriage, climbed into one of the King's enormous travelling carriage and set off towards the capital. Instead of the usual flanking outriders in their dashing livery there were the grotesquely twisted heads of their slaughtered guards carried on pikes on either side of their carriage. 'We're bring back the baker, the baker's wife and the baker's boy!' the jubilant crowd chanted as they walked alongside this peculiar cavalcade, while behind them at Versailles the shutters were slammed shut and a heavy silence fell on the gilded rooms.

As the royal carriage drew level with the gates of Madame Élisabeth's pretty estate at Montreuil which lay off the Avenue de Paris, the princess gazed sadly up her avenue which she already realised that she would never see again. 'Are you admiring your new lime avenue?' her brother asked her with a fond smile. 'No,' she replied sadly. 'I am saying goodbye.'

Chapter 11

The Baker's Wife 1789–1791

'The abyss opening at their feet.'

It took seven long and incredibly weary hours for the royal carriage to reach Paris. Marie Antoinette, shocked and traumatised by the events of the last twenty four hours, spent much of the journey crouched on the floor of the carriage, shielding her young son from the sight of the heads being waved outside the windows and trying her best to reassure both of her terrified children. Protected, pampered and cushioned all her life, Marie Antoinette had been, until now, effectively shielded from the unpleasant realities of life for the ordinary people of France. The journey to Paris that drizzly, miserable afternoon, surrounded by thousands of shouting, jeering people, many of whom were dressed in ragged clothes, was to be a baptism of fire for her and she would never again have any trust in the intrinsic goodness of the Parisian people.

They reached Paris late in the evening and came to a halt at the Chaillot tollgate where Bailly, the Mayor of Paris was waiting to greet them. With no apparent irony, he presented the King with the keys to the city on a velvet cushion, saying with an admirable attempt at courtly grace: 'What a beautiful day it is, Sire, that has brought you and your august consort to take up residence in the capital.' Louis, who was under no illusions that he and his family were effectively hostages, if not prisoners, of the National Assembly, managed to reply with equally good grace that he only trusted that his 'coming to Paris will put an end to lawlessness and bring back peace and order to the city.'

The exhausted royal family had expected to be taken straight to the royal palace of the Tuileries but instead found themselves taken to the Hôtel de Ville where they were persuaded to appear on the balcony again as the jubilant crowds that had gathered in the Place de Grève cheered themselves hoarse and shouted 'Long live the King!' There were even a few shouts for Marie Antoinette as she clutched her son to her bosom and faced the mob, rigid with indignation and wondering when her humiliating ordeal would finally come to an end.

Eventually, the royal family, thoroughly shattered by their ordeal, were escorted to the Tuileries at around ten that evening. The dilapidated old palace, which had not been properly inhabited by royalty since the minority of Louis XV, had become a kind of grace and favour residence since the young King moved to Versailles in 1722 and was now home to a hotchpotch mix of people that included elderly courtiers, retired royal officials, artists and actors, many of whom had altered the internal fabric of the palace beyond all recognition by knocking down walls and adding haphazard staircases, partition walls and flimsy windows to suit their own requirements. The news of the royal family's imminent arrival had come that morning and immediately Mique, who was in charge of the palace, set to work evicting all of the tenants, who were naturally extremely displeased, and supervising the dozens of servants who now swarmed through the draughty old rooms to prepare them for their new inhabitants.

The royal family were to inhabit the apartment where Marie Antoinette had once or twice slept during visits to the capital in her ramshackle youth, while Madame Élisabeth was assigned rooms on the ground floor and the rest of the courtiers were expected to fend for themselves with many sleeping on sofas and floors once all the available beds had been spoken for. The rather more fortunate Comte and Comtesse de Provence, who had followed them to Paris, were allowed to go to their own much more comfortable residences, the Palais du Luxembourg and the nearby Le Petit Luxembourg on the Rue de Vaugirard, where the Comtesse was able to continue to live apart from her husband. While the adults did their best to hide their unhappiness and appear upbeat and cheerful, the Dauphin was much more forthright and looked around in horror at the shabbily furnished rooms. 'It's so ugly here, Maman,' he remarked as the family sat down to supper which the King, as usual, enjoyed enormously. '*Departure for Paris 12.30, visit to the Hôtel de Ville, dine and sleep at the Tuileries*,' he wrote, rather phlegmatically, in his Journal[1] later on.

The next morning, Marie Antoinette woke up to the sound of the market women of Paris shouting on the terrace outside her new bedchamber. They wanted to see the Queen and after a moment's hesitation she asked her ladies, who looked disheveled and tired after a night camping out on sofas, to dress her in one of her prettiest dresses and find a hat covered in flowers and ribbons. Thus charmingly arrayed, she went out on to the terrace to meet the women and answer their questions, eventually winning them over to the extent that she ended up distributing the trimmings on her hat amongst them before they let her go back inside. Later on she would sit down at her desk and write a quick note to Count Mercy: '*Things look better this morning. Don't worry, I'm quite alright. And if one could forget where we are and how we came here we should be quite pleased with the way the people are behaving.*' And to be fair, things must genuinely have seemed rather more hopeful on that first morning at the Tuileries – the people appeared gratifyingly pleased to have them in the capital and Marie Antoinette hoped that their residence in Paris would make people realise that they were really just an ordinary loving family and help dispel the ugly rumours that had spread about her. Certainly, when she was in the right mood, there could be no one more charming and charismatic than Marie Antoinette and there was every possibility that she would be able to win the Parisians back to her side if presented with enough opportunities.

Their apartments, which had seemed so ramshackle and uninviting the night before, looked much better in daylight and as the weeks progressed the Tuileries began to regain its former splendour thanks to Mique's ongoing renovations and the appearance of several cart loads of furniture, paintings and other pieces from Versailles, which did much to improve matters. The Queen was lodged in a pretty apartment that had been recently renovated at enormous expense by the Comtesse de la Marck, who was doubtless livid to find herself so summarily evicted, while the King slept on the floor above near the rooms assigned to the royal children and their governess. The aunts, who had come to join them, were lodged in the Pavilion de Marsan and Madame Élisabeth had rooms on the ground floor but quickly moved after a gang of market women clambered in through her windows while she was at breakfast. The fact that they only wanted to praise her beauty and goodness was beside the point – after the events in October, she was now very nervous and insisted that she be moved to the far less accessible Pavilion de Flore, where she whiled away the hours with over a hundred books, most of which were religious tracts, sent from her own personal library at Versailles or sadly sketching imaginary nature scenes while sitting on a window seat that looked towards the Seine.

Gradually, life returned to some semblance of normality as the stately antechambers and reception rooms of the Tuileries which, as Marie Antoinette reminded her complaining son, had once been considered a suitable residence for Louis XIV 'and we must not be more particular than him', were gradually restored to something approaching their former grandeur and hummed once again with life. The Princesse de Lamballe, who had been away from court for health reasons, returned to once again supervise the Queen's household and Axel von Fersen, who had followed the royal family from Versailles, was able to discreetly visit Marie Antoinette every day and night just as he had done before. The ladies of the court continued to attend the Queen's *levée* and *coucher* and escorted her to Mass in the royal chapel just as they had done at Versailles, with the ones fortunate enough to have a Parisian residence being issued with passes that allowed them entry to the Tuileries. After a while the usual round of suppers and receptions resumed again in the state rooms of the palace with the Queen holding court on Tuesdays, Thursdays and Sundays and dining in public on Tuesdays and Sundays. In some ways it was as though nothing had really changed.

No one, including the royal couple themselves, was quite sure if the King and Queen were indeed prisoners but for now they had no real option but to stay where they were and see what happened. To the deputies and ordinary Parisian people that she encountered, Marie Antoinette was all smiles and gracious benevolence but in private she told Madame Campan that 'Kings who become prisoners are not far from death' and often shut herself away to cry, exhausted by the effort of maintaining an outwardly calm and amiable exterior and also deeply fearful about what the future held for herself and her family.

The National Assembly had agreed that the King should have an extremely generous allowance of 25 million livres a year, as well as the revenue from his estates, for living expenses but with over seven hundred people at the Tuileries, economies still had to be made and although Marie Antoinette was still getting her hair done by Léonard and her dresses designed by Rose Bertin and Madame Éloffe, who came to see her nearly as often as they always had, she was also having a lot of her older dresses adjusted and altered in order to save some money – with particular attention being paid to white, blue, red and pink dresses which were trimmed with tricolour ribbons in the hope of appealing to the Parisians. She couldn't resist splashing some cash on a few pieces of exquisite Reisener furniture for their apartments though, which shows that she was clearly resigned to staying there for quite some time.

However, although the future seemed uncertain, there were some compensations for this abrupt change in Marie Antoinette's circumstances – for a start, thanks to the close confinement of the family, she was now free to enjoy her children just as she had always longed to do and became more personally involved in their education. She took great pleasure in supervising Madame Royale's lessons and enjoyed taking them out for walks in the famously beautiful public gardens of the Tuileries where the Dauphin, who turned five in March 1790, won all hearts with his innocent, light hearted cavorting and games and was encouraged to wave and chatter to the admiring crowds that gathered to see him. Inside the palace, the entire family enjoyed spending more time together and the royal ladies were often to be found sitting together with their books and embroidery while the King taught his children how to play billiards and draughts or look at the stars through his precious telescope which had been brought from Versailles. When someone asked the Dauphin if he preferred Paris or Versailles, the little boy replied: 'Paris, because I see so much more of my Papa and *Maman*.'

This new delight in family life can be glimpsed in the charmingly carefree painting by François Dumont of Marie Antoinette and her two children sitting beneath a tree in the Tuileries gardens. This lovely portrait looks at first glance as if it should belong to the family's pre-1789 existence at Versailles but was in fact painted in the summer of 1790 and shows just how content the happily smiling Queen had become in the new even more close maternal role that she had adopted after the departure from Versailles, even if she was wracked with anxiety behind the scenes and when apart from her children, whom she was at some pains to protect from the true uncertainty of their position. The family are also dressed extremely elegantly in the pale muslins and silks that they had enjoyed at Versailles, while the Queen's blue silk covered hat, bedecked in pale pink and white plumes, is a masterpiece of millinery. Certainly no greater contrast can be imagined to the stiff and rather unattractive Wertmuller portrait of the unhappy looking Queen and her two eldest children walking in the gardens of the Petit Trianon back in 1785.

In February 1790 there came the terrible news of Emperor Joseph's death, which was a terrible blow to Marie Antoinette who had idolised her eldest brother and had, at heart, always assumed that one day he would come and rescue her from a situation that she was finding increasingly intolerable. His successor was their brother Leopold, whom she hadn't seen since he paid a brief visit to Vienna just before her marriage. Although she and the rather starchy Leopold had never really got on, the letter that he wrote to her after Joseph's death must have allayed some of her fears, even if in time she was to be sorely disappointed by her brother's lack of assistance: '*I can picture your grief, all the greater as his late majesty was particularly attached to you and had your interests so very much at heart. Though I know such a loss is irreparable, I hope you will find in me a friendship and attachment and a real and sincere interest in everything that concerns you, which will be in no way less than that of our late brother. Please give me the same friendship, the same confidence in return, and I flatter myself that I will in every way deserve it.*' Tactfully, he made no mention of the deceased Emperor's ominous final deathbed words about his sister in France: 'I commiserate with them, but from this distance I cannot think of any means to extricate them from so bad a situation other than to show both prudence and firmness. If they have both, then everything will perhaps arrange itself. If they lack them, then I have nothing more to say.'

Keenly aware that they urgently needed to win back the love and respect of their people, Louis and Marie Antoinette began to go on occasional official visits around Paris, much like the sort of engagements that the British royal family perform today, to see hospitals, factories and poor areas like the streets of the Faubourg Saint-Antoine which had once been dominated by the now demolished Bastille prison, the fragments of which were being sported as earrings by the fashionable ladies of Paris. The royal family would turn up looking elegant but demure, wreathed in smiles, asking lots of questions and giving every appearance of being both interested and engaged. The overall effect was very successful, with both Louis and Marie Antoinette hearing nothing but cheers but there was still a long way to go before the scars of October 1789 were entirely healed. 'Behold the joy of these good people,' Bailly told the Queen when one of her appearances was greeted with particularly enthusiastic acclaim. 'Yes, the people are good when their masters visit them,' she replied icily. 'But they are savage when they visit their masters.'

To Marie Antoinette's delight, they were allowed to spend the summer of 1790 at their château of Saint Cloud where the family could indulge in such bucolic and innocent delights as picnics in woodland glades, flower picking, small concerts at which the Queen sang once again, carriage rides to Meudon and, for the King, his beloved hunting. Deprived of his daily sport, Louis had started to put on even more weight and had become even more lethargic and sluggish than before, which Marie Antoinette, unsurprisingly, found utterly annoying. She was bound to the King by ties of loyalty and affection but had never been romantically in love with him – this emotion was, it seemed, entirely reserved for the handsome Swede, Axel von Fersen who followed the court to Saint Cloud and there resumed his daily visits to the Queen, often staying until the early hours of the morning, which provoked a great deal of gossip in certain circles. Marie Antoinette, always a bit of a flirt, seemed more infatuated with him than ever while Axel's obvious devotion had apparently been inflamed by her new dramatic position as a damsel in distress. Whereas their romance had almost certainly been almost entirely chaste when she was the Queen of Versailles it would be fair, perhaps, to wonder if matters had not taken a rather more intimate turn now that she was the beleaguered not quite a prisoner of the Tuileries and in need of whatever comfort and attention he was able to provide.

However, Axel von Fersen was also besotted, and in a very obviously carnal way, with his lusciously beautiful mistress Eléanore Sullivan, who had once upon a time been the mistress of Marie Antoinette's brother Joseph before ending up with an incredibly wealthy Indian Nabob Quentin Craufurd, who set her up in considerable style in Paris. Madame Sullivan was the total opposite of Marie Antoinette – sophisticated, sensual and witty and was, furthermore, just the sort of woman that Fersen had always conducted his affairs with in the past. The sort who knew the rules of the game and how to play it which Marie Antoinette, so sentimental and desperate for affection, did not. However, besides being a bit of a rake who was well aware of his own devastating effect on women, Fersen was also a massive snob and the royal mystique with which Marie Antoinette was imbued was enough to make him her devoted slave even if their relationship was actually entirely platonic.

It is clear though that Marie Antoinette loved Axel von Fersen or was at the very least completely infatuated with his handsome face, his dashing air and, most compelling of all, his way of treating her with a dewy-eyed reverence that she currently needed more than ever. Fresen's apparently uncritical approval of her must have seemed like a balm to her soul. However, although she loved to flirt and be admired by handsome young men, Marie Antoinette was not a particularly sensual woman (remember, it was not just Louis' clumsiness and lack of ardour in the bedchamber that had been criticised by her brother) and even though Fersen was almost certainly a much more attractive prospect than poor Louis, she took her duty to her husband and his crown far too seriously to ever seriously risk hurting either. The fact that she was so hurt and appalled by the broadsheets denouncing her promiscuity and alleged affairs also speaks volumes.

There were other visitors to the Château of Saint Cloud, where courtiers and commoners alike were encouraged to visit the gardens and see their rulers at play and Marie Antoinette, who was beginning to feel quite her old self again in such congenial surroundings, received friends from the past such as the Duchess of Devonshire and entertained them to elegant supper parties on the terrace. However, one visitor, the Comte de Mirabeau, one of the leaders of the National Assembly and, in the past, one of the King's most vicious opponents, came at dead of night and in utmost secrecy for an audience with the Queen. They met in the gardens, which echoed the infamous meeting that had caused such a stir during the Diamond Necklace scandal, and talked at length about Mirabeau's plans for the King and royal family. Having been so opposed to them in the past, Mirabeau had concluded that the revolution had run its course and discreetly offered his services to the King to act as a medium between them and the National Assembly – that this deal involved the settling of his enormous debts and a royal salary of 72,000 livres a year was just the icing on the cake.

Marie Antoinette did not like the Comte de Mirabeau, whom she regarded as venal, corrupt, immoral and violent but, encouraged by Mercy who saw in him their best chance of resolving the situation, even she could not deny that he was a formidable weapon to have in their arsenal. He was a brilliant and passionate orator (as they had learned to their cost thanks to his diatribes against the royal family) and was still regarded with great respect by both the Assembly and, most crucially, the Parisians. For his part, Mirabeau had no illusions about Louis, whom he regarded as completely pathetic, but he admired the spark of defiant courage that the Queen, whom he had once dismissed as frivolous and stupid, now displayed, declaring her to be the only one of the royal family worth talking to and the 'only man' that the King had about him. Although Marie Antoinette would never quite conquer her revulsion of Mirabeau, she willingly gave him her hand to kiss at the end of their meeting and even had to blink away tears when he fell to his knees before her, declaring, 'Madame, I swear the monarchy will be saved.' However, he had not always been so sanguine about their chances of survival and had previously commented to the Comte de la Marck that: '*Can't they see the abyss opening at their feet? All is lost, the King and Queen are going to perish, and you yourself will see it. The mob will trample their bodies underfoot.*'

On 14 July 1790, the first anniversary of the fall of the Bastille, the royal family temporarily left the comforts of Saint Cloud to attend the great Fête de la Fédération, which took place on the Champs de Mars in Paris. Naturally, Marie Antoinette had been dreading this occasion which for her marked the end of a miserable year of upheaval and despair, but she pinned on a smile and appeared in public dressed to impress in white with tricolour ribbons and feathers in her hair and a pretty red, white and blue trimming on her shoes. There were enormous cheers from the three hundred thousand strong crowd when the royal family arrived that morning, sheltered from the pouring rain in their covered carriage. Annoyed to have been dragged away from a day's hunting at Saint Cloud for what he considered to be an insulting and undignified charade, Louis glowered from his throne as they watched Talleyrand, the rakish Bishop of Autun, celebrate Mass in the torrential rain before the time came for Louis to take an oath to the constitution. Pleased by his show of acquiescence, the crowd erupted into cheers again and buoyed up by this enthusiasm, Marie Antoinette lifted her son up into her arms and showed him off to the people, who shouted 'Long live the Dauphin!' in his honour.

From almost the first moment that the royal family arrived at the Tuileries there had been talk of their escape. Even Mirabeau had encouraged them to consider either retreating to either Compiègne or Fontainebleau or travelling even further afield to Normandy, which still remained overwhelmingly royalist. His plan was that the royal family should leave openly but remain in France but other voices counselled a far more bold manoeuvre whereby the King and his family should leave the country and join forces with the émigrés who were massing beyond the borders of France, champing at the bit to kick start a counter revolution.

At first Louis was unwilling to leave, preferring instead to put his faith in the National Assembly and the French people, but this trust was rapidly beginning to wane and hit a steep nose dive at the end of 1790 when the National Assembly decreed that from now on all church affairs were to come under their jurisdiction rather than that of Rome and that all priests had until 1 January 1791 to make an oath of loyalty to the Assembly, with those who refused being summarily defrocked and banned from office. Louis, who had been extremely devout his entire life, was appalled by this but had no option but to give his assent to this measure even if he privately detested it. His aunts, however, were more forceful in their condemnation and in February 1791 left Paris with the intention of travelling to Rome where they would be free to follow their faith in peace. The old ladies, who had done so much to damage Marie Antoinette's reputation in France, were briefly apprehended at Arnay-le-Duc in Burgundy but then, thanks to the intervention of Mirabeau, were allowed to leave the country unmolested and make their way to Italy via a visit to their nephew the Comte d'Artois, who had settled in Turin, where his wife was born, with his family. How Marie Antoinette must have envied them all.

However, the departure of the aunts gave fresh impetus to Marie Antoinette's own secret escape plans. At some point after the events of October 1789, the royal couple had vowed to each other that from now on they were not going to be separated and so all suggestions that either Louis or Marie Antoinette should leave without the other were immediately dismissed. More plausible, however, was the suggestion that Marie Antoinette should escape with her son, who would be dressed as a girl for the enterprise while the Queen herself went in disguise as a servant. However, yet again she rejected this plan, reiterating her decision to remain at the King's side no matter what happened. Meanwhile, she secretly continued to plot with Axel von Fersen, whom she trusted implicitly, and General de Bouillé, who was based at Metz near the Austrian border. It was Bouillé's plan that the royal family separate into two groups, leave Paris in two swift separate carriages and make their way to Montmédy, where a loyal royalist regiment was based and where Louis could rally more to his cause, safe in the knowledge that the border with Austria was not too far away if his plans to regain full control of the throne went sadly awry.

Excited and nervous about their plan, Marie Antoinette ordered Axel von Fersen to make the necessary arrangements. She refused to consider Bouillé's suggestion that the family split into two, arguing that she had no wish to be separated from either her husband or her children, and instead of buying two small carriages she commissioned a large and much more slow travelling carriage, known as a *berline*, in which the family would make their escape. Claiming that the commission was for a former mistress, the Baronne de Korff who would also be providing the fugitives' identity papers, Fersen spared no expense and overlooked no detail when it came to the planning of this huge and cumbersome vehicle which would have to be both commodious and comfortable for their long journey. The outside was a discreet green and black while the interior was upholstered in sumptuous white velvet and equipped with such conveniences as a small cooker, leather chamber pots and a concealed table that could be raised at mealtimes.

Marie Antoinette's all important *toilette* was not to be neglected either and the Queen decided to treat herself to a lavish *nécessaire*, a travelling dressing case of beautiful walnut wood, inside which reposed a silver teapot and candlesticks as well as everything that Marie Antoinette could possibly require in order to beautify herself, all of which was fashioned out of the most exquisite crystal, silver and tortoiseshell. She also ordered new clothes for herself and her children and entrusted her hairdresser, the delightfully catty Léonard, who was to follow her to Montmédy to ensure that she looked her very best at all times, with her jewels. Madame Campan was bewildered by this attention to sartorial matters and tried to remonstrate with the Queen, pointing out that 'a Queen of France should be able to procure whatever she needed wherever she went' but Marie Antoinette, completely carried away and elated by her clandestine plans which served as such a delightful distraction from the mundanity of life at the Tuileries, would not listen.

In April 1791 the furtive escape plans received further impetus from the sudden death of the Comte de Mirabeau who passed away after years of dissolute excess. His final words, whispered to Talleyrand were: 'I am taking with me the last vestiges of the monarchy'. Marie Antoinette, who had grown to rely on his support even if she never warmed to him personally, wept when she was informed of his death, knowing that they had now lost one of their most powerful supporters. He was accorded the signal honour of the first state burial in the Panthéon, which from then on was intended to be the final resting place of the great men of France. Shortly after this, the royal family were prevented from leaving for their planned Easter holiday at Saint Cloud by a large and ferocious mob who suspected them of trying to escape and rioted until Lafayette turned up with his troops and dispersed them. The fact that they had been allowed to move relatively freely around Paris and had been able to spend the previous summer at Saint Cloud had done much to reconcile Louis and Marie Antoinette to their situation and even allowed them to pretend to themselves that they were not really effectively the prisoners of the National Assembly. However, this unfortunate incident served to emphasise their effective powerlessness and increased their resentment after they returned in great disappointment to their apartments in the Tuileries.

'*The event which has just occurred confirms us more than ever in our plans*,' Marie Antoinette wrote to Mercy, who had left for Brussels in October 1790. '*Our position is dreadful. We absolutely must flee from here next month. The King wishes this even more vehemently than myself.*' Plans continued to be made for the escape despite the reservations of Bouillé about both the mode of transport, which he rightly considered too slow and cumbersome for a journey whose success relied on its speed and efficiency, and the passengers. It had been decided that the King, Queen and royal children should be accompanied by Madame de Tourzel and Madame Élisabeth, who remained in total ignorance of the plan, but Bouillé would have preferred Tourzel and Madame Élisabeth (who would then travel with the waiting women Madame de Neuville and Madame Brunier, who would be following the *berline* in their own carriage) to be replaced by two capable officers with the resolution and quick intelligence to be able to cope with any emergencies that might arise along the way. However, Marie Antoinette insisted that her children could not manage without their governess and that there was no way that a Princess of the Royal Blood could be expected to travel with her servants and that was apparently the end of the matter.

'*The departure is now finally decided for June 20, midnight*,' Axel von Fersen wrote to his fellow conspirator Bouillé. '*A treacherous nurse of the Dauphin who could not be dismissed and who will not be leaving before Monday night, makes it necessary to postpone the journey until then; but you can be assured that it will take place.*' All was ready for the great escape which, incidentally, had been mostly financed by Fersen himself who had got much of the money from his mistress Eléanore and her lover, both of whom were loyal royalists.

To the courtiers and servants milling around the Tuileries, Monday 20 June must have seemed like an ordinary day just like any other. Marie Antoinette spent the morning listening to her children having their lessons then went down to the chapel with them at midday for Mass, where they met the King, who had spent the morning reading in his study. They then took luncheon, after which the family gathered in the salon and Louis quietly told Madame Élisabeth that they were planning to leave Paris that night. 'What should I bring with me?' the princess asked Marie Antoinette. 'Bring nothing,' was the reply. 'I can lend you anything that you need from my own trunks.'

Louis and Marie Antoinette then played billiards before going off to the King's rooms on the ground floor where a short while later Fersen joined them to deliver a final briefing about their plan. He was to act as coachman for the first leg of the journey before leaving them in order to ride ahead to Brussels. He would have preferred to stay with them for the entire journey but Louis, although he was grateful for Fersen's help, was adamant that he had to leave, which has been taken to suggest that he suspected that the dashing Swede was having an affair with his wife and had no desire to arrive at Montmédy in the undignified position of having him acting as their coachman. An alternative theory is that the King was put off by the fact that Fersen was not French and having made the decision to remain in France, had no wish to look as though he was accepting any foreign assistance.

Later on the Queen, feeling weepy and emotional after her interview with Fersen, took her children for their customary walk in the Tuileries gardens where the Dauphin, who was kept in total ignorance of the secret plans, waved and smiled at the crowds that had gathered as usual to see him. After the royal children had gone to bed, the Provences came over from the Palais du Luxembourg to have supper with Louis, Marie Antoinette and Madame Élisabeth. They would also be leaving that night but being blessed with more common sense than the Queen and Fersen had followed Bouillé's instructions to the letter and purchased two light carriages in which they would travel separately, taking different routes and leaving most of their belongings behind. Louis and his brother had had many clashes over the years but they were seen to be visibly moved when the time came to say goodbye. If their plan worked then they would soon be reunited but both were very well aware that if anything went awry then they would most probably never see each other again.

At ten, Marie Antoinette went upstairs and woke up the children, who were then dressed by their governess Madame de Tourzel. Madame Royale wore a brown dress patterned with white and yellow flowers while the little Dauphin, who had insisted that he wanted to wear his sword and soldier boots to impress the troops that were due to meet them, was instead dressed as a girl, much to his disappointment. The children and Madame de Tourzel, bearing a note stating that she was taking the Children of France away on the King's orders, were taken down to Axel von Fersen who was waiting in the Carrousel courtyard before the Queen returned to the drawing room as though nothing untoward had happened[2].

The family went to bed at their normal time. Élisabeth was accompanied to her rooms in the Pavilion de Flore by a National Guard who left her at her door and later testified to hearing her push the bolts across. Meanwhile Marie Antoinette impatiently endured the traditional *coucher* ceremony before dismissing her maids and getting quickly dressed again in a plain grey silk dress and a black hat with a veil which could be pulled down to conceal her face. She then left her apartments and went down to the courtyard where her bodyguard, Monsieur de Malden was waiting to escort her to the carriage that was to take them to where the *berline* was waiting for them outside Paris. Disaster almost struck when Lafayette's carriage went past, but he did not recognise the Queen, who quickly pulled down her veil, and all was well. Malden then escorted Marie Antoinette through the warren of streets surrounding the Tuileries, getting a bit lost along the way, until they reached the carriage rather later than they had been expected.

They drove to the Saint Martin barrier at two in the morning, thankfully unmolested, and changed from the carriage to the magnificent *berline*, which had been furnished with every possible comfort including a delicious picnic lunch of roasted pigeon, veal, cakes and wine. Fersen then drove them at a spanking pace to Bondy, where he was to leave them and go on alone to Brussels. Again he tried to persuade Louis to let him stay with the royal party until they reached Montmédy but he was gently turned down and was powerless to do anything other than watch as the massive coach, already three hours behind schedule, went on its way. At this point Fersen should really have taken the initiative, disobeyed the royal orders and either ridden behind the *berline* or, even better, gone on ahead to let the young Duc de Choiseul, who was waiting with his troops to escort the royal family on the final leg of their journey, know that they would be late. He did neither though but instead turned his horse's head towards Brussels and rode off, leaving them to their fate.

The *berline* was already well on its way and was crossing the Marne river at La Ferté-sous-Jouarre at around the time that their departure was discovered by the servants at the Tuileries, who immediately rose the alarm and alerted the National Assembly, whose temporary president at the time was Alexandre de Beauharnais, the first husband of the future Empress Joséphine. At this point no one knew where the King, who had left behind a terse letter listing the various injustices that had led to his departure, had gone and it was feared that the royal family had either been abducted by counter-revolutionaries or had gone to join forces with the Austrians – however, all became clear when Louis' farewell letter was discovered and they realised just how much they had been duped by the mild-mannered King and his wife. It's likely that many of the deputies had no great desire to see the royal family brought back again – this departure had, after all, played right into the hands of the extremists who wanted the monarchy abolished altogether, but even so the order was made to send troops in hot pursuit.

Meanwhile, the happy little band were now travelling towards Metz and, believing themselves safe, had begun to relax and even enjoy their adventure. It had been decided in advance that Madame de Tourzel should play the part of the Baronne de Korff while Marie Antoinette, keen as mustard as always to indulge in a little role reversal, masqueraded as her waiting woman Madame Rochet, the King played the part of her valet Durand and Madame Élisabeth played the nurse Rosalie. The royal children were to be the Baronne's daughters, Agläié and Amélie. Having seen very little of France beyond the Isle de France, Marie Antoinette gazed rapturously out of the carriage window at the beautiful countryside and insisted upon walking alongside the coach while her children, glad to be freed from the *berline*, chased butterflies and picked flowers in the fields. Meanwhile, Louis, also beaming with delight, stopped to chat about the harvest with the peasants that they passed and struck up conversations with the postillions and other patrons at the various posting stations along the way, apparently not caring when he was recognised, while in the coach he joked about wishing that he could see Lafayette's face when he realised that the royal chickens had fled their glittering coop.

Each little chat, each stop to pick flowers and each slowing down of the *berline* so that Marie Antoinette and her children could take a walk beside it, cost them precious minutes. However, the King and Queen naively believed that they had put enough distance between themselves and Paris for it to be pretty much impossible for them to be successfully pursued and captured and so saw no need to make any great haste to reach the meeting place. They were also totally untroubled by the fact that they were so obviously being recognised in every town and village that they passed through – after all, no one had made any effort to detain them and in fact they were being hailed with cheers and offers of accommodation and refreshments wherever they went, which they took as proof that outside Paris they were as well loved and popular as ever. This was not really the case though and even as they drove tranquilly on towards Metz, things were beginning to go wrong.

The first hint that disaster had struck came at the Somme Vesle bridge, where the Duc de Choiseul, who was the successor of the now deceased Choiseul who had been chiefly responsible for brokering Louis and Marie Antoinette's marriage, was supposed to be waiting for them with his troops. However, there was no one there and so the coach carried on towards Sainte-Menehould where they were once again recognised, this time by a postmaster Jean-Baptiste Drouet[3], who set off in hot pursuit after they left and eventually managed to overtake them and alert a local contingent of National Guardsmen who put together a rudimentary ambush in the town of Varennes, which he correctly guessed was to be the next stop on the journey. The royal party, worn out by the excitement of the day, were fast asleep in their luxurious carriage when they were be rudely awakened by the triumphant shouts of Drouet and his new soldier friends as well as the insistent ringing of the tocsin bell on the local church, which quickly gathered a crowd of concerned residents, who stumbled out of bed, armed themselves and gathered in a hostile crowd around the carriage. The procurator of the commune, a Monsieur Sauce, who also moonlighted as a grocer, was called upon to check that the now awake and anxious passengers' papers were all in order, which he duly believed them to be.

However, the postmaster Drouet's stubborn and increasingly irate insistence that the carriage carried the King and Queen of France and their family could not be ignored. In vain did Louis and Marie Antoinette protest that they were in fact merely the maid and valet of the Baronne and insist that they should be allowed to continue their journey unmolested – not realising that their outspoken behaviour only served to create more suspicion as no genuine servants, outside the works of Monsieur Beaumarchais at least, would ever speak so out of turn while their aristocratic mistress remained so nervously silent. If Monsieur Sauce had been left to himself he would probably have waved them on but Drouet was annoyingly insistent and the crowd was getting ugly so he asked the royal family to get out of the *berline* and come into his grocery store while he sent for a local resident who had, providentially, once lived in Versailles. The royal cover story was completely blown when this gentleman, clearly overawed to be in the presence of majesty once again, fell to his knees in reverence before the King, who with typical kindness embraced him and admitted his true identity, saying: 'Yes, I am your King'. Louis and Marie Antoinette then tried in vain to persuade Sauce to let them continue on their way but he stood firm, more scared of the National Assembly's reaction should they find out about his actions than worried about offending his King. His wife, although sympathetic, also refused to help. 'Well, Madame, you are in a very unfortunate position but *my* husband is not responsible,' she said to Marie Antoinette, who was weeping with chagrin. 'I don't want him to get into any trouble.'

At this point, the scene outside, where a crowd of curious townsfolk were still gathered, descended into chaos as the Duc de Choiseul's hussars appeared at long last, along with some other loyal troops that had raced to Varennes as soon as they heard the news. It turned out that Choiseul had waited for the *berline* for quite a while before concluding that the escape had been foiled at the outset, if it had even been attempted, the message that the royal escape was a few hours behind schedule having failed to reach him. Choiseul and another officer forced their way through the crowd and into the grocery shop, where they asked Louis, who was naturally delighted to see them, for orders. 'I have forty hussars with me,' Choiseul told him before outlining an impromptu escape plan which involved them cutting their way through the crowd outside and whisking the entire family away to safety on horseback. Choiseul had also sent a message to Bouillé, telling him where the family were and asking him to make haste with his troops.

Indecisive as always, Louis could not make up his mind what to do and so Choiseul turned to Marie Antoinette, begging her to make a decision and put her trust in the brave hussars waiting to take them to freedom. 'I do not want to take the responsibility for this,' she replied. 'It is up to the King to make the orders and my duty is to follow them.' When Choiseul admitted that he could not absolutely promise their safety, Louis finally decided to turn the scheme down, saying that he had no wish to put any lives at risk and was content to wait until Bouillé arrived with his troops as then they would be able to proceed by carriage.

However, it was two representatives of the National Assembly who arrived next in Varennes, dusty and dishevelled after their long journey from Paris and bearing an official decree that ordered the royal family to return to the capital immediately as their prisoners. 'There is no longer a King in France,' Louis said in sad resignation after he read it and dropped the paper on to the bed where the Dauphin and Madame Royale were still fast asleep, worn out after their adventure. 'I will not let my children be contaminated by this thing,' Marie Antoinette shrieked, crumpling the order into a ball and petulantly throwing it on to the floor. 'What audacity, for subjects to have the temerity to pretend to give orders to their King.'

The royal couple still had faith that Bouillé would arrive to save them but despite their best attempts to delay departure by feigning illness and the like, they were forced to give in and at half past seven in the morning sulkily clambered back into the *berline* to make the journey back to Paris, surrounded by a hostile mob of armed countryfolk. Bouillé and his much longed for troops arrived in Varennes almost two hours later to find them well and truly gone and their last chance to escape at an end.

Chapter 12

The Prisoner 1791–1792

'Do not feel sad for me.'

Whereas it had taken the royal family less than twenty four hours to reach Varennes, the journey back to Paris took four long, miserable days during which they were harangued by angry crowds that swarmed like furious wasps around the *berline* whenever it stopped. At Epernay they were spat at and had their clothes torn by an angry mob, an experience that reduced Marie Antoinette and Élisabeth to tears. The weather had become unbearably hot and they had not been permitted to change their clothes since they were apprehended at Varennes nor were they allowed to close the carriage's windows which meant that the dust from the roads got inside and they had no respite from the violent threats and curses of the crowd that ran alongside waving guns and pitchforks in the air. The high spirits and optimistic cheerfulness of their journey from Paris had completely vanished and been replaced by a melancholic despair as, at last, they considered the consequence of their actions and bemoaned the mistakes that had led to their capture so tantalisingly close to their final destination.

Just outside Epernay, they were joined by representatives of the National Assembly, who had travelled out to meet them and accompany them back to the capital. Although Marie Antoinette had every reason to distrust the two men Barnave and Pétion (a third representative, the Marquis de Labour-Maubourg travelled with the waiting women in their carriage) who clambered without ceremony into the *berline*, squeezing themselves between the members of the royal family, she was also relieved to have their protection for the rest of the journey as the crowds, which had turned out in their hundreds to stare at the royal family and shout insults at the as they went by, were becoming increasingly acrimonious and threatening the closer they drew to Paris.

However, although Pétion and Barnave were absolutely not the royal family's greatest fans, they were still taken aback by how different they were to a popular mythology that made the King out to be an oafish imbecilic buffoon led by the nose by his haughty wife. Instead, they found the royal couple to be polite, touchingly affectionate towards each other and their children and not at all stupid, although they were undoubtedly ignorant. Pétion wrote afterwards: '*I noticed simplicity and a family air which pleased me… there was ease and domestic bonhomie. The Queen called Madame Élisabeth 'ma petite soeur'. Madame Élisabeth did the same … The Queen danced the prince up and down on her knees.*' He was exceedingly taken with Madame Élisabeth, Louis' pious and virginal sister and believed her to have taken a bit of a fancy to him in return, encouraged by the fact that her arm occasionally pressed against his when they were thrown together by the movements of the carriage. *'Madame Élisabeth foxed me with melting eyes, with that languishing air that unhappiness gives and which inspires a lively interest... The moon began to shine softly... She sometimes interrupted her words, in such a manner as to agitate me. I replied...with a kind of austerity... She must have seen that the most seductive temptations were useless. I noticed a certain cooling off, a certain severity, which women often show when their pride is wounded.'* Or more likely, she had realised that her overtures of polite friendliness had been completely misinterpreted and was trying to give him a tactful brush off, although she would later write to a friend that: '*The deputies were really quite pleasant and Monsieur Barnave in particular behaved extremely well.*'

Meanwhile, Monsieur Barnave, much to his surprise, was quickly falling under the spell of Marie Antoinette. A nice boy from a decent middle class and Protestant family who'd trained as a lawyer after being homeschooled by his mother, he'd grown up with an absolute hatred of the aristocracy whom he saw as the chief architects of the country's ruin. He had not been looking forward to this rendezvous with the royal family and had, in particular, been feeling some trepidation about finding himself in close quarters with the Queen, who was the very worst of the whole worthless lot as far as he was concerned. At first he did his best to ignore Marie Antoinette, wincing when she sprinkled her perfume around the carriage in order to make the fetid air more pleasant, avoiding eye contact with her and speaking only to Madame Élisabeth, who was keen to engage him in a lengthy political debate. However, as the hours dragged on, he found himself unexpectedly enthralled and fascinated by the Queen as she chatted most unaffectedly with her husband and sister-in-law and fussed like any other fond mother over her grizzling children, who were now sitting on the knees of the adults in order to make room for the deputies.

Although she was visibly worn out, travel soiled and distressed by the events of the last few days, Marie Antoinette still retained the gentle charm that had won Mirabeau to her cause and made men like Fersen willing to risk their lives to save her from the indignities of her situation. Like many people, Barnave had become so accustomed to the swirl of terrible rumours, gossip and calumny that surrounded Marie Antoinette that he'd forgotten that she was a real woman behind it all and he rapidly began to fall beneath her spell.

They stopped at Meaux on the third night and after supper Marie Antoinette spent several hours talking to Barnave, quietly winning him over to her cause. That the young deputy was exceedingly handsome, had lovely manners and was extremely eloquent merely boosted his appeal in the eyes of a Queen who had once scandalised Versailles by choosing her footmen purely on the basis of their good looks and height rather than their ability to do the job. It was only natural that she was keen to have the dashing Barnave as her new champion in the debating hall of the National Assembly.

The next morning they got up early to begin the final stretch to Paris. It was one of the hottest days of the year and as Marie Antoinette gazed listlessly out at the angry crowds that lined the road to the capital, she may well have thought back to the journey by stages, following a very similar route, by which she had first approached Versailles over twenty one years before. It's more likely though that it was the horrible present and uncertain future that weighed on the beleaguered Queen's mind as she smiled wanly across the *berline* at Barnave and tightly held her weeping daughter's hand. At one point she pulled down the window and offered a piece of beef to one of the guardsmen riding beside the carriage but then recoiled in tears when a woman in the crowd shouted, 'Don't take it! She's probably poisoned it!' Instead, she pointedly gave the meat to the Dauphin to eat and made no further attempts to speak to the guards.

Despite the terrible heat of the day, they had been forbidden from closing the blinds and so were exposed to the hostile stares of enormous crowds that swelled in size as they got nearer to Paris. Although Barnave was quick to open the window and demand that the worst offenders stop shouting insults, he could not prevent them all and so the *berline* lumbered slowly past a menacing mob of screaming, shouting people, their faces contorting with fury as they yelled curses into Marie Antoinette's very face, threatening to cut off her head, make pies from her intestines and lace from her fine white skin. The Queen kept her composure as best she could, determined not to lose control in the face of such hostility, but her children screamed with fear, terrified as much by the angry faces of the mob as by their horrible words.

Things only got worse when they entered Paris at around six in the evening and began the slow drive through the crammed and noisy city streets, where it seemed like almost everyone had turned out to see their King and Queen's ignominious return. '*Anyone who applauds the King will be flogged; anyone who insults him will be hanged*,' threatened the dozens of placards that had been placed along the route and so they entered the city to a hostile silence, broken only by a few shouts of '*Vive la nation*!' Lafayette had also ordered that all heads should remain covered to signify that the King was no longer considered worthy of respect and so the crowds kept their hats and caps on while the National Guard lining the route kept their crossheads high as if they were the guard of honour at a funeral.

It was late in the evening when the *berline* finally pulled up at the Tuileries where Lafayette was waiting to greet them, his air of smug triumph annoying the Queen so much that she could hardly bear to look at him as she whisked past on her way to her rooms where her ladies were waiting to prepare her bath and would make the sad discovery that their mistress' hair had gone completely white[1] during her brief absence. Louis, however, politely stopped to talk to Lafayette, who asked him if he had any orders. 'It seems to me, Monsieur de Lafayette, that it is you who are giving the orders now,' the King said with a sad smile before he too departed with relief to his rooms.

As soon as she was able to snatch a few moments alone, Marie Antoinette sat down to write to Axel von Fersen. '*I am alive. Oh, the anxiety that I have been feeling for you and the sorrow I feel for all that you must have undergone in not hearing from us. God grant that this reaches you. Do not write to me, this would compromise all of us and above everything do not come back under any circumstances. Everyone knows that you helped us to escape and should you show yourself, all would be lost. We are guarded night and day, I do not care. Do not feel sad for me, nothing will happen to me. The National Assembly will be forgiving… I am able to tell you that I love you and have time only to do that. I am well. Suffer no pain for me… Let me know where I should send my letters so that I can write to you, for without them I cannot survive. Farewell my most beloved and loving of men. I embrace you with all my heart.*'

The news that both the Comte and Comtesse de Provence, who had followed Bouillé's instructions and separated into two small carriages before taking different routes (no doubt with great thankfulness as they had been living in a state of polite and perfectly amicable separation for years), had both managed to successfully leave the country without any hindrance was just salt in Marie Antoinette's wounds, although naturally she outwardly expressed relief that they had managed to make their escape even if it highlighted the mistakes that had made their own attempt such a dismal and total failure. Officially the National Assembly let it be known that the whole incident had been due to an abduction attempt by the now thoroughly discredited Bouillé along with his accomplice Axel von Fersen and that the royal family had been taken against their will but everyone knew the truth and as always the blame was placed squarely on Marie Antoinette's shoulders. It didn't matter that both she and the King frequently made it plain that they had no intention of actually leaving France – no one really believed them and matters only grew worse when a group of protesters who had gone to the Champs de Mars to sign a petition demanding the deposition of the King, who was now suspected of being in cahoots with the counter-revolutionaries abroad, were fired upon by the National Guard, which just served to inflame the situation even further.

When Marie Antoinette arrived back in her sumptuous rooms at the Tuileries that sad day in June 1791, it was to find guards posted on every door and security arrangements tightened throughout the palace where visitors, including Marie Antoinette's ladies, were now searched upon entering and the Queen was attended by four guardsmen wherever she went, including out to the Tuileries gardens which had now been closed to the public. She also had her mail opened and read before it was passed on, which meant that she now had to use intermediaries to get her coded letters out without detection. Any pretence that the Tuileries was not in actuality a gilded prison and they were perfectly at liberty to leave at any time had been dropped and the royal family were now left in no doubt at all that they were captives, although they were constantly reminded that the precautions were as much for the sake of their own safety as they were to prevent their escape. In retaliation, Marie Antoinette rebelled by giving up the patriotic tricolour ribbons with which she had taken to bedecking her gowns and instead ordering dresses in green and purple, both colours strongly associated with the royalist cause.

Marie Antoinette continued to make contact with Barnave, who had joined forces with Alexandre Lameth and Adrien Duport, both of whom shared his belief that a constitutional monarchy of limited powers, much like that in Britain, was now the best hope for France's recovery. However, as Louis sunk even further into depression and apathy and also, it was rumoured, the oblivion of the bottle, it was to the Queen that they turned for support and once again Marie Antoinette found herself having to literally struggle to comprehend matters of which she had very little understanding as she read through the political reports that Barnave obligingly sent to her in the Tuileries. Although she was far from being stupid, Marie Antoinette was undoubtedly ignorant and had very little political acumen and understanding beyond her own narrow interests and those of her friends – the bigger picture was, alas, not one that she was at all equipped to view. She was also fatally unable to compromise and although she strung Barnave along with her half promises, she had no real intention of ever fully accepting the Constitution as he urged her and Louis to do, believing this to be the only way to save any vestiges of the monarchy.

At the same time, she was maintaining her dangerous links with the counter-revolutionary leaders and keeping up a clandestine and voluminous correspondence with her brother Emperor Leopold, sisters in the Netherlands, Parma and Naples and other foreign leaders, whom she begged for help and support, receiving in return the usual flurry of vague promises intended to raise her hopes while at the same time delivering no actual concrete assistance. Although they all sympathised with the plight of Marie Antoinette and her family, there was a general feeling that they had brought a lot of their problems on themselves. There was also a feeling that revolutions, like the dreaded smallpox, had a tendency to be contagious and so no one really wanted to make any definite moves to get involved on the behalf of the embattled French King and Queen. However, even though she was undoubtedly well aware of the true feelings that lay behind the soothing words from the other European courts, Marie Antoinette, who had so hated writing as a girl, still continued to work late into the night wearily writing her coded letters in lemon juice and painstakingly puzzling over the cyphered replies which were smuggled back to her.

On 14 September, feeling himself caught between a rock and a hard place, Louis officially accepted the Constitution as he had been urged to do by Barnave and his cohorts, a decision that would seriously limit his powers, make him King of the French rather than King of France and meant that he no longer had the treasury income to drawn upon but would instead receive a fixed Civil List income. An impassive Marie Antoinette watched from a private box as her husband mounted a podium at the Salle de Manège, the riding school in the Tuileries gardens where the National Assembly held their meetings. Eager to please as always, Louis removed his hat and stood up to deliver his speech before realising that the deputies had remained sitting down and kept their hats firmly on their heads. Thrown and rather offended by this, the King threw himself down on his chair and read out the rest of his speech in a dull and barely audible monotone. However, despite this lack of enthusiasm, he was soundly cheered for his efforts before he returned to the palace to collapse weeping on his wife, bemoaning that she had come to France in order to be a Queen and instead had witnessed the end of the monarchy. Later on though they went out to preside over the official celebrations, which included a performance at the ballet and a firework display in the Place Louis XV.

In return for this humiliating capitulation many of the guards were removed from the Tuileries, security was stepped down a few notches and the gardens were once again opened to the public, while the remaining courtiers began to return to the Tuileries. The royal family were also once again free to leave the palace and go for drives around the capital and even ride in the Bois de Boulogne as before. There was even a suggestion that trips to Marie Antoinette's beloved Saint Cloud might well resume again in the near future.

While Marie Antoinette redoubled her efforts to win the fickle Parisians over by appearing in public with her children at every opportunity and making sure that she looked like a model of affectionately smiling benevolence at all times, her private life was proving to be rather less comforting than it had been before. Her husband had become even more withdrawn and uncommunicative since the events of September 1791 and her sister-in-law, Madame Élisabeth was consoling herself by keeping up a correspondence with her favourite brother the Comte d'Artois, who had surrounded himself with schemers and counter-revolutionaries and was plotting with foreign powers to overthrow the revolution. It's not certain how far Élisabeth went – some believe that she was also a key figure in the counter-revolutionary plots but others think that her nature was too conciliatory and peaceful for this to have been possible.[2] However, Marie Antoinette was sufficiently alarmed to write that Élisabeth was '*so indiscreet, surrounded by intriguers, and, above all, dominated by her brothers outside (France), that it is impossible for us to speak to one another, or we would quarrel all day*' and miserably added that it was '*hell at home*'.

However, there was one small comfort in the person of Madame de Lamballe, who had returned from her exile in England and moved back into the Tuileries, bringing with her a pet spaniel called Thisbée who was intended as a present for the Queen. Marie Antoinette had begged her friend not to consider returning to Paris but was nonetheless delighted to be reunited with her. Silly and affected though the Princesse de Lamballe undoubtedly was, her loyalty to Marie Antoinette could not be faulted and her sensitive sighs and flutterings and uncritical admiration were a definite balm to the Queen's low spirits while her presence reminded her of happier times spent at the Petit Trianon. In early 1792, there was to be further consolation when Axel von Fersen, risking his life now that he had been denounced by the Assembly as one of the chief architects behind the flight to Varennes, returned in disguise and with a fake passport to Paris. He was quickly reunited with his Queen in her private apartments where she poured out everything that had happened during their separation and he told her that he had come as the emissary of the King of Sweden who wished to assist with another escape attempt. They remained closeted alone together for twenty four hours before Louis came in to join their discussion. 'I know the people tar me with weakness and irresolution but no one has ever found himself in such a difficult situation,' he told Fersen sadly. 'I had one chance of escape and I missed it. That was over two years ago after the fourteenth of July. Such a chance never came again and now the world has abandoned me.' He now firmly rejected Fersen's new plan, reminding him that he had given his word to the National Assembly to make no further escape attempts and intended to stick to this. Fersen had no option but to withdraw. Marie Antoinette never saw him again.

Less than a month after Fersen's clandestine visit, the news arrived that Marie Antoinette's brother Emperor Leopold had died and been succeeded by his twenty-four-year-old son Francis, who had never met his aunt and so was even less invested in helping her. However, he was also definitely not a friend of the revolutionary regime in France, which he immediately made plain by refuting a French ultimatum and letting it be known that he intended to initiate hostilities between the two nations with the backing of his new ally, the King of Prussia. Marie Antoinette, like most of the National Assembly, was keen for France to go to war with Austria but unlike them she was desperate for the Austro-Prussian forces to win, writing to Mercy that: '*There must be war, so that we may be at last revenged for all the outrages committed in this country.*' Although she naturally made every appearance of patriotically desiring a French victory, she actually pinned all her hopes on her nephew's forces destroying those of France then putting her husband back on his throne again and with this goal in mind, even sent her nephew some little snippets of military information that she had become privy to – an undoubted act of treason.

However, despite her efforts to appear supportive of the French side, the declaration of war in April 1792 dealt an unsurprising blow to Marie Antoinette's already rock bottom popularity and once again she heard herself being booed and threatened when she went out in public, while in the National Assembly the Girondin Vergniaud declared that: '*From here I can see the windows of a palace within which counter-revolution is at work, where there is being planned details to thrust us back into the horrors of servitude... Let each one of those dwelling therein realise that our Constitution allows inviolability to the King alone. Let them know that the law will stretch out without the slightest discrimination to all the guilty, and there is not one single head which, once convicted, can escape its sword.*' His meaning was clear – the Austrian Queen was not to be trusted and the Constitutional laws that protected the King did not extend to his consort who could be removed and punished at the slightest hint of treachery, regardless of the fact that it was obvious to everyone that the war was effectively pitting the nation and monarchy against each other. She could not even rely on the faithful Barnave for support any more for he had been removed from the National Assembly several months earlier. '*I am afraid that I place little hope in the success of the plan you now follow,*' he despondently wrote to her in his final letter[3]. '*You are too far away from any outside help, and you will be lost long before it can reach you. I only pray that I may be mistaken in my gloomy presentiments. I myself have no doubt that I will pay with my head for the interest that I have shown in your misfortunes. All I ask in recompense is the honour to kiss your hand.*'

Matters reached a head on 20 June when a protest at the Tuileries ended with the palace being stormed by an immense armed crowd who swarmed through the royal apartments shouting threats against the Queen. Marie Antoinette took refuge in the Dauphin's bedchamber while her husband, who had been trapped in a room with his sister, did his best to pacify the intruders who at first thought that Madame Élisabeth was Marie Antoinette and then became much less aggressive when they realised their mistake. When the rioters began to ransack the Queen's rooms below where she was hiding, Marie Antoinette hurried with her children to the King's apartments and then on to the Council Chamber where a large table was placed in front of them as a barricade, protecting them from the angry crowd that streamed into the room. A battalion of National Guard kept desultory watch as for over two hours the mob screamed their insults in the face of the Queen, who remained utterly impassive while her terrified son and daughter sobbed at her side. Finally, the crowd was dispersed late in the evening and the royal family, shattered by their experience, cried together with relief. '*I still live, but only by a miracle,*' Marie Antoinette wrote to Axel von Fersen. '*The 20th was appalling. It is no longer against me that they hurl their fury but against my husband's very life and they do not disguise it.*'

Although life in the Tuileries appeared to continue as normal after this, in private the King and Queen had almost reached breaking point, having finally realised the full extent of their unpopularity as well as accepted the fact that it was almost certainly only a matter of time before the palace was invaded again. Marie Antoinette's secret correspondence with foreign courts continued apace as she hoped against hope that Austrian forces would invade and rescue her from a life that she was finding increasingly intolerable. Meanwhile, outside the Tuileries the pamphlets denouncing the Austrian Queen's lecherous behaviour and treachery against France were increasing in number while at the same time the deputies of the National Assembly were beginning to wonder if they might do better without the King. Many of the deputies would have preferred to do away with the monarchy altogether but some were more in favour of forcing Louis to abdicate in favour of his son, who could be removed and carefully moulded by specially appointed tutors into the perfect malleable Constitutional King. Their fears were only increased by the disquieting news from the front, where the Austro-Prussian armies were easily getting the better of the disorganised French troops while counter-revolutionary troops led by well-trained aristocratic *emigré* officers were reported to be preparing for invasion. While the National Assembly panicked about what appeared to be imminent invasion, Marie Antoinette secretly prayed for it and even optimistically confided in one of her ladies that: 'When I see this moon again in a month's time, I will be freed of my irons.'

On 14 July the royal family appeared as usual at the celebrations for the anniversary of the Bastille's fall. Louis was wearing a bullet proof vest beneath his suit while beside him Marie Antoinette, who had proudly refused body armour while telling Madame Campan that it would be a blessing if the insurgents murdered her, blinked back tears as the crowd booed during his speech. Matters worsened just weeks later when the Duke of Brunswick, commander of the Austro-Prussian allied army, issued a terrifying manifesto addressed to the citizens of Paris. '*Their aforesaid Majesties (the King of Prussia and Emperor of Austria) declare… on their word and honour as Emperor and King, that if the Tuileries Palace be insulted or invaded, that if the least injury, be inflicted on their Majesties the King, Queen and the Royal Family, and if measures are not at once taken for their safety, preservation and security, they, their Imperial and Royal Majesties, will wreak exemplary and unforgettable vengeance by yielding the town of Paris to military execution and utter subversion, and the guilty rebels to deserved death.*'

Marie Antoinette had already been warned about the manifesto by Fersen, who felt compelled to advise her when Lafayette suggested that the royal family remove to the comparative safety of Compiègne. '*Your bravery will be much praised and the King's steadfast behaviour also,*' he wrote. '*It is essential to maintain this, and above all else to remain in Paris. This is absolutely essential. Thus it will be simple to reach you, and this the Duke of Brunswick is planning to accomplish. Before his actual entry he will publish a powerful manifesto from the allied powers making all France, Paris especially, responsible for the lives of the royal family.*' Both Louis and Marie Antoinette had actually approved the wording of Brunswick's diatribe before it was made public, evidently hoping that its forceful language and threat of imminent menace would intimidate the unruly Parisians into behaving better. However, yet again they managed to woefully misjudge the mood on the streets of their own capital and failed to realise that the Parisians, whom they clearly regarded as little more than unruly children who could be threatened into obedience, were in no mood to be ordered around by foreigners. They ought to have realised that the manifesto, intended to cow them into frightened submission, would only make the Parisians, already so fed up and simmering on the brink of violent outburst, all the more angry and resentful, particularly of Marie Antoinette who was naturally assumed to be behind the whole thing. The arrival of Brunswick's manifesto just confirmed what everyone has been suspecting for months – that for all their pretence at patriotic fervour, the King and Queen weren't on the side of France at all but were clearly in cahoots with the enemy and had been so all along.

While in the past, Louis had managed to escape most of the opprobrium directed at his wife things had gradually begun to change and now it was he who was viciously denounced during the sessions of the National Assembly, with increasingly violent demands being made for his overthrow, particularly by Robespierre and his followers who believed that France would be better off as a republic. Meanwhile, tensions were rising on the streets of Paris where the people were beginning to arm themselves again and there was an almost palpable atmosphere of fear and distrust, mostly directed towards the royal family in the Tuileries and inflamed by the denunciations of the National Assembly and the ever-increasing stream of pamphlets accusing both Louis and Marie Antoinette of being traitors to the nation and living in the lap of luxury while they sold their own country out. It was only a matter of time before Paris erupted into violence again.

Inside the Tuileries both Louis and Marie Antoinette were well aware of the danger that they were in and were bracing themselves for the next invasion. The Queen was suffering from insomnia again and looked like a worn out shadow of her former self as she paced her rooms in the early hours, worrying about the future and praying that the Austro-Prussian troops would arrive in Paris before matters worsened any further. For security reasons, she had left her rooms on the terrace and was now sleeping on the first floor, next door to her husband who spent most of his time fretting that he was about to be put on trial. Both knew that invasion was imminent and began to take protective measures – calling in nine hundred Swiss Guardsmen to join their existing palace defenders of gendarmes and two thousand National Guardsmen of dubious loyalty. The loyalty of the Swiss Guards was unimpeachable however and it was upon them that the hopes of the King and Queen rested when on 9 August the news arrived that the faubourgs of Paris were rising up against them and attack was imminent.

As the royal family retreated to the safety of their apartments they could hear the tocsins, the warning bells, of Paris, being rung all over the city to call the people to arms. Meanwhile, the grand apartments of the Tuileries swarmed with hundreds of noblemen who had arrived, armed to the teeth, to defend their King and Queen. However, they must have wondered why they had bothered when they saw Louis shambling from room to room with his hair un-powdered, his suit in urgent need of a pressing and his expression blankly terrified. It was hard to feel any confidence when it seemed as though just when Louis most needed to be decisive and bold he had once again become even more irresolute and weak than ever. Marie Antoinette however was as brave as a lion and had a grateful word and a tight-lipped smile for everyone as she personally distributed food and drink to the men who had willingly come to lay down their lives for her – or rather the institution that she and her husband represented.

The tocsin bells stopped in the early hours of the morning and the courtiers inside the Tuileries seized the chance to get some rest, camping on sofas and floors and trying to snatch some sleep in the intolerable heat of that August night. Marie Antoinette and Madame Élisabeth couldn't bring themselves to go to bed and instead napped on sofas in a little closet overlooking the courtyard, watched over by their ladies in waiting and the faithful Princesse de Lamballe, who had refused to leave the palace. Unable to sleep, Madame Élisabeth got up and went to the window to watch a red and pink streaked dawn rise over the Tuileries gardens. 'My sister, come and see the beautiful sunrise,' she said over her shoulder to Marie Antoinette, who came to stand beside her and gazed up in wonderment at the crimson sky.

After a hurried breakfast, Louis, Marie Antoinette and Madame Élisabeth made a tour of the Tuileries' defences to make sure that everything was ready and to speak encouraging words to the troops. The tocsin had begun to ring again in the early hours and any hope they may have had that the invasion had been abandoned faded when news arrived that the people were marching in their thousands towards the palace. Marie Antoinette watched from the safety of a window embrasure as the mob, who had brought several cannons along with them, began to swarm in front of the palace gates. Louis went down to give a pep talk to the waiting troops but while he was greeted with cheers by the faithful Swiss Guards, the National Guardsmen, who had been fraternising with the crowd that was growing behind the palace gates, booed him and shouted 'Down with the King!' and 'Down with the fat pig!' until he went away again. His wife, who was watching from a window above, broke down in tears and could hardly bear to look at him when he shambled into the room and threw himself down on a sofa, declaring that he had given his orders and they had been told to hold their fire until the insurgents shot first. 'He has done more harm than good,' Marie Antoinette angrily muttered to Madame Campan.

While the crowd outside grew and became more ferocious by the minute, the atmosphere inside the palace became increasingly strained and anxious as the assembled courtiers gazed apprehensively out of the windows and wondered when the attack would start. The jeers of the National Guardsmen seemed to have drained all of the last vestiges of fight out of both Louis and Marie Antoinette and they both slumped miserably on sofas, apparently incapable of making a decision about what to do next. Some of the courtiers advised the Queen to take her children to the Assembly and ask for their protection. 'I would rather be nailed to the walls of the palace than seek the protection of those who have behaved so badly towards us,' she replied with magnificent hauteur.

The Comte de Roederer, the public prosecutor, then stepped in and made a direct appeal to Louis, telling him that there was not a minute to lose and that his family's only hope of safety lay with the Assembly. Louis hesitated and looked wildly at his wife, clearly hoping that she would make the decision for him. 'We have a considerable force ready and willing to defend us,' she said angrily. 'We cannot leave our loyal nobles and gallant Swiss to die without us.' Roederer sighed. 'Madame, you are hopelessly outnumbered,' he said patiently. 'They are still arriving in their thousands. In staying here, you are endangering not just the life of your husband but also those of your children.'

Louis sighed and stood up. 'Let us go,' he said before walking away, leaving his wife staring after him. 'We will be back soon,' she assured the assembled courtiers before taking her children by the hand and following her husband from the room. The sad little procession was joined by Madame Élisabeth and also the Princesse de Lamballe, who had demanded to be allowed to accompany them even though she was sure that they were all about to meet their deaths. 'We will never return to the palace again,' she whispered to Madame de Rochefoucauld[4], one of the several faithful courtiers left behind at the palace to save themselves as best they could.

'What will happen to all those who are left behind?' Louis asked Roederer as they made their way across the gardens to the hall where the National Assembly had its meetings. 'They will not be able to resist for long,' was the frank reply. Marie Antoinette remained tearful but silent as she walked across the garden, leading her son who was delightedly kicking his way through the fallen leaves. 'The leaves are falling very early,' his father sighed with a melancholy look. Behind her there walked Madame Élisabeth who was doing her best to comfort the terrified Madame Royale.

When they finally arrived at the National Assembly the door was closed against them and they were kept waiting for half an hour in a corridor while a debate raged inside as to whether they should be allowed to enter. Finally, the doors were opened and they walked inside – the Queen with every appearance of dignity and serenity, determined to give no sign that she was either insulted or afraid of the mob that had gathered to scream insults at her. Her self-control cracked only once when a guardsman took the Dauphin out of her arms to protect him from the mob and she began to scream, terrified that the boy was being taken away from her.

The royal family were crammed in the tiny and uncomfortable '*loge du logographie*' which was used by the editor of a newspaper to record details of the debates. They remained there for sixteen long and hideous hours while outside the screams of the attacked and dying filtered into the hall. A huge mob had invaded the palace, slaughtering and mutilating the Swiss Guards who received an order to lay down their arms too late for it to be of any use. Another order from the National Assembly, letting the populace know that there was no reason to attack the palace now that the royal family had left, had also gone astray – not that the enormous crowd, inflamed by righteous rage and bloodlust, would have paid much attention as it now rampaged through the gilded rooms of the Tuileries, killing anyone who stood in their way and looting anything and everything that came to hand, including the famously fabulous contents of Marie Antoinette's wardrobe, much of which was now being triumphantly worn by the market women. The usually serenely lovely Tuileries gardens now reeked of blood, burning, gunpowder and death as the battle raged along the terraces and on the surrounding streets.

Over a thousand people died in the Tuileries that day, all of them needlessly, while all the while the royal family sat crammed in their tiny box at the Manège listening to the debates raging on and the sound of gunfire and screams outside. They had nothing to eat but a few biscuits and some wine provided by a kind hearted porter, which the King enjoyed before having a chat with the artist David about the portrait that he was to paint of him and the Dauphin, which was destined never to be completed, and then falling asleep in his chair. The children also eventually fell asleep but Marie Antoinette, who spent most of the day in tears, remained awake and relatively alert, determined not to let death creep up on her while she slept. Finally, at nearly two in the morning, they were allowed to leave and escorted to the nearby Feuillants convent on the Rue de Saint-Honoré where they were to spend the next three nights.

Madame Campan and some other attendants who had managed to escape the carnage at the Tuileries were allowed to offer their services to the unfortunate Queen, whom they found lying on a narrow bed in her green painted cell. 'We are lost,' she cried out to Madame Campan when she entered the room. 'We are all going to die.' The family had lost virtually everything in the sack of the Tuileries, escaping only with the clothes on their backs and forced to rely on the kindness of their supporters to lend them fresh linen and money while the Countess of Sutherland[5], wife of the British Ambassador, sent over some clothes for the Dauphin, who was inconsolable over the presumed loss of his pet dog Citron, who had been left behind in the palace and not seen since.

The royal family were depressed, exhausted and thoroughly demoralised. They were taken every morning to the Mènage to listen to the deputies argue for hours over their fates until nightfall when they were escorted back to their cells in the Feuillants. Finally on the 13 August they were informed that they were to be taken to the Temple, a large fortified complex close to where the Bastille had once stood and which had once been a *pied à terre* of the Comte d'Artois and Prince de Condé, who liked to entertain actresses and courtesans in a special little love nest in one of the towers. '*You will see, they will put us in the tower, and they will make it a veritable prison,*' Marie Antoinette whispered in dread to Madame de Tourzel when she was told that they were to be taken to the Temple. '*I have always had such a horror of that tower, that a thousand times I begged the Comte d'Artois to have it pulled down; it must surely have been a foreboding of all that we would suffer there... you will see if I am not mistaken.*'

Chapter 13

Widow Capet 1792–1793

'Living and dying had become all the same to her.'

They left the Tuileries for the last time at quarter past seven in the evening on the 13 August, all crammed together in one of the state carriages. The malicious Jacobin deputies gave orders that the vehicle should drive slowly so that the people could get a good look at the royal family and warming to this task, the coachman made sure that he took a detour through the Place de Vendôme so that Louis and Marie Antoinette could see the once proud statue of Louis XIV that had been pulled down from its plinth during the riots and now lay in pieces on the ground.

At first they thought, quite understandably, that they would be lodged in the main part of the residence, which was still rather opulently appointed, but after supper they were taken instead up the narrow spiral staircase to the apartments that had formerly been inhabited by the Keeper of the Archives of the Order of Malta, Monsieur Berthélemy who had been hastily evicted just an hour earlier. Luckily for the royal family, Monsieur Berthélemy had expensive tastes and so the apartment, which was arranged over three floors, was not quite the hideous hell hole that they might have been expecting when they first got down from their carriage and stared despondently up through the pouring rain at the tower that was to be their new home.

On the ground floor there was a porter's lodge; on the first floor: an antechamber, dining room and library; on the second floor there were rooms for the Princesse de Lamballe, Madame de Tourzel and the Dauphin and also the Queen and Madame Royale as well as a privy and guard room. On the third floor there was another guard room, a kitchen where Élisabeth and Pauline de Tourzel slept, a room for some servants, the King's bedroom, a study and a room for the King's valets. After Mesdames de Lamballe and Tourzel were taken away, Élisabeth moved down to the Dauphin's room which she then shared with Madame Royale while the little Dauphin moved in with his mother. All of the rooms had been decorated very tastefully in bright, cheerful colours and vibrant patterned wallpaper and had plenty of small luxuries such as a clavichord and a well-stocked library so they all had to agree that it could have been much worse, even if Louis did not at all approve of some of the racier books and insisted upon taking down some of the erotic engravings and paintings that hung on the walls because he didn't want his innocent sister and daughter to see them.

The royal prisoners did not know what to expect and spent the next few days awaiting more drama. It came at midnight on 19 August when the guards arrived in their rooms and took the two Tourzel ladies and the Princesse de Lamballe away to La Force prison. Marie Antoinette broke down in tears as she said goodbye to the Princesse, who had been one of her best friends ever since her first arrival in France twenty two years earlier. Although Madame de Lamballe had frequently got on her nerves with her silly affectations and nervous laugh, Marie Antoinette had never ceased to be fond of her and had come to truly love her in recent years thanks to her true and wholehearted loyalty, which must have thrown the perfidy of many others into sharp relief. 'Take care of my dear Lamballe,' Marie Antoinette whispered to Madame de Tourzel as they were being taken away. 'Try to prevent her from having to reply to any awkward and embarrassing questions.'

Once the ladies had gone, life at the Temple settled into a dull and monotonous pattern broken only by the occasional snippets of precious news from outside, which were brought to them by a loyal kitchen boy Turgy and Louis' personal valet Jean-Baptiste Cléry, who had formerly been the valet of the Dauphin at Versailles and the Tuileries. When they were banned from talking aloud about current affairs, Turgy, Cléry and Madame Élisabeth resorted to the medium of coded hand gestures, all under the watchful eyes of the Tisons, an unpleasant couple who had been brought in to look after (and spy on) the royal family.

The three royal ladies got up at six every morning and in the absence of servants helped each other to dress in the simple morning gowns of plain white cotton and bombazine that had been ordered from Mademoiselle Bertin and their other favourite *modistes*, before Cléry came in to help them simply arrange and lightly powder their hair which they then covered with white linen bonnets. Rather surprisingly, the Assembly had authorised the royal ladies to order a large amount of fashionable new clothes to replace the ones that had been lost in the sack of the Tuileries and Marie Antoinette had taken great pleasure in ordering three new dresses of brown floral toile du jouy and puce and 'Paris mud' coloured taffeta; shoes; linen and muslin shifts; petticoats; capelets in white linen and black taffeta; nine fichus and two white bonnets for herself as well as clothes for Madame Élisabeth and Madame Royale, while the King ordered for himself two pale brown suits, ten pairs of black silk breeches, a black hat and some white waistcoats as well as a riding coat in the once fashionable '*cheveux de la Reine*' shade that had mimicked his wife's strawberry blonde hair that was now so sadly faded and streaked with white.

Marie Antoinette would help the Dauphin to dress and at nine they went to the King's room for a breakfast of hot chocolate, coffee and rolls and jam before they all went downstairs to Marie Antoinette's room where the royal children had their lessons. Marie Antoinette and Madame Élisabeth had taken over the lessons of Madame Royale and did their best to instruct her in religion, music, drawing and maths while Louis took full charge of the Dauphin's education which in their restricted circumstances involved a lot of looking at maps as well as teaching him how to read and write with the help of the books in their limited library.

At midday, the royal ladies went off to change into their day clothes before they went out to take a very heavily guarded walk in the gardens where the little Dauphin could play with his ball or with Marie Antoinette's little dog Thisbée, her gift from the Princesse de Lamballe, until it was time to go in again for luncheon, which was very nearly as lavish as the meals they had been accustomed to in better times with several courses and plenty of meats, cakes and other treats. As usual Marie Antoinette barely touched her food while Louis was observed to have as good an appetite as ever and also enjoyed several glasses of wine and champagne with his meal while Marie Antoinette only ever drank her favourite mineral water from Ville d'Avray, which continued to be supplied to her in prison. After luncheon, the family settled down to a game of backgammon or cards before the King settled down to his four o' clock nap and the royal ladies either knitted, did embroidery or read to each other quietly while Cléry gave the Dauphin his handwriting lesson and took him off to play in Madame Elisabeth's room where he would not disturb the King's sleep.

When Louis woke up, the family would gather together again and either played the clavichord or read aloud to each other until supper, which the children took in Madame Elisabeth's room while the King read them riddles from a book he had come across in the library. There was sometimes a rare treat at around this time in the form of some loyal newspaper vendors who deliberately positioned themselves close to the tower in the evening and called out the latest news, which the family, who otherwise felt themselves almost entirely cut off from the outside world, would strain to hear. After this the royal children would say their prayers then go off to bed escorted by the faithful Cléry, who had been the Dauphin's valet before he was transferred to the service of the King, and the adults would have their supper together, which was often interrupted by the Dauphin who, like many children his age, found it difficult to settle down to sleep and would demand that his aunt and mother come in to sit with him until he nodded off. After supper was over the King would say goodnight to the rest of his family then head off to his study where he would shut the door on his problems and read until late at night. Marie Antoinette and her sister-in-law would then remain together for as long as they could in Madame Élisabeth's room, perhaps reading one of Frances Burney[1]'s two novels *Evelina* and *Cecilia* or a devotional tract to each other or working on their embroidery. Madame Élisabeth, whose thoughts had clearly taken a rather depressed turn, was working on a morbid device of a pansy shaped like a death's head with '*Elle est mon unique pensée*' (This is my only thought) embroidered underneath. They would remain together until the guards came at around eleven to escort the Queen back to her own bedchamber, where she would be locked in for the night.

Despite the enormous strain that the royal family were under, life in the pretty pale blue apartments of the Temple was ordered and intimate and there must have been a small amount of ironic pleasure for the royal captives in the fact that they had finally been granted the quiet family life that they had always so desperately craved while on show at Versailles. The Dauphin in particular flourished thanks to this sudden closeness to his parents, even if the lively little boy was also frustrated by the restrictions of his new life. Louis seemed perfectly content with the new status quo as well and was more than happy to spend hours quietly reading his way through the library that the unfortunate Monsieur de Berthélemy had left behind. He read two hundred and fifty seven books during the next five months and, perhaps rather optimistically, ordered several more.

Meanwhile, Marie Antoinette was intensely worried about the fate of her friends, in particular the Princesse de Lamballe who had been taken off to the La Force prison in the Marais district of the city. During their time at the Temple, Madame de Tourzel and her daughter Pauline had become accustomed to keeping an eye on the always nervous Princesse, who had long been prey to fainting spells and fits which may have been caused by undiagnosed epilepsy. However, Tourzel later noted that while they were in the dank and awful La Force prison Madame de Lamballe had actually '*not been in such good health for a long time*' which seems quite remarkable considering the terrible stress and fear that they must have been existing under. La Force was primarily used to imprison prostitutes and so the three court ladies found themselves assailed day and night by crude songs, jokes and remarks. '*The least chaste ears would have been offended by everything (we) continuously heard, night and day*,' Madame de Tourzel would later recall.

On 2 September, things began to change and their gaoler told them not to leave their cell, warning them that there were rumours that the Prussians and Austrians were advancing on Paris with the result that the streets were becoming restless and even dangerous as mass panic spread throughout the Faubourgs. The aristocratic ladies must have thought themselves relatively safe within their unpleasant but nonetheless reassuringly unassailable prison but forces were already conspiring against them. That night Madame de Tourzel was woken up by a mysterious stranger creeping into their cell. To her alarm he went to the bedside of her young daughter and shook her awake, asking her to come with him at once. Powerless to disobey or indeed make a fuss, Madame de Tourzel instructed the girl to go with the stranger – who luckily for them both turned out to be a Scarlet Pimpernel like rescuer known only to posterity as Monsieur Hardy.

The next morning, Madame de Tourzel and the Princesse de Lamballe prayed for Pauline, whose fate was still unknown, and then climbed up on to the Princesse's bed which afforded them a small view onto the street below, where they saw that there was already a large mob gathered around the prison door. A few hours later, at eleven o clock in the morning, a gaoler came to fetch the Princesse de Lamballe. Madame de Tourzel's presence had not been requested but she decided to accompany her friend all the same. They walked behind the gaoler to the prison records office where a rudimentary court had been set up. The two ladies sat together and watched the proceedings which all followed more or less the same method – the prisoner was briefly interrogated for about ten minutes and then either found innocent with a cry of 'Vive la Nation' or pronounced guilty. The innocent were carried from the prison, congratulated and embraced by all before being whisked away to freedom while the guilty were passed over to a pair of sans culottes who led them out into the courtyard to be summarily despatched by the waiting mob who had armed themselves with whatever rudimentary weaponry they had managed to lay hands upon.

When Madame de Tourzel's turn came, it turned out that the intrepid and mysterious Monsieur Hardy had somehow managed to get the judges and their henchmen so completely drunk that they proclaimed her innocent when she agreed to declare 'Vive la Nation' and he was able to get her away and reunite her with her daughter. She later noted with a certain amount of irony that while she was being handed into the carriage that was waiting to whisk her away, the same blood splattered men who had been murdering her fellow prisoners all day took special care to tell her coachman which route he should take so that she would avoid seeing any of that day's carnage.

However, her friend the Princesse de Lamballe had no brave rescuer on hand and was not to be as fortunate as the Tourzel ladies. To the surprise of absolutely no one, she was found guilty by the tribunal even though she denied any knowledge of treasonous plots emanating from the royal court. She then sealed her fate by refusing to take an oath proclaiming her hatred of the king, queen and monarchy although she accepted the oath of loyalty to Liberty and Equality. She was then led out to the courtyard where the mob awaited her. What happened next is open to some debate. We are all familiar with the horrific accounts of gang rape, evisceration and so on, but did any of this actually really happen? Axel de Fersen was to write to the Duke of Södermanland that '*the Princesse de Lamballe was most fearfully tortured for four hours. My pen jibs at giving details. They tore off her breasts with their teeth and then did all possible, for two whole hours, to force her back to consciousness, to make her death the more agonising.*'

We are told by numerous sources that the Princess was either hit from behind and felled to the ground or run through with a sword and then eviscerated. In an orgy of violence she was then apparently stripped, tortured and terribly mutilated by the gleeful crowd who were keen to enact their loathing of the queen on the body of one of her closest friends. After this her head and according to some accounts also her heart and genitalia were placed on pikes and then paraded through the streets with her naked mutilated body before being waved in front of the windows of the Temple so that Marie Antoinette could see them.

However, later that same day a group of men, including two members of the Parisian National Guard, reported to the administrative office of the Quinze-Vingts Section with what the clerk noted to be '*the headless body of the former princesse de Lamballe, who had just been killed at the Hôtel de La Force.*' The clerk, who must have felt much put upon to be expected to deal with such a gruesome matter, then went on to dispassionately note that the lady's head was elsewhere and also helpfully itemised the contents of her pockets which included '*a gold ring with a bezel of changeable blue stone, in which was some blond hair tied in a love-knot with these words above it: 'Whitened through misery'* which had been sent to her by the Queen after the return from Varennes, '*a sort of double-faced image, on one side representing a bleeding heart surrounded with thorns and pierced by a dagger, with these words below: 'Cor Jesu, salva nos, perimur,' on the other a bleeding heart with a fleur-de-lis above and below the words: 'Cor Mariae unitum cordi Christi*'' and '*a medallion on light blue cloth, on which was painted a bleeding heart pierced by a dagger, embroidered in blue silk*'. There is no mention of mutilation other than decapitation nor any reference to nakedness (the pockets are a clue that the corpse arrived fully dressed) or anything else that fits in with the usual lurid descriptions of the violence enacted against the Princesse. Could it therefore be that they had been exaggerated, perhaps by those loyal to the royal family who wished to discredit their enemies? Shortly afterwards, head and body were reunited and, apparently unimpeded, servants of the Penthièvre family arrived to take them away for proper burial in the family chapel.

Marie Antoinette first became aware of the prison massacres when the royal family's daily walk was cut short on 2 September and they were hurried inside while the now dreaded tocsin began to ring once again to call the populace to arms. The royal family were forced to remain in their rooms for the next few days, enduring the sweltering heat and terrible noise from the crowds outside while their guards were doubled and were even jumpier than usual, well aware that it was only a matter of time before the mob, who had stormed the city's prisons and massacred most of the prisoners, turned their attentions to the most prestigious captives of all. Devoid of all information about what was going on outside, the royal family spent the days in silent anxiety and prayer, tormented by the shouts of the crowd and the sinister grins of their most hostile guards.

Finally, on the 3 September they thought that the end had finally come when they heard shouts and screams from the courtyard below their tower. 'What is happening?' Louis asked one of the guards, who replied that they had brought the head of Madame de Lamballe so that the Queen could give it a kiss. Marie Antoinette screamed and fainted as Cléry sprang forward to close the curtains, sparing her the grisly spectacle of her friend's head stuck on a pike.

Although the royal family were not directly harmed during the prison massacres, they were to mark a turning point in their treatment at the Temple. Although their captors had treated them surprisingly well up until now, matters now took a distinct nose dive as their lives became more uncomfortable and restricted and their guards became increasingly disrespectful and downright hostile, speaking rudely to the King, openly ogling the royal ladies and scrawling crude graffiti about the Queen[2] where the royal children would be sure to see it. Marie Antoinette did her best to stoically ignore all of this as she was still pinning her hopes on an allied victory against the French, heartened by the little snippets of news that Cléry managed to winkle out of the other servants and Turgy gleaned during his trips to the local markets. The Duke of Brunswick's troops had finally crossed the border and the Queen fully expected to hear the news that the French army had been crushed and rescue was on its way.

When a group of officials and guards entered their rooms in the Temple on 21 September, she may well have expected them to come with the news of another French defeat and the imminent fall of Paris to the Austro-Prussian armies but instead was dismayed to learn that they had instead come to inform the prisoners that by order of the Assembly, the monarchy had been abolished, France was now a republic, the National Assembly had been replaced by a National Convention and from now on the King was to be known as simple Louis Capet, a reference to a much older French royal dynasty. To the annoyance of the officials the King greeted this news with an indifferent shrug before he continued reading his book while Marie Antoinette hid her chagrin and continued her embroidery. However, she went off to bed to cry in private as soon as the men had gone. Her deep despair only worsened when the news of the French victory at Valmy and Brunswick's retreat back over the frontier arrived later on.

Just over a week later the officials were back again to confiscate all of the royal family's paper and writing implements (they would later have all sharp objects such as knives and scissors taken away too) and then to take the King away to the main tower of the Temple, an altogether more forbidding place than the comfortable quarters that they had now been inhabiting for well over a month. Marie Antoinette pleaded in vain to be allowed to accompany her husband to his new prison but was told that she must remain where she was. After a few days apart, the family were allowed to take their meals, which were still as extravagant as ever, together again and then after a month they all moved across to the main tower to share the King's imprisonment. Although the family's new quarters were not nearly so comfortable as the ones that they had just left, they were still far from being the miserable, gloomy cells described by later monarchist writers and were actually freshly decorated and furnished and relatively cheerful with blue and green striped wallpaper and pretty flower sprigged fabrics in the room that Marie Antoinette shared with her daughter. However, they were boiling hot in the winter and freezing cold and damp in the autumn and winter, which meant that the royal prisoners fell prey one after the other to colds, fevers and all manner of aches and pains. Madame Élisabeth was stricken with a terrible toothache, while both the Dauphin and the King caught severe colds and had to be nursed by the Queen, who was malnourished and far from well herself.

We get a glimpse of Marie Antoinette in the period after the September Massacres in a painting by the Polish artist Kucharski, who replaced Madame Vigée-Lebrun as the Queen's favourite portrait painter after the latter's flight from France in 1789. It's not known when Kucharski visited the Temple but two paintings exist from this time – the most striking of which was painted at some point after September 1792 and depicts the Queen in mourning for the murdered Princesse de Lamballe. It's a stark and moving piece of work in which Marie Antoinette, who turns huge red rimmed eyes on the viewer, looks closer to sixty than thirty-six and is a complete contrast to the pretty little pouting Dauphine of Drouais' paintings or the majestic matron depicted by Vigée Le Brun. However, dejected though she clearly is, there is still defiance in that erect carriage and a hint of challenge in that unsettlingly direct gaze. The Queen's rather luxurious garments make an interesting and rather startling contrast to the bleak misery of her expression though: she wears a very lovely flounced, lace trimmed and beribboned cap on her powdered hair and the fichu that she wears over her plain black taffeta gown is exquisitely embroidered and almost certainly one of the ones that she ordered from Rose Bertin after moving to the Temple.

While the royal family got used to their increasingly restrictive imprisonment, the deputies at the National Convention were continuing to row about what to do with the now deposed King with the Jacobins and several others being in full favour of putting Louis on trial. Louis Antoine de Saint-Just, Robespierre's handsome but entirely charmless left hand man argued in early November that the King was an enemy of France who must either 'reign or die' and added that 'no man can reign innocently'. A point of view that seemed entirely justified when just over a week later Louis' secret strong box was discovered in its hiding place in the Tuileries where he had hurriedly stashed it just before leaving the palace for the last time. When opened, the box was found to contain voluminous correspondence between the former King and various foreign powers, his brothers, several counter-revolutionaries and, most disturbingly of all, Mirabeau who was still being hailed by many as a hero of the revolution but was now revealed to be a two-faced schemer who sold his republican principles out in return for some royal gold and a chance to kiss the Queen's hand. However, Mirabeau was already dead and safe from the vengeance of the Convention and Parisian mob and so it was Louis who bore the full brunt of their fury as his duplicity was publicly unveiled in all its glory and the contents of his letters revealed what everyone had suspected all along – that he was a traitor to France who had betrayed his own people by putting on a show of being a true patriot while all the time he apparently had been egging the country's enemies on and encouraging them to invade.

At the start of December Cléry, who was now the family's sole source of information from outside, let them know that the Convention was planning to put Louis on trial. Marie Antoinette, who was already barely sleeping and eating and had become a thin, anxious shadow of her former self, was distraught at the thought of her husband being taken away but Louis was much more sanguine even though he knew that a trial would almost certainly end with his execution. On 11 December, the King had lunch with his family and then started to play a game with his son before being interrupted by the entrance of several guardsmen and the Mayor of Paris who informed him that he was to be taken away. Cléry went at once to the Queen to tell her that her husband had been taken to the Convention but any hopes that she may have had that he would be returned to them at the end of the day were cruelly dashed when Louis failed to come back to their rooms and she was brusquely informed by the guards that he was forbidden to have any contact with his family until the end of the trial. Louis had, in fact, been told that he could have Madame Royale and the little Dauphin live with him in his rooms below those of the Queen so long as the children didn't see their mother and aunt but Louis, although he would have loved to have had their company, refused to separate them from their mother and so lived alone in his rooms at the Temple, totally cut off from the rest of his family whom he could hear walking about overhead but was unable to communicate with, for the next six weeks.

He wasn't even allowed to see them on Madame Royale's fourteenth birthday on 19 December or on Christmas Day, which caused them all great distress. Marie Antoinette spent the day in tears while Louis, completely resigned to his fate, sat down and wrote his last will and testament with the future fate of his family, particularly his wife, clearly very much on his mind. '*I recommend my children to my wife. I have never doubted her tenderness as a mother. I particularly recommend her to raise them as good Christians, promote their minds to virtue, make them regard worldly pomps, if they are condemned to experience them, as a perilous and transitory heritage, and to deflect their thoughts to the only solid and lasting glory, that of eternity. I entreat my sister to continue her love for my children, and to be their mother should they tragically be deprived of their own.*' He then added: '*I entreat my wife to forgive me all the evils now inflicted upon her because of me, and whatever troubles I may have caused her throughout our marriage; as she may be absolutely certain that I secrete nothing against her, should she imagine anything with which to reproach myself.*' To his lawyer, Malesherbes he admitted sadly that his wife '*was a child when she first came to France and had no one to help her, not even my own relatives.*'

Louis was sentenced to death by a small majority on 16 January and to his distress he learned that his own cousin the Duc d'Orléans, who now preferred to be known as Philippe Égalité, was amongst those who had voted for his death. There was still a slim chance that he might be reprieved and perhaps banished from the country instead but this was rejected and on the afternoon of Sunday 20 January, Louis was given the news that he was to be guillotined the very next morning. His distressed family had had very little news of him for the last six weeks other than a few coded messages from Cléry and a few of their more sympathetic guards, the ones who didn't shove their fingers into their bread to search it for hidden letters or deliberately blow pipe smoke in their faces. Marie Antoinette found the long weeks of separation deeply distressing and spent most of her time in floods of tears as she fretted about her husband. It was the longest time that they had been separated since she first came to France and she missed him terribly.

Marie Antoinette and Madame Élisabeth learned of Louis' death sentence from the news vendors outside the Temple who shouted the news up to the tower where they were being held. At first the Convention decreed that the former King should not be allowed to see his family before he was taken away to die but then relented and agreed that he could be reunited with them for one last time. At eight in the evening the family were escorted downstairs to Louis' rooms by a group of guardsmen and some officials who were supposed to keep an eye on the family but were so distressed by the dreadful sobs of the royal family as they clung together that they turned their backs to give them some much needed privacy.

Marie Antoinette clung to her husband for the next two hours, crying piteously. Although they had never been lovers in the romantic sense, she had grown to love and care for Louis, the shy, awkward boy that she had first met in a sunny clearing at Compiègne less than twenty three years before, most sincerely and the thought of carrying on without him was completely devastating. She begged him to let them stay with him for the night so that they could have a little more time together but Louis gently refused, telling her that he wanted to be alone so that he could properly prepare himself for death. When she continued to plead with him, he relented and promised that he would send for them to come and see him before he left the next morning so that they could say a proper last goodbye. 'Do you promise?' Marie Antoinette asked, still crying. 'I promise,' her husband said.

He did not send for them. Unable to bear the distress of his children and unwilling to make his family, whom he loved more than life itself, suffer the horror of saying a last goodbye, he went to his death without seeing them again. 'Tell the Queen, my dear children and my sister that I had promised to see them this morning, but that I wanted to spare them the pain of such a cruel separation,' he told Cléry before he left the Temple for the last time, handing him his wedding ring and seal. 'It grieves me very much to go without receiving their last embraces and so I give to you the task of making my farewells. Please tell my wife that I leave her with sorrow.' He left just before nine in the morning in a closed carriage. His wife waited in the rooms above for the summons that never came, refusing all food and sustenance before dressing in white, the traditional colour of mourning for the Queens of France, and lying down on her bed where she cried helplessly for the next hour until the cheers and shouts of the crowds outside told her that the deed had been done. 'The monsters!' Madame Élisabeth cried, distraught with grief as her niece screamed with distress, knowing that her father was dead. 'I hope that they are satisfied now.'

Marie Antoinette was completely devastated by her husband's death and according to her daughter fell into a 'near catatonic state', refusing to eat or leave her room, getting barely any sleep and sitting in total silence for hours on end. Already thin, she now became absolutely scrawny to the extent that she was virtually unrecognisable and looked much older than her thirty-seven years while her hair, which she was always prone to lose in times of stress, began to fall out in handfuls. In vain did her family implore her to eat, sleep and get some exercise but it seemed as if life had lost all meaning for the beleaguered former Queen. Gradually though she became to recover, buoyed up by the fact that her children, particularly little Louis Charles who was now hailed by the faithful remaining monarchists as King Louis XVII, still needed her. She requested black taffeta mourning apparel for herself and her family and some additional chic black accessories from Rose Bertin: a fan, two pairs of kid-skin gloves, one pair of silk gloves, three fichus and two rather fetching mourning bonnets with trailing black ribbons. The intrepid artist Kucharski returned, disguised as a guardsman, to the Temple at about this time and sketched what was to be the final portrait of the Queen, broken but never beaten, looking mournful in her mourning clothes.

The conditions in which the prisoners were kept gradually worsened over the next few months as their living quarters became more restricted with Marie Antoinette and her children jammed in one room, Madame Élisabeth in another, their warders, the Tisons, in a third and two guards on constant duty in a fourth. Their meals were no longer quite so splendid as they had been while Louis was still alive, not that Marie Antoinette noticed for she wasn't eating much anyway. They had also lost the services of the faithful Cléry, who was dismissed after Louis' execution and banished from the Temple. Their unhealthy lifestyle began to quickly take its toll on the already thoroughly demoralised prisoners and a doctor eventually had to be called in to look at Madame Royale, who developed painful ulcers on her leg, and also her mother who was now so weak that she was prone to fainting fits and had also begun to suffer terrible haemorrhages, caused either by stress, early menopause, fibroids or something much more sinister. Although several of the guards delighted in being as rude and insolent as possible towards the royal family, they were not all bad and one in particular called Goret seems to have taken them under his wing. He tried to persuade the Queen to eat and even nagged her into going outside to take some exercise. 'I don't want to walk past the door that my husband crossed for the last time,' Marie Antoinette protested, only for Goret to suggest that instead of going down to the gardens she should go up to the top of the tower where there was plenty of room to walk about and she would not have to go past her husband's door.

Completely cut off from the world, Marie Antoinette had no way of knowing that the execution of her husband had sent shock waves through all of Europe and that the very next day England had declared war on France. She did not know that Axel de Fersen was equally devastated by Louis' death and terrified that a similarly brutal fate awaited the rest of the royal family, had been travelling from court to court trying to get support for another escape attempt. Mercifully she also didn't know just how uninterested her own family, whom she assumed would be pulling all possible strings to save her, were in getting her out of the Temple although her sisters Maria Carolina and Maria Amalia were frantic with worry about her and would have undoubtedly helped if they could.

However, the long, dark, miserable days in the Temple tower were lightened by a vague hope of rescue when another sympathetic guard Toulan joined forces with the Chevalier de Jarjayes, a monarchist and passionate admirer of the Queen, whose wife had managed to get inside the Temple disguised as a laundrywoman. Enlisting a second faithful guard Lepître, they formulated a plan to whisk the disguised royal family away from Paris and take them by carriage to the Normandy coast where they could set sail for England. They had the funds to pay all the necessary bribes and had theoretically even managed to secure false passports but their plans went sadly and catastrophically awry when the increasing unrest in Paris caused the city barriers to be closed and forced the authorities to increase their vigilance over the royal family. Lepître, who had always been the weakest link in the plan, lost his nerve at this point and backed out but the undaunted Jarjayes and Toulan now tried to persuade Marie Antoinette, who was rightly judged to be the most endangered member of the royal family, to leave alone without her sister-in-law and children. However, although Madame Royale and Madame Élisabeth begged her to take this chance, she refused to leave and sadly wrote to Jarjayes that: '*We have dreamt a pleasant dream, that is all… I know that you have my interests at heart and that the chance we are now missing may never come again. But I should never have a moment's happiness if I abandoned my children. And therefore I have no regret.*'

Toulan and Lepître were dismissed shortly afterwards thanks to the Tisons, who spied on the royal family and reported the two guards for behaving in a suspiciously familiar way around them. The defeated Jarjayes, deeply distressed to have been unable to rescue the Queen, left Paris but thanks to Toulan he took with him Louis XVI's wedding ring and seal which were destined for the Comte de Provence and Comte d'Artois, who were still in exile abroad. He also had a message for Fersen as well as a printed impression of the words on a signet ring that he had given to Marie Antoinette in exchange for one of her own rings. '*They are more true than ever*,' the Queen sadly told Jarjayes before his departure. '*Tutto a te mi guida*.' Everything leads me to you.

Frustrated and depressed, the royal ladies now took solace in their books, spending hours reading the religious tracts that they had with them and forgoing the light hearted society novels of Frances Burney that they had enjoyed before the King's execution. Marie Antoinette's only thoughts nowadays were for her son, who was now eight years old. He had become sickly and understandably fractious thanks to the close confinement of the royal family and although his mother and aunt did their best to continue his lessons, he was clearly in need of a proper tutor and a lot more exercise and stimulation. The Convention evidently agreed but instead of appointing someone worthy of the task like the philosopher and mathematician Condorcet who offered his services, they instead decided to place him under the guardianship of Simon, a former shoemaker who was now employed as general factotum at the Temple where he ran errands for the royal family and oversaw their treatment. Their reasoning was that the boy needed to have all of his royal pretensions drummed out of him and what better way to do this than to have him brought up by a proper man of the people.

On the evening of 3 July, several officials came to the Queen's room where the boy was already asleep in his bed and his mother, aunt and sister were quietly reading together. The family had been enduring random night time searches since the King's death and at first assumed that this was yet another such imposition until one of the men stepped forward and began to read out the official decree from the Convention which announced that Marie Antoinette and her son were to be separated and from now on the boy would reside in the former King's rooms downstairs where he was to be looked after by Simon and his wife. Horrified, the Queen took her son, who had woken up crying, into her arms and refused to hand him over, finally only relenting when the officers threatened to use force if she didn't let them take the boy away.

Weeping, Marie Antoinette then dressed her son for the last time and gave him one final kiss before the officers took the sobbing, terrified boy away from his family. For the next few days they could hear him crying in his rooms downstairs as he begged to be taken back to his mother. However, although royalist legend paints the Simon couple as cruel monsters who mistreated the boy King terribly, they were not nearly so bad as they have been painted and, admittedly in their own rough way, even treated him with a certain amount of brusque kindness even if they followed the instructions of the Convention to the letter and did their best to transform the little princeling into a 'child of the nation' by teaching him revolutionary songs, giving him the occasional sip of alcohol and encouraging him to use rough language and swear. His guards were also kind and relatively indulgent to the boy and tried their best to cheer him up until finally the tears that his family could hear gave way to boyish laughter and the cheerful singing of republican songs.

Already shattered by the death of her husband, Marie Antoinette was almost completely destroyed by the loss of her son, her *chou d'amour*, whom she had cherished and idolised ever since the moment of his birth. For days she could only listlessly lie on her bed, weeping constantly and straining to hear his voice in the rooms below. When Madame Élisabeth realised that they could catch brief glimpses of the boy playing in the gardens from an arrow slit on the stairs that led to the top of the tower, she roused herself and went up the stairs to keep watch, hoping to see her son for herself. For the rest of her stay in the Temple this became her chief occupation and only pleasure in a life that was otherwise devoid of all happiness. As her daughter would later recollect: '*living and dying had become all the same to her*.'

Chapter 14

The Martyr 1793

'Everything leads me to you.'

As Marie Antoinette sank into a deep depression that neither her daughter nor sister-in-law could rouse her from, she had absolutely no idea of the forces that were ranging against her in the outside world. Another failed escape attempt planned by the Baron de Batz put the authorities on high alert and had the effect of tightening surveillance on the three women cooped up in their tower rather than, as had been hoped, liberating them. Attempts were also made by members of the Convention to negotiate an exchange of the former Queen for French prisoners but these also came to nothing thanks to the apathy of her nephew, the Austrian Emperor. It was a series of defeats against the rapidly advancing Austrian-Prussian forces, however, that eventually forced the hand of the Convention when it came to the fate of their former Queen. Calls were made to have the 'Austrian Woman' tried for her crimes against the nation and so the decision was made to have her separated from her remaining family and taken into closer confinement while a case was prepared against her.

At 2am on the morning of 2 August, the prisoners were woken by a loud hammering on the door to their rooms at the Temple before a group of officials and guardsmen entered and informed the terrified women, who had been in bed and were dressed only in their nightclothes, that they had come to take 'Widow Capet' away to the Conciergerie. The men then watched as Madame Élisabeth, with shaking fingers and many tears, dressed her sister-in-law for the last time before begging in vain to be allowed to go with her and share her prison – a request that was denied. Marie Antoinette then had her pockets roughly searched and was permitted to give her daughter one last tearful embrace before she picked up the small bundle of belongings that she had been allowed to hastily throw together and left forever. She struck her head on a doorframe as she walked out of the Temple for the last time, after passing by the closed door behind which her son lay asleep and through which her husband had left for his execution. 'Never mind,' she murmured in response to one of the officers who asked if she was alright. 'Nothing can hurt me now.'

It was still the dead of night when Marie Antoinette was taken by carriage across the slumbering city to the Conciergerie on the Quai d'Horloge. She had doubtless seen the forbidding old palace countless times over the years but had almost certainly never once set foot inside the older parts of the building which were used as a prison and currently housed around three hundred prisoners. Once as pretty as a fairytale castle in a Medieval book of hours, its age blackened towers had long since taken on a more sinister aspect as they loomed gloomily over the murky Seine. Marie Antoinette would have seen none of this though as her carriage pulled up in the courtyard and her guards led her inside the prison where the turnkey Larivière was waiting to take her to her cell. First though she had to be entered in the register. 'Look at me,' Marie Antoinette, now formally designated as 'Prisoner 280', said when the nervous young registrar asked for her name.

She was then taken to her new quarters – a cell that recently briefly housed General de Custine[1]. It had formerly been used as the Council Chamber of the old palace and was fifteen square metres inside and very meagerly furnished with just a table, two chairs, a bucket and a camp bed which the jailor's kindhearted wife Madame Richard had made up with her own best linen and some lace edged pillows. Madame Richard and her shy young maid Rosalie Lamorlière were to have the chief care of Marie Antoinette and filled with understandable curiosity, hastened to greet her as soon as she arrived in her cell. There they found the Queen hanging her little watch, a present from her mother that she had brought with her from Vienna all those years ago, from a nail protruding from the wall. Along with her wedding ring, a diamond ring and a locket containing her children's hair, it was one of the few jewels that still remained to her from the fabulous collection that she had once commanded as Queen of France.

Overawed to be in the Queen's presence, Rosalie shyly asked Marie Antoinette if she needed help to undress. It was just after three in the morning and the exhausted Queen, whose sickly and bedraggled appearance shocked the other two women who had no idea just how much she had changed over the past twelve months, was obviously in need of some sleep. 'Thank you but no,' she said gently to Rosalie. 'I will look after myself from now on.'

After the relatively tranquil life that she had experienced at the Temple, it must have been a shock to Marie Antoinette to find herself in an actual prison. Although she was kept in strict isolation and forbidding from mixing with the other prisoners, Marie Antoinette would still have been able to hear them chattering and laughing in the corridors and singing popular songs out in the women's yard, where they gathered every day. Perhaps it even lifted her depressed spirits just a little to know that she was not entirely alone and to be able to feel for the first time in months as if life, even if she couldn't see it, was still going on around her.

She continued her habit of getting up at six every morning, after which Rosalie would bring her a breakfast of coffee and rolls and help her to dress. Shortly after her arrival a parcel had arrived from Madame Élisabeth containing some fine lace edged underclothes, black stockings, fichus, caps, a white dress and a pair of satin shoes, which meant that the former Queen was still able to array herself with relative elegance even if her wardrobe was a long way off the sumptuous one that she had enjoyed in her glorious heyday at Versailles. Her enormous wardrobe had once filled entire rooms beneath the eaves of the palace but was now so small that it could be kept in a small cardboard box donated by the kind hearted Rosalie and was darned, patched and mended over and over again by the turnkey's mother Madame Larivière rather than an army of maids and seamstresses. To her credit though, Marie Antoinette rarely uttered a word of complaint and expressed no regret about a way of life that she now had to accept was vanished forever. Instead, she calmly accepted everything that happened to her, enduring changes of guards, stricter rules, searches and interrogation without protest and with every appearance of quiet resignation.

Isolated from the other prisoners and seeing only a few people, Marie Antoinette found the long hours difficult to fill although Rosalie and Madame Richard did their best to cheer her up with little chats (they would eke out their tasks as long as possible in the evening to delay the moment when the Queen would be left alone for the night), occasional presents of flowers and even some treasured rare snippets of news about her children. Forbidden to possess paper or writing implements, the woman who had once found reading such a terrible chore now devoured the few books that she had been allowed to bring with her. In the Temple she had enjoyed the translated light hearted novels of Frances Burney but in the Conciergerie she showed a marked preference for travel memoirs such as *The Stories of Famous Shipwrecks* and *The Travels of Captain Cook*, which allowed her captive imagination to fly free of her damp and mouldy cell walls during the long, empty hours of confinement.

Both Madame Richard and Rosalie were excellent cooks and did their best to tempt the Queen's waning appetite with special little treats to supplement the simple diet of roast chicken, vegetables and noodle bouillon soup which she existed on. They were aided in this by several market women who insisted upon donating choice morsels such as the plumpest chickens and sweetest grapes to the Queen's table. Her supply of Ville d'Avray mineral water also continued, much to her relief as the weather became unbearably hot and made the conditions inside the Conciergerie intolerably humid and malodorous, so much so that Rosalie had to burn juniper in Marie Antoinette's cell to hide the terrible smell that seemed to saturate the mouldering stone walls of the old prison by the Seine. While her guards would on occasion volunteer to scrape off the mould that grew on the bottom of the Queen's shoes.

Two guards kept watch over her at all times of the day and night and a small screen was provided to conceal her when she got dressed and undressed and performed her natural bodily functions, which were made more difficult now by the increasingly dreadful haemorrhages that she was enduring. As usual she was quietly courteous to her keepers and for the most part they returned her politeness and did their best not to invade her privacy. However, her main jailor Monsieur Richard was not averse to making a bit of extra money out of his most famous prisoner and soon had a healthy little sideline going in charging people to come in and take a peek at the former Queen in her miserable little cell. Marie Antoinette was accustomed to being stared at and would sit in impassive silence, focusing all of her attention on her books or the backgammon and card games that the guards would play to while away the long hours and making no attempt to speak to these random visitors who came to gawp at her. She even managed to maintain her silence when some of these unwelcome visitors quietly offered to help her escape.

She paid a little more attention though when one gentleman visitor, the Chevalier Rougeville whom she had briefly met at the Tuileries during the terrifying invasion on 20 June 1792, threw a clandestine note wrapped around a carnation on the floor of her cell as he was leaving, offering her enough money to bribe her way out of the Conciergerie should she wish to make an attempt to escape in a carriage which he would endeavour to have waiting for her outside the prison. Marie Antoinette tried to reply by picking out a message with a pin but the plan was quickly discovered after one of her guards blew the whistle and it all came to nothing. Rougeville fled the city and once again it was Marie Antoinette who bore the brunt of the failure of others when she endured an arduous and humiliating two day interrogation, had her mother's watch and few remaining pieces of jewellery confiscated and lost the right to have light in her cell after dusk. When the investigation was over it was decided that Marie Antoinette should be moved to a more secure cell and the Richard couple replaced by Monsieur and Madame Bault, who were judged to be far less indulgent and could be relied upon to put a stop to the stream of visitors to the Queen's cell. However, although they were more strict than the departed Richard couple, the Baults were also extremely kind in their own way and did their best to make Marie Antoinette's life as comfortable as possible by making sure that she still got decent food and had fresh linen, often risking official censure in the process.

Marie Antoinette was moved to her new cell on 11 September. It was the former dispensary of the prison and still smelt strongly of medicines, which wasn't helped by the fact that the one window, which overlooked the women's yard, was permanently closed to prevent conversations between the Queen and the female inmates, some of whom she had known in happier times. She could still hear them though as they gathered outside to do their meagre laundry in the giant stone tub in the corner of the yard every morning and took their dinner together in the afternoon, chattering, laughing and singing as if they hadn't a care in the world as it was considered very bad form to show the least sign of fear of apprehension about the fact that you were facing certain death on the scaffold. Not for nothing was the Conciergerie known as the Guillotine's Waiting Room as prisoners were brought there from the other prisons in Paris and beyond when it was time for them to face trial and then almost certain death on the scaffold.

The other prisoners spent a great deal of time speculating about the former Queen whom everyone knew was locked up alongside them, wondering what sort of conditions she lived under and whether she would ever be allowed to walk free or even just fraternise with everyone else. Marie Antoinette also wondered if she would ever be able to leave her prison and confided to Rosalie that she still had faith that her nephew would somehow manage to negotiate her release, little knowing that he had more or less washed his hands of her predicament and she was not considered of enough diplomatic importance to exchange for prisoners – although some desultory attempts had been made to negotiate her release, all of which had come to nothing. While the Queen waited and prayed for her relatives to come to her rescue, her fate was eventually sealed during a secret late night meeting at the Committee of Public Safety, during which it was decided that Marie Antoinette should be put on trial and then executed as her husband had been.

Meanwhile, her eight-year-old son was caught playing with his genitals, a common enough pastime for boys of his age and one that his mother and aunt had frequently tried to put a stop to. Ashamed, the boy, whose habit of lying to get out of trouble had often exasperated his mother and governess, told his 'guardian' Simon that he had been taught to do so by his mother and aunt. Delighted by this revelation, Simon scurried off to let Jacques-René Hébert, Marie Antoinette's greatest enemy and editor of the scurrilous newspaper Le Père Duchesne, know what had happened, clearly believing that here at last they had some concrete evidence of the former Queen's famous debauchery. The unfortunate Louis Charles persisted in his tale when interrogated at length by a group of officials although he was, rather tellingly, unable to provide much in the way of actual details other than a vague reference to it happening in the mornings when either his mother or aunt would take him into their beds. He was even sufficiently buoyed along by the extremely gratifying interest that the officials were taking in his tale to persist in his allegations when confronted by his sister and aunt, both of whom naturally denied that any such thing had ever occurred. In fact, the gently reared and innocent Marie Thérèse did not even understand what any of them were talking about. Her aunt Madame Élisabeth did though and furiously turned on the unrepentant boy, calling him a 'little monster'.

Marie Antoinette was woken up in the early hours of 12 October and taken to a secret cross examination in the court room of the Palais du Justice, which formed part of the Conciergerie complex and where the Kings of France, including her own husband, had once held their formal *lit de justice* meetings. Here she was confronted by Hermann, the President of the Revolutionary Tribunal, Fouquier-Tinville, the Public Prosecutor and a clerk called Fabricius. The exhausted Queen was then assailed by a barrage of accusations that dredged up virtually every calumny, real and imagined, that she had ever been charged with. She was accused of encouraging her husband in his treachery against the French people, of sending money to her brother in Austria and of encouraging the counter-revolutionary movement, all of which Marie Antoinette strenuously denied. Realising that they were getting nowhere, Hermann and Fouquier-Tinville brought the session to an end and asked the Queen if she would like them to appoint two defence lawyers for her trial which they informed her was due to begin in two days time. Marie Antoinette agreed to this and was taken back to her cell where she was visited the following day by her newly appointed defence: Tronçon-Ducoudray and Chauveau-Lagarde, who had unsuccessfully defended Charlotte Corday[2] a few months earlier.

Both men were rather thrown by the almost indecent haste with which the trial was being put together and immediately beseeched the Queen to write to the Revolutionary Tribunal and beg them to delay the trial by a few days so that they would have time to put together a proper defence. They both knew, of course, that Marie Antoinette was already doomed and that the trial was just a charade intended to blacken the Queen's name even further while at the same time appeasing her relatives by giving the whole miserable episode at least the vaguest semblance of justice. However, they still couldn't believe that they hadn't been given more time to look at all the relevant documents, especially as preparations for the King's trial had gone on for months. Marie Antoinette grudgingly agreed to write to the Tribunal but her letter was completely ignored and she was escorted from her cell the following morning, Monday 14 October, as planned.

Once again Marie Antoinette was taken through the prison to the court room, which this time was packed to the rafters with people – an off-putting and doubtless nervewracking sight after so many months of solitary confinement. The judges in their heavy black robes and medallions saying 'La Loi' were already arrayed in their seats along with a hastily assembled and decidedly shady looking jury, while the rest of the hall was crammed with a great noisy mob of spectators who had come to get a glimpse of the former Queen. If they had been expecting the haughty mistress of Versailles to appear in their midst then they must have been exceedingly shocked when instead a wan faced woman in black widow's weeds, aged almost beyond all recognition by her terrible experiences walked slowly and with the heavy tread of someone in terrible pain into the room and took her place opposite Hermann and Fouquier-Tinville. Wracked by another haemorrhage, the Queen was suffering terrible abdominal cramps and was so weak with pain that she could not stand for long periods of time and indeed sank gratefully into the waiting armchair after she had taken her oath, giving her age as 'almost thirty eight' which must have stunned the onlookers who saw what appeared to be an elderly woman in front of them. She drummed her fingers on the arms of her chair as the clerk of court read out the indictment, which had dredged the worst depths of the libellous pamphlets about Marie Antoinette to come up with a distorted tissue of lies, misrepresentations and calumny.

The following cross examination was not much better as over forty witnesses stepped up to add further lurid colour to the Tribunal's indictment, repeating every dreadful lie that they had heard about the Queen and making up a few more besides. The hapless Marie Antoinette was accused of leading her husband astray, of plotting to murder the Duc d'Orléans, of smuggling vast sums of money out of the country to her brother and a whole other array of alleged crimes. With a deft mixture of contempt and humility, the Queen defended herself against every charge but fell silent when Hébert stood up to deliver a denunciation that included mention of Louis Charles' accusations towards his mother, adding that, 'this criminal sexual intercourse was not dictated by pleasure, but by the calculated expectation of enervating the physical condition of the child, whom they still liked to think of as destined to occupy a throne and over whose mind, therefore, they wanted to be sure of having power… Now that the child has been taken from the mother, he has become healthy and strong.'

When one of the jury members heartlessly prodded the Queen for a response to Hébert's monstrous charge, she stood up and with tears in her eyes replied that, 'If I did not reply, it is because nature refuses to answer such a charge against a mother.' She then turned towards the crowd that had gathered in the courtroom, many of whom were female. 'I appeal to every mother here.' There was a stunned silence followed by a roar of indignation from the spectators who harangued Hébert, the judges and the jury for trying to blacken the Queen's reputation with what was obviously a horrible lie. They had come with the full intention of seeing the former Queen condemned to death but this, it seemed, was a step too far even for them and Hermann was forced to stop the trial for several minutes so that order could be restored. Meanwhile, Marie Antoinette turned to one of her defence lawyers and anxiously asked if perhaps her reply had not been too dignified. 'Madame,' he replied kindly, 'just be yourself and you will always be perfect.'

There was a brief break at half past four during which Marie Antoinette had a few mouthfuls of soup before she was once again forced to take her place on the stand and listen as more witnesses were called in to discredit her. The fifteen hour long session finally came to an end at ten in the evening when the exhausted Marie Antoinette, barely able to walk due to blood loss and terrible agonising cramps, was escorted wearily back to her cell for the night. She was back in court again at eight the next morning, the guards coming to collect her before Rosalie had even had a chance to serve her breakfast. Again terribly weakened by pain and loss of blood, the Queen faced her accusers and the enormous crowd without any form of sustenance until the afternoon break when Rosalie made her some bouillon soup which alas was mostly lost when one of the guardsmen let his girlfriend give it to the Queen instead and the star-struck girl was so nervous that she managed to spill most of it down herself on the way.

The second session followed much the same lines as the first with the same miserable parade of lying, embellishing witnesses and the vicious cross examination of the judges who were doggedly determined to run her into the ground. Marie Antoinette listened in dispassionate silence to their questions and denied everything when prompted for a response. She was even interrogated about the Diamond Necklace Affair and yet again denied having ever met Madame de la Motte-Valois[3] or having any involvement whatsoever in the incident. Much was made of her alleged extravagances at the Petit Trianon and also the huge financial rewards that she had showered upon the Polignac family but time and time again they returned to the same old theme – that Marie Antoinette had been the true power behind the throne of France and a malign and scheming influence on her husband Louis who, in a reversal of the accusations levelled against him at his own trial, was now portrayed as a weak minded and susceptible fool for the purposes of fully incriminating his wife for his alleged crimes against the French people.

Finally at the very end, the Queen was asked if she had anything that she wished to say in her defence. 'I will finish by observing that I was only the wife of Louis XVI and I had to submit to his will,' she said with quiet dignity. There was a brief adjournment before Fouquier-Tinville made his closing statement, declaring her to be 'the avowed enemy of the French nation' who had syphoned off the country's assets to be disposed of amongst her friends, Austrian family and upon her own extravagant excesses as well as being the chief architect of the bloody unrest that had soiled the first years of the glorious revolution and furthermore imposing her own stronger will upon that of her feeble and apathetic husband King Louis, enticing him with her womanly wiles into betraying the interests of his people. Her lawyers then took the stand and did their best to present a case for the defence but they were utterly unprepared and completely dispirited by the knowledge that nothing they could say would make the slightest bit of difference to what was an obviously completely rigged trial. Nonetheless they put up such a reasonably spirited defence of their client that she was moved to thank them both before she was escorted out, doubtless aware that both men had put their own lives[4] at risk by doing so.

After Marie Antoinette had left the court room, Hermann took the floor once again to sum up all the evidence, such as it was, for the jurors who were then asked to consider if they believed that Marie Antoinette had plotted and conspired with foreign powers, counter-revolutionaries and émigrés and given them monetary assistance with the aim of helping them invade France, cause a civil war and overthrow the republic. No actual proof of any such activities had been given and the Queen herself had most strenuously denied these allegations, even though she *had* indeed done so although not to the extent suggested by the prosecution in her trial, but the Tribunal were not going to let these minor details stand in their way. Hermann ended by reminding the jurors that they were making history by putting the Queen on trial. 'Nature and reason, outraged for so long, are finally satisfied as equality triumphs. A woman once surrounded with all the brilliant splendour that royal pride and slavish servility had been able to invent, today occupies in the National Tribunal the place occupied two days ago by another woman, and this equality assures her impartial justice. This matter, citizen jurors, is not one of those in which a single deed, a single crime, is submitted to your conscience and intelligence. You have to judge the accused's entire political career since she came to sit beside the last King of the French.'

At three in the morning, the jury went off for an hour to pretend to deliberate before Marie Antoinette was brought back into the court room. She had given her lawyers the impression that she expected to be deported and they had gently let her go on thinking this even though it was clear to everyone else where the trial was inexorably heading. Shattered but still dignified she listened in impassive silence as Hermann announced that she had been found guilty on all counts and Fouquier-Tinville informed her that she had been sentenced to death and would be executed later that morning. When asked if she had anything to say, Marie Antoinette simply shook her head and was observed to look stunned but not afraid as, flanked by guards, she made her way slowly out of the court room, lifting her chin proudly as she ignored the cheers and catcalls of the spectators who now rushed out into the chill morning air and raced to the Place de la Révolution in order to secure the best spots around the scaffold.

It was half past four in the morning and outside the damp walls of the Conciergerie the first purple and pink glimmers of the approaching dawn were starting to appear above the slumbering city. Completely shattered and weakened by lack of food, pain and blood loss, Marie Antoinette stumbled on the steps leading down to the cells and a young guardsman called Louis-François de Busne took hold of her elbow to steady her then, with a courtesy that she had not seen for a very long time, politely removed his hat and offered her his arm for the rest of the way. He would be denounced and arrested [5]the next day for this kindness.

There were candles, paper and a pen waiting for her in her cell when she got back, the first time she had been allowed writing materials and light for several months. Unable to sleep, desperately lonely and crying with fear and longing for her children, Marie Antoinette sat down and pulled the paper towards her, words tumbling through her mind as she considered who to write to before finally settling upon her sister-in-law Madame Élisabeth who was still imprisoned in the Temple. Sadly, the letter was never to reach her as it was stolen by Robespierre, who hid it beneath his mattress along with other relics of the royal family.

> '*It is to you, my sister, that I write for the last time. I have just been condemned, not to a shameful death, for it is shameful only for criminals, but to rejoin your brother. Like him innocent, I hope to display the same firmness as he did in his last moments. I am calm, as one is when one's conscience holds no reproach. I regret deeply having to abandon my poor children. You know that I lived only for them and for you, my good and kind sister. In what a situation do I leave you, who from your affection sacrificed everything to be with us. I learned from the pleadings at the trial that my daughter was separated from you. Alas! Poor child, I dare not write to her, she would not receive it. I do not know even if this will reach you. Receive my blessing on them both. I hope that one day, when they are older, they will be able to join you again and profit to the full from your tender*

care and that they both remember what I have always tried to instil in them: that the principles and the execution of their duty should be the chief foundation of their life, that their affection and mutual trust will make it happy.

Let my daughter remember that in view of her age she should always help her brother with the advice that her greater experience and her affection may suggest, and let them both remember that in whatever situation they may find themselves they will never be truly happy unless united. Let them learn from our example how much consolation our affection has brought us in the midst of our unhappiness and how happiness is doubled when one can share it with a friend – and where can one find a more loving and truer friend than in one's own family? Let my son never forget his father's last words, which I distinctly repeat to him, never try to avenge our death. I have to mention something which pains my heart. I know how much distress this child must have given you. Forgive him, my dear sister, remember his age and how easy it is to make a child say anything you want, even something he does not understand. The day will come, I hope, when he will be all the more conscious of the worth of your goodness and tenderness towards them both. I now have only to confide in you my final thoughts. I would have liked to write them at the beginning of the trial, but apart from the fact that I was not allowed to write, everything went so quickly that I really would not have had the time.

I die in the Catholic, Apostolic and Roman religion, in the religion of my father, in which I was brought up and which I have always professed, having no expectation of spiritual consolation, and not even knowing if there still exists any priests of that religion here, and in any case the place where I am would expose them to too much danger if they should enter. I sincerely beg pardon of God for all the faults I have committed during my life. I hope that in His goodness He will receive my last wishes, and those I have long since made, that He will receive my soul in His mercy and goodness. I ask pardon of all those I know, and of you my sister in particular, for all the distress I may, without wishing it, have caused them. I forgive all my enemies the harm they have done me. I say farewell here to my aunts and to all my brothers and sisters. I had friends. The idea of being separated forever from them and their troubles forms one of my greatest regrets in dying. Let them know, at least, that up to my last moment I was thinking of them.

Farewell, my good and loving sister. May this letter reach you! Think of me always, I embrace you with all my heart, together with those poor, dear children. My God! What an agony it is to leave them forever! Farewell! Farewell! I shall henceforth pay attention to nothing but my spiritual duties. As I am not free, they will perhaps bring me a (conformist) priest, but I protest here that I shall not say a word to him and that I shall treat him as a complete stranger.'

Unlike her husband it did not occur to Marie Antoinette to write a will but then again, now that virtually everything had been stripped from her she had precious little left to leave. When her cell was searched after her departure only a few meagre belongings were found: a sponge, a box of powder, a small box of pomade, some handkerchiefs, garters, two sets of pockets to be worn beneath her dresses, a black crepe mourning gown, some linen undergarments, a bonnet and two pairs of black stockings, all stored in the box donated by the kindly Rosalie who also gave her a small mirror backed with red lacquer that she had picked up from a market stall for a few coins.

The Queen spent the next few hours lying on her bed, unable to sleep and weeping silently as the dawn broke outside her windows and the two guardsmen watched silently, muffling their yawns behind their fists, from the other side of their screen. At seven, Rosalie came in and asked her if she felt able to take some food, gently reminding the Queen that she had barely eaten since the trial began and would have need of all her strength to get through the ordeal that lay ahead, but Marie Antoinette refused. 'My child, I need nothing now,' she said sadly. 'Everything is over for me.' However, she relented when she saw how genuinely distressed the little maid was and agreed to have some left over *bouillon* soup and noodles, only managing a few mouthfuls before she pushed it to one side and they embarked on the important business of dressing her for her final public appearance.

Marie Antoinette had lost a lot of blood overnight and was desperate to change into fresh underthings but when Rosalie attempted to discreetly remove her petticoats and help her change into clean ones, one of the guards stepped around the screen and made it clear that he intended to watch. 'For the love of God, Monsieur, let me change my chemise in private,' Marie Antoinette begged but he insisted that orders were orders and refused to move, leaving the two women to do their best to hide the Queen's bloodstained linen by rolling it into a ball and shoving it into a gap in the wall before pulling a black petticoat over her clean chemise. However, if she hoped to be allowed to wear a black dress that would hide the worst of her bleeding, she was to be disappointed for the Committee of Public Safety had sent over an order that the Queen was not to be allowed to wear mourning for her husband but instead could wear any other colour to the scaffold. Marie Antoinette, who had once owned dresses in all the colours of the rainbow and a few more besides, had only one dress that wasn't black and that was the plain white piqué morning gown[6] that her sister-in-law Madame Élisabeth had sent over from the Temple. Perhaps Marie Antoinette allowed herself a small sad smile as Rosalie helped her into the dress, remembering as no one else seemingly had that the long ago Queens of France, including her ancestress Mary Queen of Scots, had traditionally worn white when mourning their husbands. She completed her last *toilette* with a white *fichu*, plain white lawn bonnet decorated with black ribbons, black stockings and a pair of purple shoes.

At some point Abbé Girard, a priest who had sworn the oath of allegiance to the Constitution, was brought to her cell but, as she had promised her sister-in-law, Marie Antoinette refused to acknowledge him, offended that, unlike her husband who had gone to his death accompanied by his Irish confessor Abbé Edgeworth, she was not permitted to have a priest who had not sworn the oath but instead had someone of whom she could not approve foisted upon her at this most spiritually critical time. It probably also hurt that while Louis had been permitted to say goodbye to his family there was clearly no intention of allowing her the same privilege and that she would be going to her death without so much as a glimpse of the faces that she loved best in all the world and would never get the opportunity to forgive her son for his childish rashness.

When the turnkey Larivière and the judges Fouquier-Tinville and Hermann went to Marie Antoinette's cell at ten in the morning, they found her kneeling beside her bed and deep in prayer. The court clerk read out the indictment again, ignoring the Queen's gentle protest that she had already heard it and then stepped aside as the executioner

Sanson entered with a length of rope. The Queen recoiled in horror. 'You did not tie Louis XVI's hands,' she protested, obviously distressed, but with the judges of the Tribunal watching he had no choice but to follow orders and tie her hands behind her back as she fought to hold back her tears. There was then further indignity when his assistant fetched his scissors and he roughly cut off what was left of her prematurely grey hair.

There was barely time to say one last farewell to Rosalie before the Queen was led up the nine stone steps to the Cour du Mai of the Palais du Justice where a horse drawn cart was waiting for her rather than the closed carriage which had been provided for her husband's final journey to the scaffold. Appalled by the terrifying prospect of being driven through the streets, exposed to the violent abuse and insults of the crowd, Marie Antoinette lost control of her bladder and had to retreat behind a wall to relieve herself before she felt able to clamber on to the cart, where she was instructed to sit with her back to the horses so that everyone could see her. Abbé Girard, determined to remain beside her until the very end even if she repudiated his attempts to comfort her, climbed up and sat beside her while Sanson and his assistant hitched a ride at the back of the cart. It had been freezing cold overnight in the Conciergerie but the weather had become warmer in the morning and was now reasonably pleasant as they set out on their journey, which would normally take less than an hour but took twice as long this morning thanks to the huge crowds that had gathered to see the former Queen go by for the last time.

The small procession made its way out through the gilded gates of the Palais du Justice at eleven and turned on to the Rue de la Barillerie and then rumbled over the Pont au Change. The route was lined with over thirty thousand guardsmen who had been hastily deployed overnight to restrain the rabble and prevent any last minute attempts to rescue the Queen. They held back the enormous crowds that had begun to gather on the streets as soon as the verdict was announced in the early hours of the morning and which were now shouting and shrieking at the silent Queen, who stared straight ahead as if she simply could not hear them. An actor called Grammont rode ahead of the cart, waving his sword in the air and shouting 'Here she is at last! It's Antoinette, my friends, going to her death! She's finished!' Many watched her go by with silent sympathy though and as she passed one doorway a young mother held up her little boy, who waved and blew the Queen a kiss, almost reducing her to tears.

The tumbrel turned on to the long Rue Saint Honoré which Marie Antoinette had known very well in happier times. She went past beautiful old mansions where she had once danced all night, Mademoiselle Bertin's shop, the Palais Royal and the lovely Church of Saint Roch where the tumbrel halted for several minutes so that the huge group of the market women who had gathered there could scream abuse and spit at the Queen who still continued to stare straight ahead, apparently unmoved by their fury. The artist David was waiting on a wrought iron balcony at the Café de la Régence close by the Palais Royal; renowned for the intellectual insight of his portraits, he quickly produced a line sketch of the beleaguered Queen in her tumbrel, broken but never unbowed as she confronted the fury of the mob. Only once would the Queen show some spark of emotion, when the tumbrel turned down the elegant Rue Royale and came within sight of the Tuileries palace and her eyes filled with tears as she gazed up at the windows where once upon a time she had looked down at a sea of cheering faces and the Duc de

Brissac, who had perished along with the Princesse de Lamballe in the prison massacres in September 1792, had murmured that 'Madame, I hope that Monsieur le Dauphin won't be jealous when I say that you have two hundred thousand lovers.'

A few moments later the tumbrel came to a juddering halt in the Place de la Révolution, where Marie Antoinette's husband had met his end almost ten months earlier. The square was still as elegant as ever but there was a pile of rubble where Louis XV's equestrian statue had been toppled from its podium and smashed into pieces on the ground and the entire vista was now dominated by the wooden scaffold where the guillotine, that most inelegant of contraptions, awaited her. Marie Antoinette blinked with surprise as she looked around the enormous crowd, several hundred thousand people strong, that had gathered in the square to watch her die, held back by several rows of guardsmen. 'This is the moment, Madame, to arm yourself with courage,' the tenacious Abbé Girard exhorted the Queen as she was pulled down from the cart. 'Courage?' Marie Antoinette snapped, provoked into speaking to him at last. 'The moment when my troubles are about to end is not the moment when courage is going to fail me.'

The Queen hurried up the scaffold steps with the light-footed grace that had once enchanted all of Versailles, her eyes fixed on the instrument of death that loomed above her. In her haste she managed to step on Sanson's foot, making him yelp with pain and surprise. 'I am sorry, Monsieur,' Marie Antoinette murmured with a smile. 'I did not do it on purpose.' She turned and looked over the heads of the enormous roaring crowd at the Tuileries but there was no time to dwell on the past before she was roughly seized, tied to the plank then pushed down beneath the guillotine's blade. In a heartbeat, the noise and roar of the crowd and brightness of daylight all faded away to nothing and Marie Antoinette was at peace at last.

Chapter 15

The Chapelle Expiatoire

'Called to immortality.'

Tucked away on the Rue Pasquier in the 8th arrondissement of Paris, there is a small park that holds a precious secret – an exquisite little chapel behind a high wall that serves as a memorial to Louis XVI and Marie Antoinette. Above the entrance there is the following inscription:

> *'King Louis XVIII raised this monument to consecrate the place where the mortal remains of King Louis XVI and Queen Marie-Antoinette, transferred on 21 January 1815 to the royal tomb of Saint-Denis, reposed for 21 years. It was finished during the second year of the reign of Charles X, year of grace 1826.'*

After the executions of Louis XVI and Marie Antoinette in 1793, their bodies were dumped without ceremony alongside those of several thousand other victims of the revolution in the small graveyard of the nearby Madeleine church. Their bodies remained there forgotten alongside those of the Swiss Guards massacred in August 1792, Antoine Barnave (who went to his death in November 1793 with a piece from one of Marie Antoinette's dresses in his pocket), Charlotte Corday, Madame du Barry, Madame Roland and the Duc d'Orléans until 1803 when the site was bought by a loyally royalist magistrate, Pierre-Louis Olivier Desclozeaux who had been watching when the royal couple were buried and so was able to recall where the bodies lay and later do his best to discreetly mark the spots with cypress trees.

Intriguingly, in 1770 the little Madeleine cemetery was also the burial ground for the one hundred and thirty three victims of the tragic accident that occurred at the firework display to mark the Parisian celebration of Louis and Marie Antoinette's wedding. Who could ever have guessed that the royal couple would one day end up buried alongside them and in such grisly circumstances?

After the Bourbon Restoration in 1815, one of Louis XVIII's first actions was to have his brother and sister-in-law's bodies exhumed and buried with proper ceremony in the royal necropolis, the Basilica of Saint Denis. A year later, Desclozeaux sold the graveyard to King Louis who then proceeded to build a memorial chapel on the site, sharing the three million livres expense with his niece and the sole surviving child of Louis XVI and Marie Antoinette, Marie-Thérèse, who had become the Duchesse d'Angoulême when she married the eldest son of her uncle the Comte d'Artois.

As you walk up the path towards the main building, you see memorials to commemorate the unfortunate Swiss Guards who were massacred at the Tuileries in August 1792 as well as memorials to other well-known victims of the Terror buried there before the cemetery was officially closed in March 1794 after the executions of Hébert and his chief supporters. It's not known how many victims of the revolution were buried at this site, but it could be anything up to three thousand. Thousands of others, including Madame Élisabeth, Camille and Lucile Desmoulins, Robespierre, Saint-Just and the handsome Duc de Lauzun were buried at the Errancis cemetery while others, including Marie Antoinette's last *dame d'atours* Comtesse d'Ossun, Madame de Noailles and several members of her family, lie in grave pits at the Picpus cemetery.

The Chapelle Expiatoire was designed by one of Napoleon's favourite architects Pierre Fontaine and overseen by his assistant Louis-Hippolyte Lebas and took ten years to complete. By the time it was actually finished, Louis XVIII was no more and it was his brother Charles X along with his daughter-in-law niece Duchesse d'Angoulême who presided over the chapel's inauguration in 1826. The Archbishop of Paris was on hand to bless the corner stone and, perhaps rather inappropriately, took this as an opportunity to preach about forgiveness for the exiled members of the Revolutionary National Convention. Or perhaps it wasn't actually all that inappropriate – the chapel could be taken to not only be an apotheosis of the executed Louis and Marie Antoinette but also an acknowledgement that the horrors of the Terror were now in the past, sanctified and cleansed by the erection of a memorial chapel and proper remembrance of the numerous dead.

The interior of the chapel mirrors the serenity and pale glow of the exterior and is a perfectly balanced and harmonious neoclassical design that manages to be both uplifting and sombre at the same time. I think that Marie Antoinette would definitely have approved of the fact that it absolutely brings to mind the gentle serenity of both her chapel at the Petit Trianon and the dairy built for her at Rambouillet as well as the light elegance that she sought to surround herself with in private. Although the chapel is also dedicated to the memory of Louis XVI, it is clear that here as with other sites associated with the doomed couple it is his wife who is chiefly evoked and brought to mind.

On the left hand side as you enter the chapel, there is a statue of *Marie Antoinette Supported by Religion* by Jean Pierre Cortot, in which Religion has the beautifully serene features of Marie Antoinette's sister-in-law, Madame Elisabeth, who would follow her to the guillotine in May 1794. This is a beautiful statue – which contrives to be both elegant and moving as the Queen appears to almost abandon herself to religion in a frenzy of devotion with her hair tumbling down her back and eyes gazing fervently upwards. We are reminded here that although Marie Antoinette lived an apparently frivolous life before the Revolution, she found enormous comfort in her faith during her final years, when virtually all else had been stripped from her, as symbolised by the crown that rolls forgotten and abandoned on the ground by her knee.

On the right hand side is *Louis XVI Called to Immortality, Sustained by an Angel* by Francois Bosio. Poor Louis. He is anchored to the ground by his grand robes and gazes upwards with seeming relief as the light-footed angel shows him the way forward. Here is a man who never wanted to be King, but who nonetheless did his best only to die feeling like he had failed in his duty both to his people and also his family.

It is impossible to stand in the Chapelle Expiatoire and not be moved by the horrible fates of the royal couple and of the other thousands of victims whose bodies reside on that hallowed site and others throughout the city, all lying together regardless of political viewpoint. You can descend to a vault below the main chapel and see a black marble altar that marks the spot where the royal couple's remains were allegedly originally discovered – they were identified thanks to the fact that unlike the other bodies that surrounded them, they had been buried in coffins.

On 21 January 1815, the anniversary of the King's execution, the remains of Louis XVI and Marie Antoinette were moved from their resting place close to the Madeleine in Paris to the Basilica St Denis, there to lie for eternity alongside the bodies of their ancestors although possibly not in the way that they had planned.

In the autumn of 1793, the remains of the royalty of France had been removed from their graves with a total disregard for age, sex or status and dumped together into mass graves outside the Basilica before being hurriedly replaced higgledy piggledy and with very little order all together in the crypt after the restoration of the Bourbons. At St Denis, their beautiful memorial statues by Edmé Gaulle and Pierre Petitot kneel in the basilica with regal solemnity. The statue of Louis XVI bestows the maligned and ridiculed King with a dignity that he was denied in real life, while Marie Antoinette, pleasingly, is dressed in the elegant fashion of 1815 which sadly she never got to wear. Their actual bodies, however, rest alongside those of Louis' brothers and their wives beneath plain black marble slabs in the crypt below the main church, close to the memorials for Madame Élisabeth, whose body was never recovered despite attempts to find it, and their children, Louis-Joseph, Sophie Béatrice and poor little Louis XVIII, who died in the Temple prison in June 1795 and whose heart was laid to rest in Saint Denis in 2004.

Notes

Chapter 1

1. After inheriting the majority of the Habsburg empire from her father in 1740, Maria Theresa (1717–1780) was ruler of not just Austria but also Hungary, Bohemia, Croatia, Transylvania, Milan, Galicia, the Austrian Netherlands, Mantua and Parma.
2. The traditional Catholic day of mourning and therefore not an especially auspicious date for the arrival of any baby, let alone a princess. For many years afterwards, Marie Antoinette's birthday would therefore be officially celebrated a day earlier.
3. François Etienne de Lorraine (1708–1765) was voted Holy Roman Emperor in 1745 according to the wishes of his late father-in-law. However, although the title was nominally his, everyone knew that it was his wife who was actually in charge.
4. A few days after the christening, news would arrive that the Portuguese capital Lisbon had been completely destroyed by an earthquake and subsequent tsunami on the day before Marie Antoinette's birth. Naturally this would later be seen as a rather hefty portent of future disaster.
5. Marie Antoinette's eldest brother Joseph (1741–1790) would succeed his father as Emperor Joseph II in 1765.
6. Maria Anna (1738–1789) was the eldest surviving daughter of Maria Theresa and Francis. As she suffered from poor health she never married and remained with her family.
7. Joseph Weber (1755–1830) remained close to Marie Antoinette for the rest of her life and would later write a memoir about their friendship.
8. Leopold (1747–1792) was the imperial couple's second surviving son and would eventually succeed his elder brother Joseph II as Emperor Leopold II.
9. Maria Luisa of Spain (1745–1792) was the second surviving daughter of Charles III of Spain and his wife Maria Amalia of Saxony, whose younger sister Maria Josepha was Dauphine of France and mother of the future Louis XVI.
10. Isabella of Parma (1741–1763) was the eldest daughter of Philip, Duke of Parma, son of Philip V of Spain and his wife Louise Élisabeth de France.
11. Frederica Caroline (1752–1782) would marry the Grand Duke of Mecklenburg-Strelitz and have numerous children, including Queen Louise of Prussia and Frederica, Queen of Hanover. After her death in childbirth, her younger sister Charlotte married her widower and then herself died shortly after having his son.
12. Louise (1761–1829) married her cousin, Louis I, Grand Duke of Hesse in 1777 and was an ancestress of Empress Alexandra Feodorovna of Russia.
13. Charlotte was born just a few days after Maria Antonia on 5 November 1755. She would marry her elder sister's widower, Charles II of Mecklenburg Strelitz and died after giving birth to his son in 1785.
14. Sadly, Mimi's notes to Isabella have not survived as she ordered them to be destroyed after her death.
15. Maria Luisa of Parma (1751–1819) would eventually marry the heir to the Spanish throne and become Queen of Spain. She is probably familiar to art lovers from her not especially flattering portraits by Goya.

16. Ferdinand (1751–1825) was the third son of Charles VII of Spain and brother of Maria Luisa, wife of Maria Theresa's second son Archduke Leopold. He was made King of Naples at the age of eight when his father succeeded to the throne of Spain and abdicated from Naples and Sicily in his favour.
17. Ferdinand of Parma (1751–1802) was the only son of Louis XV's daughter Louise Élisabeth and her husband Philip, who was the second son of Philip V of Spain. He had become Duke of Parma at the age of fourteen.
18. Charles II of Zweibrücken (1746–1795) would eventually marry Amalia of Saxony, a first cousin of Louis XVI via his mother, who was her aunt.

Chapter 2

1. Jean-Georges Noverre (1727–1810) is often regarded as one of the inventors of what we now know as ballet.
2. Antonia Esterházy von Galántha, Princess Paar (1719–1771) was a member of the highly important Esterhazy family from Hungary.
3. Maria Amalia of Austria (1701–1756) was the eldest daughter and heiress of Maria Theresa's uncle Emperor Joseph I, which technically gave her a better claim to the throne until Maria Theresa's father inherited the title after his brother and engineered it so that his own daughter would inherit the empire if not the actual title, which could only be held by a man, instead.

Chapter 3

1. Anne Claude Louise d'Arpajon, Comtesse de Noailles (1729–1794) was also Duchesse de Mouchy by marriage but she and her husband preferred to be known as Comte and Comtesse de Noailles. They would be guillotined in 1794 along with three other female relatives.
2. Amable Gabrielle de Noailles, Duchesse de Villars (1706–1771) was a relative by marriage of Madame de Noailles.
3. Marie Anne Julie Le Tonnelier de Breteuil, Comtesse de Clermont-Tonnerre (1716–1793).
4. Adélaïde Diane Hortense Mancini-Mazarin, Duchesse de Cossé-Brissac (1742–1808), would be the dame d'autours from 1771 until 1775.
5. Marie Éléonore de Lévis-Châteaumorand, Marquise de Saulx-Tavannes (1739–1793) would become Duchesse when her husband inherited the title.
6. Louise Charlotte de Noailles, Marquise de Duras (1745–1832), who became Duchesse de Duras when her husband inherited the title, was the daughter of Madame de Noailles.
7. Marie Jeanne de Talleyrand-Périgord, Comtesse de Mailly-Haucourt (1747–1792) would later become Duchesse de Mailly when her husband inherited the title. She would also be Marie Antoinette's Lady of the Wardrobe (Dame d'Autour) from 1775 until 1781.
8. Marie Paule Angélique de Luynes, Duchesse de Picquigny (1744–1781) would later become Duchesse de Chaulnes when her husband inherited the title.
9. Louis René Édouard de Rohan (1734–1803) would eventually succeed his uncle as Bishop of Strasbourg in 1779. We will meet him again.
10. Jeanne Antoinette Poisson, Madame de Pompadour (1721–1764) had been the most significant fan of the Viennese match along with her great friend, the Duc de Choiseul. Sadly, she died before she was able to welcome an Austrian Archduchess to Versailles.
11. Louis (1729–1765) was the only surviving son of Louis XV and Marie Leszczynska.
12. Maria Josepha of Saxony (1731–1767) was the daughter of Augustus III of Poland and Maria Josepha of Austria, who was a first cousin of Empress Maria Theresa.
13. Anne 'Ninon' de L'Enclos (1620–1705) was a celebrated Parisian salonniere and courtesan who was an early patron of both Voltaire and Molière. Her lovers included some of the influential men in France.

14. Maria Teresa Rafaela of Spain, Dauphine of France (1726–1746) was daughter of Philip V of Spain and Elisabeth Farnese. Her elder sister Mariana Victoria had been raised at Versailles as fiancée of Louis XV.
15. Marie Louise Geneviève de Rohan, Comtesse de Marsan (1720–1803) was the latest in a succession of Rohan royal governesses.
16. Marie Adélaïde de France (1732–1800) was the sixth child and fourth daughter of Louis XV.
17. Marie Louise Thérèse Victoire de France (1733–1799) was the seventh child and fifth daughter of Louis XV.
18. Sophie Philippine Élisabeth Justine de France (1734–1782) was the eighth child and sixth daughter of Louis XV.
19. Louise Marie de France (1737–1787) was the youngest child of Louis XV and consequently known as 'Madame Derniere' for most of her childhood.
20. Louis Philippe I, Duc d'Orléans (1725–1785) was a cousin of Marie Antoinette's father.
21. Louis Philippe II, Duc de Chartres (1747–1793) would inherit the title Duc d'Orléans in 1785.
22. Louis Alexandre de Bourbon, Prince de Lamballe (1747–1768) died of a venereal disease at the age of just twenty.
23. Maria Teresa Luisa of Savoy (1749–1792) was the daughter of Louis Victor of Savoy, Prince of Carignano and his wife Princess Christine Henriette of Hesse-Rotenburg.
24. Louis Stanislas Xavier, Comte de Provence (1755–1824) would eventually succeed as Louis XVIII.
25. Charles Philippe, Comte d'Artois (1757–1836) would eventually succeed as Charles X.

Chapter 4

1. Now known as the Place de la Concorde.
2. Marie Adélaïde de Savoie, Duchesse de Bourgogne (1685–1712) was the granddaughter of Henrietta Anne of England, Duchesse d'Orléans and mother of Louis XV.

Chapter 5

1. This is a very strange way to describe a nose and it isn't clear what Louis XV meant by this – my interpretation, however, is that he was leaning into a very unpleasant anti-semitic trope that was unfortunately prevalent during the 18th century. Or perhaps he was once ripped off at cards by someone who had a similar nose and was genuinely triggered by his grand-daughter-in-law's facial features. We don't know.

Chapter 6

1. I do not in general approve of historical figures being definitely diagnosed with disorders unless it is absolutely provable – however, my own personal familiarity with the autistic spectrum does make me wonder about Louis XVI.
2. Almost certainly due to short sight but could facial blindness, where he genuinely struggled to recognise even people who were familiar to him, also have been an issue for Louis XVI?
3. Similarly, in the case of Marie Antoinette, as someone who has been diagnosed with ADHD, I do often find myself relating to various aspects of her character. Once again though, I would not even attempt to actually diagnose her with ADHD or any other disorder but it is certainly something to consider.
4. She did not. Although, as we will see, she considerably modified her appearance after her thirtieth birthday, believing that she was now too old for certain colours, patterns and embellishments.
5. Only one of Marie Antoinette's wardrobe books, for the year 1782, still exists. It is full of fabric swatches for each of her dresses and provides a fascinating glimpse into her preferred style.

6. Henriette-Lucy Dillon, Marquise de la Tour du Pin (1770–1853) was the only child of one of Marie Antoinette's best friends, Madame Dillon and would be a lady-in-waiting at the royal court in its final days. Her lively memoirs of the period are an invaluable resource for anyone wishing to know more about life at Versailles.
7. Thérèse-Lucie de Rothe married her cousin, the Anglo-Irish nobleman Arthur Dillon in 1768. Although, not especially noble compared to the rest of the Queen's circle, Marie Antoinette was fond enough of her to give her a position at court. She was the mistress of the Prince de Guéméné. Her daughter Lucie would, as Madame de la Tour du Pin, also join the Queen's household.
8. Yolande Martine Gabrielle de Polastron, Comtesse Jules de Polignac and later Duchesse de Polignac (1749–1793) was usually referred to by her middle name Gabrielle.

Chapter 7

1. In 1775, the position of Dame d'Autours to Marie Antoinette was passed from the Duchesse de Cossé-Brissac to Laure-Auguste de Fitz-James, Princesse de Chimay and then finally to Marie-Jeanne de Talleyrand-Périgord, Duchesse de Mailly, who remained in the post until 1781, when it was taken over by Geneviève de Gramont, Comtesse d'Ossun.
2. It is clear from portraits of this era that the ladies of Versailles were no longer caking their faces with white lead paint and thick circles of unblended red rouge – but instead moving towards a more natural and attractive use of cosmetics that accentuated rather than concealed.
3. Although it is clear that Versailles was no way near so appallingly dirty and malodourous as popular legend describes, it could still, like a busy underground train at rush hour in the height of summer, a teenage boy's bedroom or a packed club at 4am for example, have its unpleasant moments.
4. Lady Georgiana Spencer was married to the Duke of Devonshire on her 17th birthday in June 1774 and would not give birth to her first child, a daughter, until July 1783.
5. The royal assistance to this family was enough to enable Armand's brother, Denis to train as a musician and become a cellist in the royal orchestra, while doweries were provided for his sisters Louise Marie and Marie Madeleine. However, Armand Gagné would repay her generosity by turning on his royal patrons during the revolution and would eventually be killed at the age of twenty fighting for the Revolutionary Army at Jemappes.

Chapter 8

1. Adrien-Louis de Bonnières, Duc de Guines (1735–1806) was so fat that he had two types of breeches made – one that could be worn while sitting down and tighter ones that he could only wear on days when he was expecting to spend the day standing and which required the assistance of two footmen to get him into. 'Will Monsieur le Duc be sitting today?' his valet would politely enquire every morning before he dressed him. It's hard to imagine Marie Antoinette finding this anything other than absolutely hilarious.
2. Louis' compliance in this matter has led to some speculation that he either had a crush on Madame de Polignac or was actively having a full blown affair with her. The former theory is not altogether unlikely as she was very lovely and they spent a lot of time together but it is highly improbable that a man like Louis XVI would have an affair with his wife's best friend.
3. Marie-Philippine Lambriquet, known as 'Ernestine' (1778–1813), was a few months older than Madame Royale and was raised alongside the princess as her constant companion. The two girls were dressed and treated in the exact same way and shared their lessons and meals. Marie Antoinette formally adopted Ernestine in 1788 after the death of her mother. Her father was guillotined during the Terror but Ernestine, who remained loyal to her royal patrons, survived and would eventually marry.

4. Louis Philippe (1773–1850) would indeed eventually succeed his father as Duc d'Orléans and would also preside over the new Orléans dynasty as King Louis Philippe between 1830 and 1848.
5. It's probable that this match would have been a better one for Madame Royale than the one that she eventually made, with her first cousin, the Duc d'Angoulême. Louis Philippe d'Orléans was much better looking, more amusing and very bright and if she had married him then she would have followed in her mother's footsteps and been Queen of France between 1830 and 1848. Instead, he married her first cousin Maria Amalia of Naples and Sicily, one of the daughters of Marie Antoinette's favourite sister Maria Carolina, Queen of Naples. Maria Amalia had previously been betrothed to her cousin Louis Charles, the second son of her aunt Marie Antoinette.
6. Joseph Bologne (1745–1799) was born in Guadeloupe in the French West Indies and was the son of a plantation owner and an enslaved Créole woman. He was the first biracial composer to achieve significant success in Europe. He was also a notably talented fencer and dancer.
7. Until recently, royal babies were not immediately baptised but instead were officially known by their titles until they were considered old enough to be officially christened, often alongside their siblings. Louis XVI was baptised in the same ceremony as Provence and Artois. Due to her frailty, his youngest sibling, Élisabeth was baptised on the day of her birth, however and it seems that from this point onwards most royal babies were also baptised straight away.
8. The King's livery, worn by his household, was blue with red braiding while that of the Queen's household was the opposite – red with blue braiding.
9. Gustav III of Sweden was almost certainly at least bisexual if not entirely gay.

Chapter 9

1. This delightful little residence still exists today.
2. Geneviève de Gramont, Comtesse d'Ossun (1751–1794) was a highly respected and very well connected member of court. She was appointed as mistress of Marie Antoinette's wardrobe in May 1781, replacing the Duchesse de Mailly.
3. Meudon was one of the most beautiful royal residences of this era but sadly very little of it has survived.

Chapter 10

1. Louise Élisabeth Félicité Françoise Armande Anne Marie Jeanne Joséphine de Croÿ d'Havré, Marquise de Tourzel 1749–1832 was the daughter of the Duc d'Havré and via her mother, a granddaughter of the Maréchal de Luxembourg, which made her very well connected. Her husband had died in 1786 as the result of falling from his horse while out hunting with the King.
2. It is tempting to say that it looks much the same nowadays during the summer when the palace is full of tourists.
3. Marie Charlotte Pauline du Bouchet de Sourches (1771–1839) was the youngest daughter of Madame de Tourzel. She would later become Comtesse de Béarn and write a fascinating memoir of her youth.

Chapter 11

1. Louis XVI's journals get a lot of criticism which I think is unfair – they were never intended by him to be a verbose outpouring of his thoughts but instead a simple record of his day to day life.
2. In a story that is replete with tragedy, perhaps one of the greatest is the fact that due to the timings involved, if Louis and Marie Antoinette had consented to let their children go without them that night, they would almost certainly have escaped.

3. Drouet would be significantly rewarded for his role in the capture of the royal family and became a politician, which enabled him to later vote for Louis XVI's execution. Much later, he would be captured by the Austrian army and would form part of an exchange of French prisoners for Madame Royale, the only surviving member of the royal family.

Chapter 12

1. Known today as canities subita or 'Marie Antoinette syndrome' it is apparently possible but still very rare for someone's hair to turn completely white due to stress or trauma. It seems likely that Marie Antoinette was already going grey and the stress simply speeded the process up.
2. This question will obviously be addressed more fully in my biography of Madame Élisabeth.
3. Poor Barnave (1761–1793) would be guillotined in November 1793 with a piece of one of Marie Antoinette's dresses, allegedly the one she wore during the return from Varennes, in his pocket.
4. Alexandrine Charlotte Sophie de Rohan-Chabot, Duchesse de la Rochefoucauld (1763–1839) survived the Terror but her husband (who was also her uncle) was less fortunate as he was murdered during the Prison Massacres of September 1792.
5. Lady Elizabeth Sutherland (1765–1839) was Countess of Sutherland in her own right. Her husband was appointed Ambassador to France in 1790 and they would remain in Paris until 1792.

Chapter 13

1. Frances Burney (1752–1840) was a very successful novelist during this period and was also very well connected as she held the post of Keeper of the Robes to Queen Charlotte. She would later marry a French émigré, Alexandre d'Arblay.
2. If you're also interested in the Romanovs, you're probably seeing parallels in the treatment of Louis XVI and his family and that of Nicholas II and his family in 1918. Which goes to show that people have always been absolutely horrible.

Chapter 14

1. Adam Philippe de Custine (1740–1793) was a liberal aristocrat who later became General in Chief of the republican Army of the Rhine before falling out of favour. He was tried and executed at the end of August 1793. His gorgeous daughter-in-law Delphine de Sabran attended every day of his trial and was so distracting that Fouquier-Tinville accused the jurors of deliberately extending the trial just so they could stare at her.
2. Marie Anne Charlotte de Corday d'Armont (1768–1793) was a upper middle class girl from Normandy who assassinated the Jacobin leader Marat in July 1793 and was guillotined just a few days later. I love her.
3. Madame de la Motte-Valois would almost certainly have been called as a witness for the prosecution had she not died in 1791 when she fell (or was perhaps pushed) out of a window in London, where she had fled after escaping from prison.
4. Marie Antoinette's lawyers were both interrogated after her verdict but were released without charge. Chauveau-Lagarde would later defend her sister-in-law Madame Élisabeth at her trial – again without success.
5. He would later be exonerated and freed.
6. Anyone who has ever menstruated will understand why Marie Antoinette was not keen to wear a white dress on that day.

Bibliography

Allen, Rodney, *Threshold of Terror: The Last Hours of the Monarchy in the French Revolution*, 1999.

Andress, David, *1789: The Threshold of the Modern Age*, 2009.

Andress, David, *The Terror: Civil War in the French Revolution*, 2006.

Angoulême, Marie-Thérèse de France, Duchesse d', *Mémoire écrit par Marie-Thérèse-Charlotte de France sur la captivité des princes et princesses et ses parents depuis le 10 août 1792 jusqu'à la mort de son frère*. Jacques Brosse, Mercure de France, 1968.

Béarn, Pauline de Tourzel, Comtesse de, *Souvenirs de quarante ans (1789–1830)*. Jean Chalon, Mercure de France, 1986.

Bernet, Anne, *Madame Élisabeth: Soeur de Louis XVI*, 2022.

Bernier, Olivier (editor), *Imperial Mother, Royal Daughter: Correspondence between Marie Antoinette and Maria Theresa*, 1986.

Bertière, Simone, *Marie Antoinette l'insoumise*, 2002.

Blanc, Olivier, *Last Letters: Prisons and Prisoners of the French Revolution 1793–1794*, 1987.

Blanc, Olivier, *Portraits de femmes: Artistes et modèles à l'époque de Marie Antoinette*, 2006.

Cadbury, Deborah, *The Lost King of France*, 2012.

Campan, Jeanne-Louise Genet, Madame, *Mémoires*. Jean Chalon, Mercure de France, 1988.

Castelot, André, *Marie Antoinette*, 1957.

Castelluccio, Stéphane (editor), *Le Journal de la Cour 1723–1785*, 2022.

Chalon, Jean, *Chère Marie Antoinette*, 1988.

Chrisman-Campbell, Kimberly, *Fashion Victims: Dress at the Court of Louis XVI and Marie Antoinette*, 2014.

Cronin, Vincent, *Louis and Antoinette*, 1989.

Dunlop, Ian, *Marie Antoinette: A Portrait*, 1993.

Dunlop, Ian, *Royal Palaces of France*, 1985.

Dunlop, Ian, *Versailles*, 1970.

Farr, Evelyn, *Before the Deluge: Parisian Society in the Reign of Louis XVI*, 1994.

Farr, Evelyn, *Marie Antoinette and Count Axel Fersen: The Untold Love Story*, 1995.

Feydeau, Élisabeth de, *A Scented Palace: The Secret History of Marie Antoinette*, 2021.

Fife, Graeme, *The Terror: The Shadow of the Guillotine: France 1792–1794*, 2003.

Foreman, Amanda, *Georgiana, Duchess of Devonshire*, 2004.

Fraser, Antonia, *Marie Antoinette: The Journey*, 2001.

Haslip, Joan, *Madame du Barry: The Wages of Beauty*, 1992.

Haslip, Joan, *Marie Antoinette*, 1987.

James-Sarazin, Ariane and Lapasin, Régis, *Gazette des atours de Marie Antoinette*, 2023.

Jones, Colin, *The Great Nation: France from Louis XV to Napoleon*, 2003.

La Tour du Pin-Gouvernet, Lucie Dillon, Marquise de, *Journal d'une femme de cinquante ans*. C de Liedekerke-Beaufort, Mercure de France, 1979.

Lever, Évelyne, *Louis XVI*, 1985.

Lever, Évelyne, *Marie Antoinette: The Last Queen of France*, 2000.

Louis XVI, *Journal de Louis XVI*. Louis Nicolardot, 1873.

Moorehead, Caroline, *Dancing to the Precipice: Lucie de la Tour du Pin and the French Revolution*, 2010.

Nagel, Susan, *Marie-Thérèse: The Fate of Marie Antoinette's Daughter*, 2009.

Oberkirch, Henriette-Louise de Waldner de Freudenstein, Baronne d', *Mémoires sur la Cour du Louis XVI et la société française avant 1789*. S. Burkard, 1970.
Sabourdin-Perrin, Dominique, *Les Oubliés du Temple*, 2022.
Salmon, Xavier and Arrioli-Clementel, Pierre, *Marie Antoinette* (exhibition catalogue), 2008.
Spawforth, Tony, *Versailles*, 2010.
Thomas, Chantal, *La Reine Scélérate. Marie Antoinette dans les pamphlets*, 1989.
Tilly, Pierre-Alexandre, Comte de, *Mémoires du Comte Alexandre de Tilly, ancien page de Marie Antoinette*. C. Melchior-Bonnet, Mercure de France, 1969.
Tourzel, Louise-Félicité de Croÿ d'Havré, Marquise de, *Mémoires de Mme la Duchesse de Tourzel, gouvernante des enfants de France pendant les années 1789 à 1795*. Jean Chalon, Mercure de France, 1969.
Trey, Juliette, *La mode à la cour de Marie Antoinette*, 2014.
Vial, Charles-Éloi, *Marie Antoinette*, 2024
Vigée Le Brun, Élisabeth, *Memoirs*, translated by Siân Evans, Indiana University Press, 1989.
Walter, Gérald (editor), *Actes du Tribunal révolutionnaire*, 2005.
Weber, Caroline, *What Marie Antoinette Wore to the Revolution*, 2006.
Yalom, Marilyn, *Blood Sisters: French Revolution in Women's Memory*, 1995.
Zweig, Stefan, *Marie Antoinette: The Portrait of an Average Woman*, 1984.